The Kingsleys in 1870s Colorado

A Very British Desire for
Adventure, Investment, and Community

The Kingsleys in 1870ˢ Colorado

A Very British Desire for
Adventure, Investment, and Community

Tamara M. Teale

℮ast of the Mountains and West of the Sun™

RHYOLITE PRESS LLC
Colorado Springs, Colorado

———◆———

The Kingsleys in 1870s Colorado:
A Very British Desire for
Adventure, Investment, and Community

First edition - October 1, 2021
ISBN 978-1-943829-35-4
Library of Congress Control Number: 2021942110

Publisher's Cataloging-in-Publication data

Names: Teale, Tamara M., author.
Title: The Kingsleys in 1870s Colorado: a very British desire for adventure,
· investment, and community / Tamara M. Teale.
Description: Includes bibliographical references and index.
Colorado Springs, CO: Rhyolite Press LLC, 2021.
Identifiers: LCCN: 2021942110 | ISBN: 978-1-943829-35-4
Subjects: LCSH Kingsley family. | Kingsley, Rose Georgina, 1844-1925. | Kingsley, Maurice, 1847-1910| Kingsley, Charles, 1819-1875. | Colorado Springs (Colo.)--History. | British Americans--West (U.S.)--History. | Frontier and pioneer life--West (U.S.) | BISAC HISTORY / United States / State & local / West (Colorado) | HISTORY / Great Britain / Victorian Era
Classification: LCC F784.C7 .T43 2021| DDC 978.8/56--dc23

———◆———

Published by Rhyolite Press LLC
P.O. Box 60144
Colorado Springs, Colorado 80960
www.rhyolitepress.com info@rhyolitepress.com

Printed in the United States of America
Cover and book design/layout by Donald R. Kallaus

Cover Image: Northwest Corner of Tejon and Huerfano, 1871
Colorado College Special Collections. Colorado Springs Area Early Views D4.

You may imagine Colorado Springs, as I did, to be a sequestered valley, with bubbling fountains, green grass and shady trees: but not a bit of it. Picture to yourself a level elevated plateau of greenish-brown, without a single tree or plant larger than a Spanish bayonet (Yucca) two feet high, sloping down about a quarter of a mile to the railroad track and Monument Creek . . . and you have a pretty good idea of the town-site as it appears in November 1871.

The streets and blocks are only marked out by a furrow turned with the plough, and indicated faintly by a wooden house, finished, or in process of building, here and there, scattered over half a mile of prairie. About twelve houses and shanties are inhabited, most of them being unfinished, or run up for temporary occupation; and there are several tents dotted about also.

— Rose G. Kingsley, *South by West*, 1874.

CONTENTS

ACKNOWLEDGMENTS

No writer can read and research for nearly eighteen years on a single topic—as I have on the Kingsleys—without feeling a sense of indebtedness to many people. An early love of 19th-century British and French literature put me on the path to an undergraduate year at the University of East Anglia, Norwich, England, as an exchange student from the University of Colorado at Colorado Springs. I was a non-traditional student. At UEA, lecturers in English and American Studies alerted me to transatlantic influences that I could not have known had I remained in Colorado. A tour of 18th-and 19th-century literature and social history made me aware of the background to the mid-Victorian era and England's place in a changing Europe, an awareness of which I've tried to reflect throughout *The Kingsleys in 1870s Colorado.*

Another year in England, at the University of Essex, Colchester, gave me further background in British social history, but also showed me that the course of study which British faculty had designed for European students enabled all students—including Americans—to discuss the contemporary world political scene, and the challenges which we have inherited from the Victorians. At Stony Brook University, the topic of European travelers to the United States took hold of me, as did the attractions of writing for a general audience—as I describe in the Preface to this book.

On returning to my hometown, Colorado Springs, I discovered how little I knew of the city my parents had chosen decades earlier. Learning that Mt. Rosa was named for Rose Georgina Kingsley precipitated further investigation which revealed the role of her brother, Maurice, in the early stages of town planning. Reading about their father, Charles

Kingsley, who stayed in the Manitou Springs area for six weeks in 1874, while he was Canon of Westminster Abbey, convinced me that General William J. Palmer's desire for English influence went deeper into Colorado Springs history than had ever been studied. Moreover, Charles's brother, George H. Kingsley, M.D., played a more significant role in Estes Park, Colorado, than had been investigated previously.

In late 2002, a modest grant from the Colorado Endowment for the Humanities enabled me to attempt an account of the Kingsleys' love of landscape but I could not complete the work to my satisfaction. The challenge of telling the story of these four Kingsleys in Colorado became so daunting that I set aside the project for many years. I attempted again to at least focus on Rose Kingsley's adventure, inspired to do so by Kimberly Madsen Dill, of Great Falls, Idaho, when she selected me to sit on a panel at the annual meeting of the Rocky Mountain chapter of the Modern Language Association in 2012. Her collegiality, and the encouragement of co-panelist, Precious McKenzie of Billings, Montana, meant that an audience could form around this topic of one English family's substantial influence in Colorado.

Four years later, in the early autumn of 2016, a "Literary Walk in the Woods" organized by Lucy Bell of Colorado Springs, for the Cheyenne Mountain State Park, showed me that the Kingsleys would not leave me alone until the full story was written.

I have been deeply indebted to the Special Collections library staff and archivists of the Pike's Peak Library District, the Charles L. Tutt Library of The Colorado College, and the Stephen H. Hart Research Center of History Colorado in Denver. Most of all, my sincere regards to Patricia Lorimer Lundberg, scholar and writer, and to Peter Covey-Crump, curator of the Kingsley Family Archive.

May 2021
Tamara M. Teale
Colorado Springs and Pueblo, Colorado.

LIST OF ILLUSTRATIONS

Mr. William A. Bell, Palmer's business partner, c. 1910, Rhoda Wilcox Collection, Pike's Peak Library District Special Collections.

Mr. William Blackmore, the London-based independent financier who assisted General Palmer, c. 1868. Photo from the frontispiece of volume 1 of Herbert Brayer's book, *William Blackmore* (1949).

Dr. George H. Kingsley, M.D., c. 1865. Photo from the frontispiece of *Notes on Sport and Travel* (1900), edited by his daughter, Mary H. Kingsley.

From the Kingsley Family Archive. Peter Covey-Crump, curator.

Rose G. Kingsley in Eversley about to go riding, c. 1865.

Canon Charles Kingsley and Mrs. Frances Kingsley at the St. Mary's Rectory, Eversley, c. 1870.

Maurice Kingsley while in Mexico City on the survey expedition 1872.

A NOTE ON THE TEXT AND STYLE

Every reader trusts that the adventure on which the author has embarked—the narrative which the author would like readers to follow—is an honorable journey told with integrity. The greatest task for me has been to aid the reader in understanding how the Denver & Río Grande Railway arrived at the Colorado Springs townsite. By what inspiration William J. Palmer got the idea for his own railway project and how the financing came about was complex material which I had to simplify without diluting the basic reality of the tale. If the reader was not told the story of how the railway through central Colorado came about, then the reader would not know how traveling writers like Rose G. Kingsley arrived—and everyone after her.

To ease the reader's way through this narrative of the Kingsleys in Colorado, I have not used endnotes or footnotes to show from which books I've quoted necessary facts and ideas. I employ only in-line citations (without the cumbersome repetition of the letter 'p' for page) to refer to those publications listed in the final pages in Works Cited. My in-line (or in-text) citations follow the Modern Language Association style as much as possible. The Works Cited includes e-mails written to me from archivists and library staff in Britain who were responding to my enquiries.

As much as practicable, I've woven into the reading experience the titles of books which are readily available on internet archives, such as HathiTrust.org. In addition, I mention the titles of published works from which I did not take direct quotations but which the reader might like to see as further reading.

PREFACE

An Untold Story in Transatlantic Relations

Within the ten years immediately following the end of the American Civil War in 1865, many British people were drawn to the Pike's Peak region of central Colorado Territory. Three individuals of the Kingsley family arrived for differing but related purposes: Maurice Kingsley came in 1870 as part of war veteran General William J. Palmer's management team at the Fountain Colony Company of Colorado Springs, his sister Rose Georgina Kingsley arrived in November 1871 to write about the new town, and their father, the Reverend Charles Kingsley, Canon of Westminster Abbey and Chaplain-in-Ordinary to Queen Victoria, rested in nearby Manitou Springs at the end of his 1874 American lecture tour. A fourth Kingsley, George, a traveling physician, younger brother of Charles and residing primarily in Highgate, London, accompanied the 4th Earl of Dunraven on numerous sojourns to Estes Park. In the Kingsleys' intersecting stories, I show that there is no single factor explaining the allure of the American West even for English people who were shaped by the same mid-19th century social and economic backgrounds as the Kingsleys, rather, it is their very personal paths that make the story of travel and immigration palpably human.

While Canon Charles Kingsley's life is well-documented, his sojourn in the Pike's Peak region has never been fully presented to the public for appreciation of all its paradoxes. To a general readership, little is known of Rose Kingsley and still less of her brother Maurice. In addition, readers of Colorado history familiar with Isabella Bird's account of her travels in the Rocky Mountains at Estes Park might know that George H. Kingsley, M.D., was the first to give medical aid to Bird's "Rocky Mountain Jim" after he was shot by one of Dunraven's employees; and yet, no one has written of the doctor as an analyst of British presence worldwide, nor mentioned his daughter Mary Henrietta Kingsley's memoir of him.

In this study of four Kingsleys in Colorado, I've included two English men without whom the Colorado story cannot be told: Palmer's business partner, William A. Bell, and independent financier, William H. Blackmore. I map the trajectory of their lives in Colorado and examine their cultural predicament with compassion but not without criticism. I touch on all the subtleties of family interaction, the concept of loyalty in transatlantic business, and the interpersonal relations possible in the newly-founded town, Colorado Springs. I hope the reader will agree that Rose Kingsley's achievement has had lasting value.

Scholars of the British mystique of transculturation—of which I am one—continue to explore what propelled English people with secure social positions to leave their comfortable homes for extensive travels in America, and yet, these same scholars seldom consider that Americans had ineffable needs of those English. I trust that the reading public will have an interest in this human drama. For the sake of readers with a non-specialist enjoyment of history—but even for university scholars who want clear writing—I've become a kind of translator. I've taken clues on international business relations from heavily footnoted volumes, like Herbert O. Brayer's volume 2 of *William Blackmore*, subtitled "Early Financing of the Denver & Rio Grande Railway and Ancillary Land Companies," and made them accessible to the reader.

Though the Kingsleys, Bell, and Blackmore are the English actors in this drama, the Colorado topography determines the telling. The primary scene of the action in this tale of international investment intrigue is Colorado Springs, a resort town officially founded in late

July 1871 at the eastern base of Pike's Peak; however, the setting of the story is broadly regional including the High Plains of eastern Colorado and western Kansas, but primarily the Front Range of the Rocky Mountains from the El Paso County line along Monument Creek to Colorado Springs, then south with Fountain Creek, to Pueblo, south-central Colorado, and north-central New Mexico, and for George Kingsley's story, the secluded valley of Estes Park north-northwest of Denver.

From the late 18th-century to the eve of the American Civil War in 1861, dozens of commentators (including William Faux, Adam Hodgson, Charles Augustus Murray, Joseph Latrobe, and most notably Alexis de Tocqueville) attempted to find out how America was being made and what makes an American, while English businessmen seemed to focus on only the next deal. In the early 1870s, Blackmore's transatlantic business included placing a vast tract of land—the Sangre de Cristo Land Grant—on the international market, while Bell felt sure his plan to make a fortune in Colorado would be ruined by the Washington, D.C., demand that Britain compensate for damages caused by the Birkenhead-built Confederate States Ship *Alabama*, and that the Irish American Fenian Raids into Canada would permanently harm British and American trade relations. However, Bell encouraged three of the Kingsleys to come to Colorado as though they were members of the Mountain Base Investment Fund designed to promote Colorado Springs to British settlers.

To interweave all of these voices, contexts, and international dynamics, I employ a flexible narrative voice rather than attempt to maintain throughout an academic prose which cannot honor the story. While factual accuracy is essential to writing lucidly about the Kingsleys, my lyrical and exploratory writing style establishes the emotional truth for each person, a tone which, as a shaping force, reveals the meaning of the facts and establishes an accurate picture of each of the historical actors.

The reader can trust that I have thought and felt everything on this topic of the Kingsleys in Colorado that can be thought and felt for it.

I begin this narrative in Colorado Springs not with the romantic views of Rose Kingsley in her book *South by West* (1874), nor with the impressions of Charles Kingsley in his letters home, or William A. Bell's observations in his *New Tracks in North America* (1869), or even with Blackmore's business facts—but with Maurice Kingsley. As a man seeking his fortune but unsure, 24 year-old Maurice (for the American audience, pronounced Morris) witnessed the early development of Colorado Springs when opening mail in the Fountain Colony office. Enough facts of Maurice's life are known to warrant my deductive projections of his thoughts before contrasting him with the over-zealous financier, Blackmore, and the promoter, Bell—then addressing the engaging travel observations of his sister, Rose.

Of all the Kingsleys, and of all their English business associates attracted to this region, Maurice was the least likely to know what he wanted, and yet, because of his uncertainty, he was the most likely to know the allure of adventure, the dark side of investment, and the impossibility of community.

May 2021
Tamara M. Teale
Colorado Springs, Colorado.

INTRODUCTION

Maurice Kingsley and the making of Colorado Springs

On October 27, 1871, the track-laying crews of the Denver & Río Grande Railway Company had finished ballasting the rails up to the Colorado Springs depot, a new log cabin situated just north of the confluence of Fountain Creek with Monument Creek, which ran below a mesa on which the Colorado Springs townsite was being platted. A ceremonial train—filled mostly with Denver City newspaper men, potential investors, prominent citizens, and survey engineers—shortly followed with fanfare. Maurice Kingsley, from Eversley, Hampshire, England, was present trackside when the train arrived signaling the completion of the "First Division" of the Denver & Río Grande. For Maurice, the past few months had been exciting as the Americans around him affected him with their keen anticipation. Born in 1847, the early stages of railway development in England were over by the time Maurice was fifteen, but not in Colorado where there was everything to be done.

The thrill of watching the first train pull up to the depot reminded him how much he wanted to fit into this new post-Civil War America. Now the railway was here, a diminutive narrow gauge engine and cars inspired by Wales. Added to Maurice's hopes was a feeling of relief: His sister Rose Georgina Kingsley would arrive in Denver City in three days aboard the Kansas Pacific, and if the D&RG—as it was popularly known—had not been completed to the Springs, he would have had to make the seventy-mile trek northward to meet her in a supply wagon or in a bone-jolting stagecoach, which was not a daily service.

Maurice knew his sister had no choice in the timing of her arrival. In September, she had crossed the Atlantic with her father's friend and colleague, John Saul Howson, the Dean of Chester Cathedral, who was scheduled to attend a convention of the Episcopal Church in Baltimore as an invited Church of England representative. After a brief tour of upstate New York, and the Canadian shore of Lake Ontario, a churchman would escort Rose cross country to the Denver City depot. Maurice planned to give Rose a regular Colorado welcome; they would dine at Charpiot's, a fashionable and exclusive European-style restaurant near the depot, and several of Maurice's town planning colleagues would show Rose around Denver—a rather brief tour since the population of Colorado's capital was barely 5,000 at the 1870 Census. After resting two days, including Sunday, October 31, Maurice and Rose would take the new Denver & Río Grande Railway to Colorado Springs, accompanied by Maurice's aforementioned colleagues. A delightful surprise was planned for Rose's arrival at the log cabin station—which Maurice must not reveal beforehand. He would have to refrain from any hint that General William Jackson Palmer and the absolutely charming Mrs. Palmer were to appear suddenly in the dining room.

With two days to go before this excursion to Denver, Maurice tried to appear dignified to the laboring men who worked at the Springs's depot. Aside from the fresh excitement of the new rail service, his business day would be a desk-bound one in the Fountain Colony office, the real estate sales division of the Colorado Springs Company, an office which for the past several weeks had consisted of not much more than a small table in a hastily-built wooden shanty with a tent erected over the doorway. Of course, the mail coming down from the north would now be brought by the D&RG—weather permitting— but passenger stagecoaches would still make connections southward to the farming village of Fountain, and on to Pueblo and the South Pueblo Colony site, then the infant Walsenburg, the old dusty trading village of Trinidad, then slowly over the Ratón Pass to the Maxwell Land Grant headquarters at Cimarrón, New Mexico Territory, before crossing another pass to Don Fernándo de Taos, and on to Santa Fé. Mail would still come by coach from points to the southeast, that is, from La Junta on the Arkansas River heading westward and via Pueblo, north along Fountain Creek. Maurice grabbed a bite to eat at the station, and just as he had done for the first time the day before, slung the mail bag over his shoulder—still light enough to carry— and hiked upslope to the Fountain Colony office near the town center, mid-block between the two main streets of the four that had been marked with a horse-drawn plow.

Outside the shanty-tent office, Maurice paused to survey the scene. It was rather amazing how Americans could carve a town out of the raw prairie. Across Huerfano Street and over on Tejon was the stagecoach and freighting office and six other buildings which formed a front against the wind and snow. No one should expect sidewalks, or curbs, let alone macadam paved streets for quite some time. About three city blocks away to the north, across the dry prairie soil and clumps of long-stemmed bunchgrass, a work crew was constructing a building frame from boards delivered by rail just the day before. The sound of the hammer blows reached Maurice at off-beat intervals.

Looking eastward, he observed the survey crew guiding the plow turning a furrow to mark where a street would be, to be named Weber or Kiowa. Maurice ruminated about Kiowa Street, how Americans often name things after what they have destroyed. Of course, there was no Arapaho street though one of the most prominent summits visible from town, about six miles south of Pike's Peak, was Cheyenne Mountain at 9,565 feet. Near the top of one of the double summits of Cheyenne was a 500-foot tall crag shaped like a buffalo horn, its tip curving toward heaven, tinted pink in the afternoon light, in a way only a geologist could explain, but which only an artist could convey. The long sides of the mountain were robed in ponderosa and blue spruce in thousand-foot folds to the canyon at the base where shadows formed early in the afternoon. The somber canyon indicated a sublime place of contemplation. Maurice regretted that he'd had no time to explore South Cheyenne Cañon let alone the north one since railroad and town business was so pressing. His gaze ranged back to the pyramid-shaped summit with a scooped out face, Pike's Peak, the Sun Mountain as he'd heard Ute people call it, the first point to catch the dawn light. Maurice studied the fabled mass. At its zenith of over 14,000 feet, the mountain seemed to inspire action—and to preside over failure.

Maurice looked back to the raw town in front of him, to the streets being surveyed and staked out at perfect right angles. Construction of Colorado Springs was going forward so rapidly that in a few days, by the time he returned from Denver with his sister, nearly six more city blocks could be furrowed out by the Colorado Springs Company. The men responsible for supervising the platting and surveying were General Robert Cameron, a distinguished war veteran like Palmer, and Edwin S. Nettleton, known familiarly as E. S. Each street would be as neatly planned as the first that had broken the dry russet and dun-colored soil.

The street on which Maurice's office-shanty stood—actually the shanty and tent belonged to Palmer's English business partner William A. Bell—was named Huerfano Street for a creek in Las Animas County. The street had indeed been an orphan but was no longer so since Goodrich & True's general merchandise building was up nearby. Two blocks away to the west on Cascade Avenue was the 2-story Foote's Hall with a downstairs pharmacy. The hall was becoming the central gathering place for anyone living in the area—excluding the band of Ute Indians who were more comfortable camping on the edge of Colorado City, about three miles to the west.

From where Maurice stood, there was so much open space, especially to the south and southeast edges of the mesa top that everyone seemed extremely vulnerable, liable to blow away in the next wind storm. But the confidence of Americans was massive, Maurice thought, like mountains. Just two blocks away to the southeast on Nevada Avenue at the northeast corner of a street named Cucharras—never mind that no one knew how to spell in Spanish—the house going up was a fine English-style town home, built to the specifications of the far-sighted Alexander Cameron Hunt, the fourth governor of Colorado Territory from April 1867 to June 1869, for the purpose of highlighting the skill of Colorado workmen. The huffing and puffing of the northbound train reached Maurice, as it pulled out of the station taking away the curiosity seekers and businessmen. The sound of wagons hauling building material up from the railroad station slowed and stopped—perhaps, for a mid-afternoon break. He opened the flap of the tent, glanced one more time at the perfect pyramid-shaped mountain everyone seemed to worship, went inside, and set down the mail bag. He put the kettle on to boil, and opened a few envelopes.

With this simple action of opening the mail asking about colony lots, Maurice became the mediator between the creators of the Fountain Colony at Colorado Springs and the people who wanted to live in it. The story—or, rather the web of narratives—of English people and East Coast in-migrants in Colorado Springs indeed begins at Maurice Kingsley's desk in October 1871. Most of the mail he read was addressed to The Fountain Colony at Colorado Springs, though it was also advertised as "Villa la Font" in a prospectus widely distributed on the American East Coast and in England. The mail to the Fountain Colony Company was from people wanting to know about the progress of the platting of the downtown area called Colorado Springs, and wishing to buy a Fountain Colony lot around the perimeter of the town.

The letters of inquiry needed only simple answers from Maurice since the prices advertised by the Colony were easily explained; for example, a lot for a business building on Tejon or Cascade was $100, and a residential home lot east or north of downtown was $50. If people wanted to see the place before committing—a reasonable request—they could now be in Denver within four days from New York, and take the D&RG to the Springs, however, they would have to arrange to camp out overnight because the hotel wouldn't be finished for two months—in January 1872. In addition, the dozen small cabins going up a block away were being snapped up by Chicagoans fleeing the Great Fire of two weeks earlier. Maurice didn't want the lack of hotels to discourage new arrivals. He could recommend that interested visitors book rooms at Lydia Teachout's country inn seven miles to the north near Pulpit Rock, then take a coach into town.

When at his office desk, Maurice often felt like sitting back as a detached observer. People of financial means always wrote elegantly on fine textured paper asking about the weather and the healthy climate. Maurice was quick to respond with the company-required information while adding a sentence about the landscape. Of course, every immigration office worker like himself from Illinois to Nebraska and Kansas had written the same thing: Our destination is the most wonderful in the country. Then, there were letters on paper of lesser quality asking about work opportunities, from people who had little money but wanted to advance themselves as well-paid wage labor before moving up the scale. Maurice understood them. He had tried to do something similar in Argentina. Fleeting thoughts of his failure there in 1869 returned to him. He attempted to brush off the discomfort like the prairie dust, thankful that back in England, Bell had told him and his father about his Colorado business connections.

For Maurice, thinking of the origin of Colorado Springs was like a review of his life in the past few months. On June 26, 1871, the Colorado Springs Company had been incorporated as a joint stock company for the sole purpose of constructing the town. Then, just over a month later, the ceremonial first stake was driven at the corner of Cascade and Pike's Peak avenues to signify the birth of the town. Maurice had actually been named Assistant Treasurer of the Colorado Springs Company (Fisher, 199; Brayer, v. 2: 82-3), and yet, he felt like an outsider. He could afford neither stocks nor bonds, and, other than wages, had only the cash his father had given him. As a strange compensation, Maurice often felt that he had insider knowledge. People on the East Coast who wanted second homes, or prospective settlers from Britain who wrote asking about small farm acreages, had no idea how the town came into being nor how the numerous ancillary corporations Palmer and his associates created to facilitate the financing of the railway-to-town projects actually operated.

In the planning of his dream city, General Palmer hadn't overlooked anything. A year earlier, he and his associates had incorporated the Mountain Base Railway in addition to the South Park Railway and the Western Colorado Railway as corporations that would secure every possible right of way against competition. All were organized between February and May of 1870—before the name Denver & Río Grande Railway Company was decided upon in late October 1870. Everyone knew well the aridity of the climate, and to bring water to the mesa top, Palmer and his team organized the El Paso Canal Company on July 8, 1871 (Brayer, v. 2: 29-33, 299). Maurice had witnessed many of these developments since he had arrived at the Summit Lake stagecoach stop in October 1870 to take up his first assignment for Bell and Palmer at their small ranch near there.

Maurice knew that Palmer's business ethics had been nurtured in Philadelphia, where his work with J. Edgar Thomson of the Pennsylvania Railway assured his place in a network of business contacts in which everyone had a reputation for integrity. In fact, the Colorado Construction Company had been incorporated in Philadelphia in October 1870, as was the North & South Construction Company, for the purpose of ensuring that Palmer's dream railway south from Denver would be constructed with high standards. However, in the past year alone, several of these corporations had to be repurposed on short notice, as fast as the entrepreneurs could think. This pace and constant need to adjust railway and land development strategy—depending on economic fluctuations and perceived competition—was the post-Civil War reality. Maurice compared this situation with the England his father and grandfather knew in which social and technological change had been managed by the men selected by the working aristocracy in concert with the county-town leaders.

For over a hundred years, British financial institutions had advocated parliamentary legislation which would fine-tune joint stock partnerships with limited liability in order to encourage overseas investment and strengthen government stability, all the while nurturing national feeling symbolized by a myth-like monarchy. Knowing of the London financial district's efforts, the war veteran Palmer's railway financing plan was based on logically attracting the most judicious English financiers who were wary—and weary—of brash American entrepreneurs. Maurice believed that Palmer's adoption of William A. Bell as a business partner was based on sound evidence, but he wondered to what extent the American was simply fascinated by Bell's combination of conservative Victorian values and upper-class manners. And yet, Maurice saw Palmer's wisdom. In a faster and faster-paced American West there was little to encourage a notion of community except those Philadelphian cultural values Palmer saw reflected in Bell's type of Englishness.

Responding to the Fountain Colony mail, Maurice often paused. When he thought of his sister's arrival in two days, he knew she would assist him with the mail, all these letters on fine paper from people expressing a desire for the health and happiness, opportunity and community that had eluded them everywhere. Even in nearby Kansas, a relatively new state in the Union, George Grant was planning an English colony called Victoria, near Fort Hays, as though to welcome people escaping from England's intractable social problems, which, in fact, his father, the Reverend Charles Kingsley of Eversley, had addressed throughout his career: The health problems and death caused by improper disposal of untreated sewage, the lack of clean drinking water, and the persistence of foul-smelling, sooty air. Nervously, Maurice got up from his desk, pushed the tent flap aside and stepped out. He inhaled the air of the 6,200 foot elevation.

Glancing westward to the gentle slopes beneath Pike's Peak, Maurice reflected that Colorado Springs was not the first deliberately planned community in the Pike's Peak region. Twelve years earlier, in August 1859, Colorado City had sprung up to the west along Fountain Creek. George Bute and Anthony Bott, and about eight other men, knew that miners and freighters traveling the Ute Pass trail to Cripple Creek and into South Park needed a supply hub at the east base of the Peak. After a first attempt six months previously had failed, they went to the Denver City law office of Richard E. Whitsett to incorporate Colorado City (*Gazette*, Aug. 1, 1926; p. 2). Then, two of the ten who could ride the fastest—Rufus Cable and Melancthon S. Beach—galloped the seventy miles from Denver and staked out Colorado City from just above Camp Creek and along Fountain Creek almost to Monument Creek, not far from the future Colorado Springs townsite then undreamed of.

When contemplating the first ill-planned attempt to found Colorado City (that of early 1859), Maurice felt it illustrated the hurry that Americans were in. When Bute and Bott initially scouted out the Fountain Creek site, they called it El Dorado City—in the boastful American fashion—but were insufficiently organized to prove a title. By going to a law office to establish legal rights to the land along Fountain Creek, Bott and Bute with their cofounders, Beach and Cable, and Dr. James Garvin and Charles W. Persall both of Lawrence, Kansas, among others, were able to create on this second attempt the only community in a 150-mile stretch between Denver City and the cabin and adobe cluster called El Pueblo. Colorado City was made the El Paso County seat in early 1861, at the formation of Colorado Territory, and was briefly the capitol, though Governor Gilpin never moved his offices there. And in less than ten years, the gold madness ended and the town had declined from 360 full-time residents. In 1871, Colorado City was surviving as a stagecoach stop, and a lonely but livable village with small farms and ranches along the Fountain. The few streets of houses and businesses were languishing with only eighty people—depending on what time of year a count was taken. When Anthony Bott, and his few colleagues remaining from the original founders, heard that a new town and a railway would be constructed just to the east, they were elated. Prosperity was once again within reach. For Palmer, the fact that Colorado City was a few miles off was enough for him to welcome the manpower that it offered, while knowing that he had a substantial townsite on which to form his dream city *without* saloons and frontier riffraff.

As for Maurice Kingsley, he liked the regular townsfolk of the frontier settlement. He understood how the town had been thrown together with little money and no single dynamic personality to lead the way. As an Englishman with some college background, Maurice was expected to be discerning and abstemious, and he had been so in England, but he soon dropped most pretenses, and rode to the county town on Fountain Colony business whenever possible—perhaps popping into one of the saloons—until at some point he knew his sense of adventure had a limit. Even so, he realized that sensible and hard-working people had settled the area. He had met many of them, including all the British. Of course, any Irish Americans with good intentions were welcomed to reside, if only they could be like Scotsman Walter Galloway on his homestead a mile north of Colorado City near a canyon where General Palmer's English-style mansion was under construction. William Dixon was an English farm laborer living near Colorado City, as was John Carmen who responded to the 1870 census-taker about his stock dealing business, his wife from New York and their two children. Henry Templeton was as fine a Scottish settler as one could ask for; a courageous, early immigrant, his flour mill flourished about ten miles northeast of town on a winding road that ran through a gap between pine-covered sandstone bluffs.

While they were already settled, and were not interested in purchasing a town lot in the Fountain Colony, their persistence in the Pike's Peak region would set an example for the new Springs settlement. Even the two brothers from New Mexico, Juan and José who had either Anglicized their surname from Martínez to Martin— or let the census-taker do that—had been welcomed as all-around farm workers and stock tenders. The Cardonen family living nearby consisted of patient and reliable people Maurice recognized from either Cimarrón on the Lucien Maxwell Land Grant, or the village of Costilla at the 37-degree boundary with New Mexico Territory.

Comparing the settlers of 1859 and the newer breed of educated town planners, Maurice dwelled on his own path to Colorado with some embarrassment. As a young man, he sensed his lack of scholastic ability at Wellington College, not far from his father's Eversley Rectory. And when it was obvious at the end of one year at Cambridge University that he didn't fit in, his father agreed to let him try the Royal Agriculture College at Cirencester in October 1867. It was there that he heard about Argentina. Somewhat impatiently, he left the R.A.C. in June 1868 without a diploma (Williams, K., e-mail to author), and sailed in early July to Buenos Aires, arriving there in mid-August. Maurice cast about the Río de La Plata and the Entre Ríos province for an opportunity, but he didn't like working so hard on someone else's *estancia*. He wrote home with a sense of resignation, addressing the Canon of Chester Cathedral as "Dear old Dad" and begging him for money. A few months later, Maurice decided Argentina was not for him either (Covey-Crump, n. pag.), and made the five-week long voyage back to England to his parents' home at the St. Mary's Rectory, Eversley, arriving in late February 1870, while his father was home from his duties at Chester.

In early March, Maurice had been unwinding at the rectory for a week or two, when William A. Bell visited Eversley before another transatlantic crossing and on to Colorado. Maurice would have noticed how happy his father was to see Bell who had been a Cambridge University student from 1860 to early 1867, exactly during the years of Kingsley's tenure as a crown-appointed professor of Modern History from 1860 to 1869. Though Bell's future wife, Cara, would write decades later that Bell met Kingsley at "a place where they were both trying to cure themselves of stammering" (Bell, Cara, *Diary*, 16), it's unlikely that Bell would have met Kingsley in 1856 at Dr. James Hunt's office if Bell was only fifteen and attending the Ipswich School. What is known for certain is that when at Cambridge, Bell had been an ardent follower of Charles Kingsley's history lectures. By the time Bell stopped by the Eversley Rectory in early 1870, he was himself firmly in the Cambridge University network. For the remainder of his own life, Bell saw in Kingsley all that was good about being an Anglican representative of Victorian Britain—a topic I will detail in due course.

Maurice compared his own dismal performance with the upward trajectory of William Abraham Bell, who had gone from one strength to another, earning a First Class pass in the Natural Sciences Tripos exam in 1863, a B.A. degree in 1864, and the *Medicinae Baccalaureus*, or M.B. in 1867. After Cambridge, Bell's life really took off when he decided to completely forget further medical studies. He found a position on the Kansas Pacific survey expedition seeking a route to the Pacific from the end-of-track encampment, Phil Sheridan, Kansas— another of the topics I will develop further. Significantly, Bell wrote an adventure and travel account titled *New Tracks in North America*, and was elected to the Royal Geographical Society on June 8, 1868, a full year before the book appeared in May 1869 as a two-volume set in England. When the university awarded Bell a Master of Arts Degree in that same year, 1869, his entry into an élite network of personal and professional contacts was assured.

At the time Bell made a social call to the Kingsleys in Eversley, he had solid business connections in Colorado, while Maurice had just arrived from Argentina and was in extreme discomfort from his failure there. Bell was intelligently charming and a model when speaking of business. He suggested to Maurice that Western America was an opportunity for him to get a foothold in civil engineering, particularly with sound leadership from the best types of Americans. In a brief flash of insight, Maurice felt it, too, that his one year at Cirencester would finally pay off. He expressed interest, yet he did not sail with Bell. Evidence suggests that Maurice lingered at Eversley another week or two after Bell's departure. In sum, Maurice was in his father's rectory home only four weeks after returning from Argentina before sailing for New York. His eagerness to leave suggests he was fleeing his father, but not sailing with Bell indicates his reluctance to take up a promising opportunity; later evidence suggests that emotional stress haunted Maurice.

When Maurice embarked from Liverpool for the East Coast of America, he may have been more exhausted than he realized, nor did he completely know his frame of mind. With the latest of steamships, a person needed only eleven days—twelve at the most—to cross the Atlantic to New York or Philadelphia, then after two or three days of rest, plus another four by rail, one could be in Denver in less than three weeks. No one needed five *months* to reach Colorado—but Maurice seems to have taken them. He wrote to no one of how he had looked around and lingered, and yet, based on the known details of lone enterprising male immigrants and on the extant facts of the American context, one can make a reasonable projection about Maurice's movements. When the United States of America abounded with opportunities, it made sense for a charming person like Maurice to spend a week in New York, then, say, a week or more in Philadelphia, ten days in Pittsburgh, and more in each of Ohio's major cities plus frontier boom towns like St. Louis, Kansas City, and Omaha. A two week stay in Chicago would be advisable given its major commercial status, and railway service to Cheyenne, Wyoming Territory, from which access to the regional capital Denver was easy. Like thousands of other young men, Maurice might have worked odd jobs among the railway towns just to get by in case the money from his father ran out. Maurice didn't want to rush to the Sheridan, Kansas, field office to meet General Palmer where definite though regimented employment awaited him.

An anxious Reverend Canon Kingsley went about his parish business in Eversley, but at the end of five weeks after hearing nothing from Maurice, not even a telegram or cablegram—assuming the transatlantic system was working—Kingsley addressed a letter to General Palmer at the Sheridan station just east of the Colorado Territory line, dated May 24, 1870, carefully preserved in the collection of Tutt Library at Colorado College. Kingsley's letter conveys the worry of a conscientious father when he asks Palmer if Maurice has gone to New Mexico Territory with William A. Bell to follow up on investments in the Maxwell Land Grant or on a railway route scouting expedition. Kingsley assures the General that Maurice is a "very able and daring young man, and worthy of all confidence. . ." and that £100 had been telegraphed to an agreed-upon location. When Maurice finally met up with General Palmer, and heard about the letter, Maurice would have been embarrassed. He couldn't see why his father would write to Palmer and not to him in care of Palmer. He didn't want such a distinguished war veteran to think of him as a remittance man—even if he was.

One's curiosity about the perceptions of uncertain Englishmen (and the marvelous efficiency of the postal service) increases when we consider that Kingsley's May 24 letter went from Eversley, Hampshire, to the Sheridan station in about sixteen days, by which time, however, the Kansas Pacific Railway was no longer using the location as a base but had pushed further west to Kit Carson, Colorado Territory, where the KP would launch a massive building program to reach Denver (which had dropped the "City" by then). Maurice had an idea

13

of Palmer's work schedule as Superintendent of Construction responsible for ensuring that the KP would reach the Comanche Crossing finish line by mid-August. He could assume that Palmer didn't have time to notice the whereabouts of a twenty-three year old Englishman; and Maurice may have purposefully delayed his arrival in Denver until late August, at which time Palmer's work for the Kansas Pacific was complete, and he'd be in a new office devoting full-time to his own enterprise, the Denver & Río Grande. When Maurice arrived at Palmer's office, he could have excused his father's nervous disposition, explaining that he, Maurice, had needed time to evaluate the current situation of American business development in each of the major cities—as thousands of Englishmen had done before him.

Until further evidence comes to light (perhaps a letter in an archive), the only proof that Maurice had met up with Palmer in Denver is a late-October 1870 letter that Palmer posted to his fiancée, Mary "Queen" Mellen just before he departed for their November wedding in Flushing, New York. The letter to Queen states that William A. Bell will meet a "Mr. M. Kingsley" at Lydia Teachout's countryside hotel to take charge of their cattle and sheep operation, one of Bell's and Palmer's earliest enterprises (Fisher, 194), possibly created to supply their railway employees. Will Palmer communicated everything to his fiancée, and if he had mentioned Maurice Kingsley before, he would never have referred to Maurice as "Mr." in such a formal tone a second time.

After meeting up with Bell at Teachout's, Maurice managed the small ranch called "Monument Farms" not far from Summit Lake—later renamed Palmer Lake—and awaited the turn of business events that would result in the founding of Colorado Springs. Ranching was honorable work, guaranteed employment when the approach of winter meant a slowdown in agriculture and most aspects of railway work and mining. Within two months on the job, by January 1871, it was within Maurice's ability to see that for Bell and Palmer everything was moving forward splendidly. Even so, given that Maurice was employed by them for only about two years, one wonders if Maurice decided there was no future for him in the Springs. A scholar should make projections on historical figures' actions based on only well-researched facts and an intelligent interpretation of human motivations, as I intend to do throughout this study.

When the shipment of iron rails arrived, and construction began south of Denver, the pace of development accelerated. The route had already been surveyed and leveled out, then rails laid and ballasted; small depots were under construction at selected whistle-stops along the 75-mile route. And suddenly a year had passed, and Maurice felt he was in an office job with greater responsibility. He should be satisfied with an official title as Assistant Treasurer and to find himself in such company as the city planners Cameron and Nettleton, and William E. Pabor, Secretary of the Colorado Springs Company, who was also a promotional writer, and William Proctor Mellen, the Treasurer, and also Palmer's father-in-law. In addition, the professional atmosphere was maintained by highly-regarded railway route engineers Colonel William H. Greenwood, Colonel James P. Mersereau, and Captain Howard Schuyler.

After contemplating the recent past, Maurice glanced at his desk intending to open mail, but his thoughts shifted to the role of William Blackmore, another of the English connections in this railway enterprise. If Palmer needed an Englishman to make his Colorado Springs and Fountain Colony recognized—beyond William A. Bell's high reputation—it was William Henry Blackmore, a tradesman's son, an assertive, independent financier with international social and business ties, an intermediary who would not attach himself to just any American enterprise. Born in 1827, nine years before Palmer and almost fourteen before Bell, Blackmore moved from his childhood home in Salisbury to Liverpool where trade with the United States of America was booming. He earned a law degree and became a partner in a very active firm handling maritime merchant cases—the type of legal work which enabled him to find out which corporations were making money and by what financial strategies.

As described by scholar Anthony Hamber, Blackmore began building contacts, most notably with the private merchant banking firm of Brown, Shipley and Company, one of whose partners, William

Brown, he met through their mutual interest in historic artifacts and archaeology (Hamber, 35-9). In 1869, Blackmore had his eyes on the Sangre de Cristo Land Grant that straddled the 37-degree parallel separating Colorado and New Mexico territories, and was aware of any plans to route a railway near the land. He'd heard a rumor about General Palmer's plans for a north-south line, and if an extension could be built over La Veta Pass into the southeastern quadrant of the San Luís Valley, Blackmore could make a fortune, as Colorado archivist and historian Herbert Brayer has shown (Brayer, v. 2: 41-4). While 21st-century readers have the advantage of looking back, onlookers like Maurice Kingsley may have felt that the international investment intrigues created by insiders like Blackmore and Bell, with Palmer, in the geographic space called Colorado, could be figured out only with impressive detective skills.

In November 1870, while Maurice was less than a few weeks into his cattle-tending assignment at Summit Lake, Palmer left Denver on the Union Pacific for his wedding to Queen Mellen, as touched on earlier, after which they immediately departed for England on a combination honeymoon and railroad business tour (Brayer, v. 2: 35). Once in London, Mrs. Palmer was the leisured tourist while the General and Bell met with Blackmore. In January, they all sailed over to Amsterdam to continue their money-hunting adventure, which reached a preliminary conclusion with Wertheim & Gompertz (Brayer, v. 2: 48-51), a complex tale which I will shortly review.

Then, Palmer took a step suggested by Bell in Amsterdam that after the meetings with the Dutch financiers, he and his bride return to England to meet Canon and Mrs. Kingsley at Eversley's St. Mary's Rectory, which they did in early February—another topic I will take up in due course. Even while visiting Eversley, Palmer would make the commute to Blackmore's London office for business meetings to resolve potential misunderstandings about the distribution of shares in the Denver & Río Grande Railway Company, as well as to respond to any feasibility questions from Wertheim & Gompertz and to telegraph his colleagues in Denver and in Philadelphia. By the time the Palmers returned to the United States and arrived at the

Philadelphia office of the D&RG, Palmer's associates had exchanged telegrams with London and Amsterdam that the deal was finalized with the Dutch, leaving only minor matters to settle (Brayer, v. 2: 45-52). The Denver & Río Grande construction would go forward, thus precipitating the construction of Colorado Springs and the rapid expansion of Pueblo.

Maurice resumed opening mail but got up from his desk on hearing the approach of his friend and local news source Ike Yoho as he rode up to the Fountain Colony office shanty. In practice, Maurice never talked about money or D&RG business, but had learned of many developments from Ike, who was a very American type from Missouri, a hunter of his own age employed by Blackmore as his local property manager, a kind of steward or land agent. Maurice was content that he'd made a friend who on occasion would sit with him around the shanty's heated stove, a boon companion willing to tell what he knew of Blackmore's business affairs when Maurice felt overwhelmed at the complexity of the financial arrangements that were making Colorado take shape. Later, Rose would describe Ike's thrilling appearance, noting his "Mexican saddle with broad stirrup straps and high peak in front; and the glorious mountains" of Pike's Peak and Cameron Cone "as background" as Ike paused outside the shanty office to chat with her brother (*South by West*, 58-9). Most times, Ike's conversations with Maurice may have been brief, and he would gallop away on Blackmore's business, to the El Paso County land office in Colorado City.

As Ike vanished over the edge of the mesa, the workmen continued construction next door to the shanty-tent; the Denver & Río Grande Railway Company was building a proper office for Palmer and Bell and the D&RG management who would move down from Denver when practicable. The fact that Wertheim & Gompertz had purchased the first mortgage bonds to fund the First Division of the D&RG to the Springs, and that they would finance the second from the Springs to Pueblo (and its 700 residents) and the new South Pueblo Colony, was quite a paradox since Palmer had long been convinced that only if English money came to the Pike's Peak region would English culture follow to soften the harsh lives of the settlers while offering the upper-middle class style demanded by well-to-do travelers, health-seekers, and seasonal residents.

Maurice believed that English settlers would always come to Colorado regardless of the advertising. He recalled what he'd heard from his father about the Palmers' five day visit in early February. The Canon of Chester Cathedral was in awe of Mrs. Palmer. And Queen Palmer admired Canon Kingsley. In fact, Mrs. Palmer loved England. How fateful, Maurice thought, knowing how much he simply wanted to escape it, or—dare he say it?—put as much distance as possible between himself and his father. And this was the excruciating paradox: His father was a truly good and kind man. But Canon Kingsley had been too much in the forefront of current events, had taken too prominent a position in that informal group of Church of England ministers who—like their counterparts in politics, science, medicine, industry, and the military—were shaping the mid-19th-century consciousness.

Maurice Kingsley shrunk with embarrassment from time to time, never knowing when his father's combative personality would show itself. His dispute with Dr. John Henry Newman turned out badly for the Reverend Kingsley when Newman's book of 1864 *Apologia pro Vita Sua* (originally serialized) recounting his transformation from Anglican to Catholic was written in such a compelling style. And then, his father's comments about the United States during the Civil War were simply grotesque. Luckily, one of Canon Kingsley's best qualities was his ability to realize when he was wrong. What didn't change was the Canon's inordinate adoration of his sons, a type of overbearing attention detrimental to both. If such palpable but never discussed tension between a father and son was typical in Britain, it was no wonder so many young men left England with the intention of never going back.

The routine of responding to the mail troubled Maurice; he couldn't return to the desk. He'd light a lamp later and stay up to get it done in time for the next day's train to Denver. He left the tent and stood outside in anticipation of the stagecoach coming up from the south. Maurice's spirits lifted when he looked far away as though surveying the landscape afresh—the variety of topography from steep mountain valleys with their pockets of aspen groves, to the yellowing cottonwoods thick along the banks of Fountain Creek near the confluence with Shook's Run and Bear Creek, then the rolling prairie southward over a ridge swallowed by the earth curving away. Oh, the serene beauty of it!

But then a certain type of booster American, a newspaperman named Bowles, had called Colorado the "Switzerland of America." In effect, the land was already being turned into a commodity, not allowed to be uniquely itself. Feeling disgusted, Maurice tried to rally himself; he felt sure that William J. Palmer never stood around judging everything.

Of course, everyone had something for sale. Maurice had enough material to write numerous short stories. There was nothing like that ride over Ratón Pass on Maxwell Land Grant business for Palmer, and the occasion he met a rascally old-timer, Dick Wootten, who ran the toll booth at the summit of the pass. During fine weather, you felt you were at the top of the world, with the Spanish Peaks to the west-northwest, and the Ratóns stretching away to Trinchera Pass in the east. But in the town-building reality in front of him, there was no time for rumination, let alone fiction writing. Labor conditions were so favorable in Colorado that there was the temptation to move on to other employment every few months. Maurice sought stability, and yet he suspected that he, too, would be unable to focus on one particular type of employment due to his own unfortunate kind of idealism. Not surprisingly, he was in awe of his Uncle George, Dr. Kingsley, a world traveler and the Earl of Dunraven's expedition physician, who just happened to be northwest of Denver with the 4th Earl on an autumn sojourn to buy land in an alpine valley, called Estes Park, all the while both George and Dunraven had wives and children, and the Earl an estate in west Ireland, and a seat in the House of Lords, and yet they felt called away into the world.

The immediate reality for Maurice was that over on Tejon Street men were busy around Swisher and Holmes's Livery Stable in preparation for the arrival of the Barlow & Sanderson coach. Maurice let his gaze travel to the southern edge of the mesa, the direction from which the stage would approach, shielding his face from the low-leaning sun. Just then four men on horseback emerged over the southern edge of the mesa, less than a mile to the south where the town streets had not yet been staked out. Based on the classic riding style of one of the men, Maurice was sure it was Captain Howard Schuyler coming back at the end of the day from inspecting the track laying work done on the route to Pueblo, especially where an alkali flat meant unstable ground.

The riders do not approach the Springs town center but keep toward the mesa edge, then pause to let their horses breathe. The men nod in conversation as though discussing which of the two restaurants is best, the new one on Cascade Avenue near Matt France's office or the incomparable log cabin railway station. Howard Schuyler seems to lead the discussion. Not afraid of long hours, he is the up-and-coming type the older veterans prefer. On the Kansas Pacific, Schuyler had impressed Palmer and the managing engineer, Colonel Greenwood, with his fearless route engineering work. And Palmer had mentioned Schuyler by name and cited his work many times in his official *Report of Surveys Across the Continent*, when he was under no obligation to do so. For some reason, Schuyler had a reputation for being a ladies' man, but Maurice didn't believe a bit of it. Probably, the captain was perceived as an American aristocrat since he was a descendent of one of the Schuylers of old New York and New Amsterdam, and was a unique combination of action and education. Howard could enjoy brief leisure time, but he was too business-like to be a friend, too serious to sit by a fire and enjoy the idle chat that Maurice liked. The riders recommenced movement, turned westward, and rode out of sight downslope toward the depot restaurant.

Seeing Schuyler and his survey crew sent Maurice into further musing on how his father had let it be broadcast that he was a railway engineer—another embarrassment! He felt he could be a survey engineer one day, but on the D&RG all the top positions were taken, besides he could never travel miles in any weather checking the composition of the soil and the presence of running water. And he was not cut out for the hard labor of staking the route, nor could he—heaven forbid!—actually work with the ground crew in the leveling and the grading of the surface, the laying and ballasting of the rails. Maurice was sure his current position would yield greater opportunities.

He watched several men inspecting the building next to Swisher and Holmes's stable where a hardware store would move in, as well as a much-needed boot and shoe shop. A block away over on Cascade Avenue, work was winding up at Field and Hill's store near Dr. Gatchell's office, and on Huerfano Street's south side, men were unloading furniture at Foote's Hall. Maurice thought of his sister, how the energetic and enterprising Rose Georgina was needed to put Foote's Hall to its best use for the purpose of creating community feeling.

Rose knew how to engage in conversation without their father's rough patches; and although no one could get along with everyone all of the time, Maurice felt sure his sister could persuade the roughest ditch digger on the irrigation project to attend tea service and a music concert. Maurice had a vision of her well-chosen words calming the nerves of the most disappointed settler. Rose had become a careful observer and accomplished botanist from assisting groups of people in plant identification as they walked along the seashore near Chester with Canon Kingsley; moreover, her recent nurse's training in Chester, while her father was fulfilling his position as a canon residentiary, gave her medical knowledge and sharpened her decision-making skills. Rose's role as her father's assistant and amanuensis had taken shape due to their mother's inability to endure the hardships of foreign travel, but largely through Rose's own native energy.

Just a few blocks away, the last furrow for the day had been cut through the wild grass to indicate the location of a new street. There, the prairie recommenced stretching far and away. Maurice mused that his sister was on the passenger train somewhere in Kansas at this point, her notebook in hand with a good supply of pens and ink and drawing pencils—and hiking boots. Suddenly, he realized one of

Rose's reasons for coming to Colorado: to see Queen Palmer again. The two women had gotten along so well during the Palmers' brief visit at Eversley.

The arrival of the stagecoach ended Maurice's unquiet meditation. The sight and sound of the harried rotation of the coach wheels came to him like a portent from a gypsy fortune teller though Maurice could not have named the object of his foreboding. He looked toward the livery stable where the personnel awaiting the coach watched the horses kick up the gritty soil. The driver who held the reins like a modern Jehu—as he was often called—guided the team with dexterity. Eager to see the postal service bag, though a much lighter one coming up from the south, Maurice crossed the street and picked up his pace along a furrow that marked where one day would be a sidewalk. Leaning into the breeze, he braced for a late October chill as gale-blown gray-white clouds streamed like a veil from the summit of Pike's Peak.

At the stage stop, all the talk was about the economic future that the Denver & Río Grande narrow gauge train service would bring. Not everyone had a place in such a future. Maurice gazed at the stage driver in puzzled wonderment.

The creation of Colorado before the Kingsleys arrive

In December 1868, William J. Palmer had finished writing *Report of Surveys Across the Continent*, his summary of the Kansas Pacific expeditions across the Southwest territories to the Pacific Coast, which he handed to the President of the Kansas Pacific, John D. Perry, who then submitted it to Congress in January 1869 as persuasion for additional financing. By that time, Palmer had crossed the Pike's Peak region again on a route reconnaissance ride thinking that the Kansas Pacific would eventually build south of Denver. He had become familiar with the major wagon trails to the Pike's Peak region, usually accompanied by his personal assistant, Captain William F. Colton. Palmer had no doubt that respectable middle-class travelers could be persuaded to give up Saratoga Springs, New York, for a Colorado health-resort. He had the engineering knowledge to build a safe railway to the Manitou medicinal springs, where the dry air and the aromatic scent of the pine-covered hills would provide a healing atmosphere.

However, by March 1869, when Congress ordered the Union Pacific Eastern Division to terminate in Denver (and officially changed its name to Kansas Pacific, though the line had almost always been referred to as the KP), Palmer had already experienced the disadvantages of seeking taxpayer money. He would have noted at least two situations that spoke against congressional control. Most noticeable was that since its launch in St. Louis, construction on the U.P.E.D. (KP) had been stopped several times for months at various places in Kansas, when, in comparison, the Union Pacific was fully funded and had reached Cheyenne, Wyoming, in November 1867, and was under construction westward toward its anticipated May 1869 rendezvous with the Central Pacific at Promontory Summit, Utah (to complete the transcontinental line). Despite such proof that taxpayer money could make a railway happen, a nearly one-year hiatus for the U.P.E.D. (KP) had been necessary—for unclear or unstated reasons. And though the Board of Directors used that time wisely for the survey expeditions to the Pacific Coast, such long breaks were discouraging for the governing officers, who in addition to Perry, included Charles B. Lamborn and Palmer himself. For Palmer, the halts in construction were a warning about his own fate.

The second and most troubling development for Palmer with regard to congressional financing (and the best reason to seek private funding for his own project) was the severe criticism that two government-hired railway experts leveled at the U.P.E.D. (KP) engineering staff. One might wonder what criticism, since it's impossible to imagine General William J. Palmer's construction supervision ever being criticized. However, not long after the U.P.E.D. (KP) reached Fort Hays (after the completion of the survey expeditions and Palmer's resumption as Superintendent of Construction), the House of Representatives ordered the Department of the Interior to inspect the use of taxpayer money. The Interior Department hired two Special Pacific Railroad Commissioners, Major G. K. Warren and his assistant, Mr. J. Blickensderfer, Jr., to complete the inspection.

As the official evaluation turned out, the two commissioners found fault with every aspect of the U.P.E.D. (KP) route from the surveying work, the track-laying and ballasting of the Kansas Pacific line from Lawrence, Kansas, to Fort Hays. Their criticism was made public in a "Letter" from the Secretary of the Interior to the House of Representatives, dated January 6, 1869, and recorded for posterity in Volume 7 of the House of Representatives *Executive Documents* (recently scanned for internet archives). Warren and Blickensderfer,

Jr., wrote the Interior Department report submitted to the House of Representatives stating that though they did not yet know all the reasons for the choice of route, "it is yet apparent that the road is not located so as to take full advantage of the capabilities of the country, and as a through line its commercial value is less than it should have been." Moreover, Warren and Blickensderfer state, "If the road is to be extended to form a line reaching to the settlements at the base of the mountains [Denver], or to be part of a through line to the Pacific, much of its location requires a thorough overhauling, and parts of it probably must be abandoned" (U.S. *House, Ex. Doc.* No. 25; 4-5). In effect, the report was a complete dismissal of the work done. The criticism was so derogatory that Palmer, when thinking of his own railway project, didn't want his engineering executives Mersereau, Greenwood, and Schuyler to suffer through the analysis carried out by the congressionally-appointed railway inspectors.

Even though Palmer may not have been accountable for the surveying work from Salina to Fort Hays, Kansas, and might not have been Superintendent of Construction until after the line reached Sheridan, this kind of criticism from congressional inspectors would have stung Palmer personally since he was a KP stockholder and on the Board of Directors and the Executive Committee. In short, with congressional money came congressional owners and overseers and nay-sayers who would attempt to diminish his dream. Palmer wanted creative control. He wanted to make his own mistakes and not have to live with those of others (if indeed anyone on the Kansas Pacific was at fault). In context, members of Congress were much occupied during that session with decisions other than railway finance, as demonstrated by just a few of the topics listed in the Volume 7 mentioned. The Johnson-Clarendon convention was being crafted to settle Canadian boundary disputes dating from before the Civil War, a convention which in April (1869) Senator Charles Sumner would argue did not hold the British sufficiently accountable for their negligence in allowing the CSS *Alabama* to harass American merchant vessels. Congress was also busy with setting a fair rate for postage stamps and telegraph service, and determining contracts to carry the overland mail.

Without the constraint of Congress controlling the use of taxpayers' money to build the Denver & Río Grande, Palmer and his team would be free to find the right methods to finance the construction of the railway, to create towns along the route, and where villages already existed—like Labran (Florence), Cañon City, Pueblo and Trinidad, Ratón, Las Vegas, and Santa Fé—to engage the minds of those desiring railway transport. In essence, Palmer and his crack team of experts planned a massive privately-funded, for-profit railway system as part of a town development strategy cornering all trade along the route. For Palmer, failure was inconceivable because of his egalitarian values and the purity of his motives. Musing on his Kansas Pacific experience, he wrote to his fiancée, Queen, early in 1870, that his "dream" for the Denver & Río Grande was "not all of a new mode of making money" but to have every employee "no matter how low his rank" feel they were a part of the enterprise and that the railway company was not "some stranger soulless corporation" (Brayer, v. 2: 18-9).

In addition to building his own railway south to Trinidad and over the Ratón Mountains to Albuquerque (which the KP survey expedition had thoroughly scouted) Palmer's plan was to extend the line along the Río Bravo del Norte (as the Río Grande was called) through Belén, Socorro, and Valverde, and link all the military posts from Fort Craig, past San Diego (Hatch) to Fort Selden, Fort Fillmore and Mesilla to Fort Bliss and El Paso, Texas—even to Mexico City. In fact, in the First Annual Report of the Board of Directors of the Denver & Río Grande, dated April 1873, Palmer included a map of Colorado and New Mexico territories with the rail lines drawn to El Paso, as though the route were done and not a dream. The future was clear to him and his closest business friends, Colonel Robert H. Lamborn and his brother Charles B. Lamborn (Secretary of the Kansas Pacific), Alexander C. Hunt, William Sharpless Jackson and William P. Mellen. For them, every topographical factor indicated that a new town at Colorado Springs, and one five miles to the west called Manitou Springs would fulfill the Easterner's desire for a health resort town for upper middle-class citizens not wishing to travel to Europe.

Mere decades earlier, the fate of the region did not matter to anyone. The United States government barely had a concept of the land to the west of the Mississippi River. The area that would become Colorado was still the domain of the Ute people, the Arapaho and the Cheyenne, the Kiowa and the Apache who followed the buffalo, deer, and antelope, and tended small villages. In 1806, Lt. Zebulon Montgomery Pike was the first to write about the peak later named for him, though he did not climb to the summit. However, he got an idea as to what sort of hold the Mexico government had on its province north of the 32-degree of latitude; he was arrested near the future site of Alamosa, Colorado, and escorted to Chihuahua for questioning.

Hints at the possibility of settlement would be frequently published by pen-wielding men passing through central Colorado in the Arkansas Valley watershed. By the time Fitz Hugh Ludlow's book, *The Heart of the Continent*, was published in 1870, every railway man knew that what the writing traveler from New York City predicted was true: "When Colorado becomes a populous State, the springs of the Fontaine qui Bouille"—as Fountain Creek was then called—"will constitute its spa" (Ludlow, 178; Fisher, 3). The concept of a "spa" meant that the New Yorker was thinking like a European.

But even Ludlow and his companions learned of the landscape seventy miles south of Denver from other sources. Connecticut native and journalist Rufus Sage—not to be confused with Rufus Cable—traveled in the 1840s when nothing had a name but Lieutenant Pike's mountain and Colonel Stephen H. Long's peak. Leaving Fort Lancaster (modern Ft. Lupton) in 1844, Sage's party traveled through the future sites of Denver and Colorado City—a 100 mile stretch of wide-open nothing—and first wrote of what Cable and Beach would name in 1859 "The Garden of the Gods." Sage related that a "wall of coarse, red granite (quite friable and constantly abrading) towers to a varied height of from fifty to three hundred feet." Sage continued, "This wall is formed of immense strata, planted vertically. . . . This mural tier is isolated, and occupies its prairie site in silent majesty, as if to guard the approaches to the stupendous monuments of nature's handiwork . . ." (Sage, 1854, 171). Sage and his companions had traveled south from Fort Lancaster for the same motivation as the few early adventurers, namely to reach the collection of adobe huts or *jacales* called El Pueblo, while hunting along the way. For nearly twenty years, from 1846 on, Rufus Sage's travel accounts would run to several editions with minor revisions indicated by changes in title such as *Scenes in the Rocky Mountains*, or *Wild Scenes in Kansas and Nebraska*, or *Rocky Mountain Life*. Rufus Sage was earlier than even George Frederick Augustus Ruxton, the first pen-brandishing Englishman on the scene.

From Ruxton's account, his route to the eastern base of Pike's Peak was from the south, from Santa Fé. Heading northward, Ruxton and his companions first stopped at the village of Don Fernándo de Taos then continuing, paused to admire the Spanish Peaks near Trinidad, still inside the Mexico national boundary. Ruxton and company also took in the view of the Greenhorn Mountains near El Pueblo before traveling northward to the base of Zebulon Pike's mountain and the well-known defile out of which Fountain Creek flows. George Ruxton never mentions the obvious red rock formations just a mile to the north, suggesting that he had not actually visited much of what he described. Even at the time of publication, many of Ruxton's readers suspected that he had bluffed his way through the scenes which have insufficient detail to make them authoritative, as numerous editions of Ruxton's work reveal, particularly *Ruxton of the Rockies* edited by LeRoy R. Hafen and colleagues.

To further fuel the suspicion that Ruxton was not an eye witness for much of what he relates, it seems impossible that he didn't know of Rufus Sage's description of the "friable" red rock geological wonders which trappers and traders sought out as they traveled between Fort St. Vrain, Fort Lancaster, and El Pueblo. In addition, Ruxton assured the reader that he camped along Fountain Creek—the *Fontaine qui Bouille*—for more than a month during the winter of 1846 to 1847 because he and his fellow adventurers found plenty of deer collecting there, when, in fact, sunset is so early in the afternoon that such a location (at the east base of the Peak) is too dark and cold for winter camping, or the presence of deer, even if Ruxton conflated the upper Arkansas River with Fountain Creek. Tragically, the following year, on his return to the United States, Ruxton died of epidemic dysentery, age 28, in St. Louis, Missouri, on the edge of this new American empire, perhaps without ushering *Adventures in Mexico and the Rocky Mountains* through the final stages of publication. *Life in the Far West* was serialized in *Blackwood's* Magazine from July to November 1848, concluding with a memoir of Ruxton.

In the 1870s, the accounts written by Pike, and Stephen H. Long's expedition physician Edwin James, and by Sage and Ruxton may have seemed too recent to be considered history and yet too outdated to be relevant to the new men with their railways and telegraph systems. But everyone had to take William Gilpin into account, a transitional figure from the Age of Exploration to the post-Civil War era of nation building. In April 1860, Gilpin seemed to be firmly settled in his most recent home, Independence, Missouri, and had just finished a publishable draft of *The Central Gold Region* subtitled "The Grain, Pastoral, and Gold Regions of North America" and sent it to his St. Louis publisher for simultaneous publication in the spiritual center of America, namely, Philadelphia.

Gilpin's book was a kind of manifesto. His tone in writing about the need for a Pacific Railway system and the heroism required to build it across magnificent terrain approached the lofty language of religion. Gilpin extolled every river, mountain pass, *cordillera*, the climate, winds, rains, the basins and mesas, the high altitude mountain parks within the western Kansas Territory (to become Colorado Territory). He expounded on the "extent and characteristics of the hemp-growing region of the United States" and the new gold fields of America centered at the base of the mountain range where the South Platte River forms, visible across the prairie from Denver City. Colonel Gilpin had the authority to write of such a geographic space as the Front Range of the Rockies and the new Southwest; he had earned his rank during the war with Mexico as a diplomat and soldier traversing the Arkansas River Valley and conversing with the people in the Río Grande basin both indigenous tribes and Hispano settlers.

Born in Wilmington, Delaware, in 1813 (not 1815 as one source claims), Gilpin was a much younger brother of Henry Gilpin, an attorney with Washington, D.C., connections, who was interviewed in 1831 by French visitors Tocqueville and Beaumont. William Gilpin attended school in England briefly, while his parents were there on business. Later, in Philadelphia, after several days of interviews and oral exams, Gilpin was admitted to the University of Pennsylvania, where he graduated in 1833. William grew into this birthright of East Coast and British social and political circles before striking out on his own, maintaining family ties in England, but heading westward with the flow of exploration. As narrated by biographer Thomas Karnes, Gilpin had become well known through his association with John C. Frémont, his petitioning Washington on behalf of Oregon, and his diplomatic negotiations with the Navajo people. Gilpin was lauded as a man of "unimpeachable integrity" (Karnes, 253-4).

In the same year as the publication of *The Central Gold Region*, 1860, the looming threat of armed national conflict precipitated the making of Kansas Territory into a State of the Union, which immediately led to the formation of Colorado Territory out of western Kansas, part of Nebraska and Utah, and taking one degree of latitude away from New Mexico Territory, thus setting the southern Colorado boundary at the 37-degree latitude (contiguous with Oklahoma). By March 1861, Gilpin was so well-known that President Lincoln followed everyone's suggestion to appoint him the first territorial governor. At the time, Gilpin showed that he understood and appreciated the Hispano and *nuevoméxicano* settlers of Conejos and Costilla Counties, now in Colorado, from the earliest days when the 1848 Treaty of Guadalupe Hidalgo ceded the area to the United States. Gilpin had the text of his first legislative session translated into Spanish, spelling his own name as Guillermo Guilpin (Karnes, 266).

No matter who was appointed governor, the creation of a civil society would have been daunting. Gilpin had first to appoint supportive administrative advisors, then divide the Territory into seventeen counties, select officials, commission accurate topographical maps, organize an official census, and call for an immediate two-month legislative session. Gilpin had wisely noticed the efforts of miners and ranchers to govern themselves; he confirmed their informal laws and practices, and oversaw a smooth transition to a regular territorial court system (Karnes, 263). For much of what Gilpin needed to do, no funding was coming from Washington, D.C. He was almost fifty years old at the time. A man with less experience would have been overwhelmed.

Almost from his first day as Governor, Gilpin had to assess the strength of a group of Confederate States sympathizers in the Denver area and the potential that their presence would encourage an invasion (Karnes, 270-3). At first, a supposed Confederate attempt to take the Black Hawk and Golden City gold mines (west of Denver) for the South seemed preposterous, but, based on credible intelligence reports, Gilpin determined that the threat was real. Then, in villages and mining camps across the territory, Gilpin opened recruiting offices; volunteers came from all over the territory to form several companies, a regiment, if possible. Within weeks, the American garrison in Santa Fé had intelligence that New Mexico was in great danger of being invaded from the southern territory line adjoining the State of Texas.

By the autumn of 1861, Gilpin could no longer wait for official funding from Washington, D.C., to enable him to provision the troops he was sending to New Mexico's assistance. Hesitating further was dangerous. Without official sanction, Gilpin issued drafts to businesses supplying his troops, a move for which he would be replaced the following year (Karnes, 286), even though it turned out that Gilpin was right, as Karnes shows. As it happened, Colonel Henry Sibley's Confederate troops from Texas invaded New Mexico from Fort Bliss, defeated Colonel E. R. S. Canby at Valverde on the Río Grande, and took Albuquerque and Santa Fé, which had been deserted by Federal troops. Gilpin's commanders marched their men overnight through southern Colorado to reach Fort Union, New Mexico, and wisely did not rest there long, but continued on past the important commercial hub of Las Vegas. The First Colorado Volunteers with one company of New Mexico volunteers, and a company of informally organized men, met the Confederate troops at Glorieta Pass, and over two days in late March 1862, convincingly defeated them (Karnes, 284-5).

Though forced to resign for the unauthorized supply drafts, William Gilpin's reputation for foresight and quick action grew as he stayed on in Denver to promote Colorado. Confederate States veterans would be welcomed as settlers and businessmen with the intention of healing the wounds of the civil conflict. When General Palmer opened his Denver office in mid-1870, he would meet Gilpin and welcome any advice from the elder statesman of Colorado. Gilpin would play a role in 1870 seeking funding for the D&RG—as I will show in due course.

As is well known, the pace of development of Colorado Territory increased after the end of the American Civil War. Given that trappers and traders, and then military troops knew the path from Denver to Colorado City and beyond, one would think that the future townsite of Colorado Springs had been pointed out to Palmer—but not so. In August 1859, as noted earlier, men including Anthony Bott, Melancthon S. Beach, and Rufus Cable, selected the Fountain Creek location for Colorado City as the one most likely to interest gold miners traveling Ute Pass, and perceived any other location as too far away, including the distant mesa top—if they noticed it at all. Contrary to what seems obvious in the 21st-century (with Interstate 25), the north-south route through the Pike's Peak region to Santa Fé was actually not a main line of travel. Only fur traders and proto-business men like Rufus Sage knew of it as they made their way from the Fort Lupton area to El Pueblo, the only substantial settlement, other than Bent's Fort on the Arkansas and small ranches along the Huerfano River, to continue on to Taos and connect with the trail to Santa Fé. Similarly, the Smoky Hill Trail was used by travelers and Midwestern in-migrants en route from Kansas to Denver, while traders approaching the Pike's Peak region from southwestern Kansas came along the Arkansas River to Bent's Fort to arrive in El Pueblo.

In addition, the "historic" Santa Fé Trail never approached El Pueblo but took a curving path from Bent's Fort on the Arkansas through southeastern Colorado to Trinidad; travelers on the Santa Fé Trail could take the "Cimarrón cutoff" from the site of Dodge City,

Kansas, to Cimarrón, New Mexico Territory, and thence to Santa Fé. Stagecoach service from Denver to Colorado City and Pueblo, linking Trinidad, Cimarrón and Santa Fé wasn't feasible for Barlow, Sanderson & Company until about 1866 (Noel, 27), and even then, as the coach traveled along Monument Creek, on its approach to Pulpit Rock it would head toward Camp Creek and enter Colorado City about three miles from the future Springs townsite mesa.

Since early 1867, Palmer and a few of his Kansas Pacific railway associates had ridden several times across western Kansas and the plains of eastern Colorado Territory. They made essential exploratory digressions, detours off the well-traveled routes or side trips along the route from western Kansas to the Arkansas River, as survey engineers seeking the safest route, not thinking of locating sites for new towns. They analyzed every landscape feature on the plains—the arroyos and gullies and the washouts—as obstacles to railway routes. On one of these route reconnaissance digressions (for the Kansas Pacific Railway Company) in the autumn of 1869, Bell, Palmer, and Palmer's assistant, Captain Colton, with visitor, Nathan Meeker, took a closer look around Colorado City. A few miles further west, where the *Fontaine qui Bouille* tumbled over a waterfall into a narrow but flat valley, Palmer glanced around the ponderosa and blue spruce covered slopes, the piñón pines and yucca rooted in the rocky hills on the north side. His eyes rested on the clear-running Fountain Creek. So did Bell's.

In another canyon two miles northward, similar conditions existed; a restful, secluded valley with blue spruce, Douglas fir, and mountain mahogany secure in the thin rough soil along the lovely waters of Camp Creek beneath pale sandstone cliffs. William J. Palmer determined he would make his permanent home in the area, though he had no thought of how to do so, as explained by Herbert Brayer, the first Colorado State Archivist to extensively organize the records left by Palmer in the D&RG archives. Luckily, Meeker was looking for agricultural land and chose the site for Greeley north of Denver (Brayer, v. 2: 79). Palmer and his associates were disappointed at hearing of Meeker's choice, however, the idea of his own townsite hadn't crystallized; as construction supervisor for the Kansas Pacific Railway,

Palmer was still thinking only of advancing the KP.

Before long, while Palmer worked in his railway car office on a siding, he received mail from Colton which contained a topographical sketch (or so Palmer himself later claimed) reminding Palmer of the flat mesa of several thousand acres about two-hundred feet above Monument Creek near its confluence with Fountain Creek, and bounded on the east side by Shook's Run. Though the townsite was referred to as a mesa, Rose Kingsley would describe it as a "prairie rise" (*South by West*, 59) because there were no steep sides as the word mesa suggests in the American southwest. Colton's sketch made all the elements of railway and town synthesize in Palmer's mind, with a keen sense of the inevitable which he had missed earlier. This flat area rising high above two flowing streams was a perfect viewing platform for the range of mountain peaks to the west—especially Pike's Peak.

As soon as Congress decided that the KP should be completed to Denver only, the massive construction push was on to finish the track to the Comanche Crossing site on August 15, 1870, as noted earlier, where the outward bound track-laying crew would meet up with Palmer's west-bound crew for the completion ceremony, the location now called Strasburg. Even before the tracks were finished, fine brick buildings began springing up in downtown Denver. In addition to the 5,000 residents there, the official U.S. census for 1870 shows another 2,000 souls scattered throughout Arapahoe County (before Denver County existed), and another 2,400 throughout Jefferson County. For a resourceful and inventive Civil War veteran, already on the lookout for his own rail-to-city project, this mushroom success of Denver was proof that his own dream plan would be right.

Like a military strategist, Palmer had studied how much land south of Denver along the South Platte, Plum Creek, and Monument Creek was in the public domain. He had telegraphed Alexander C. Hunt in the Denver surveying office to begin purchasing the railway right-of-way from Denver to the Colorado Springs townsite, in an effort to discourage the competition that already threatened his project. There were a few homesteaders with small holdings on the mesa, perhaps from Colorado City or an earlier settlement attempted by other intrepid individuals from Lawrence, Kansas (Ormes, 21-2), but they didn't mind being paid a great deal to relocate when the El Paso County Clerk, Irving Howbert, inspired them to do so with his description of the new town that would be under construction according to a visionary leader's plan. Soon, Palmer and his associates formed the townsite development company and several ancillary corporations mentioned earlier in this study, and acquired over 9,000 acres (Brayer, v. 2: 20-1).

From Maurice Kingsley's experience in the weeks after the July ceremony of driving the first stake for the Springs and before his Fountain Colony desk job demanded his attention, we can imagine an ordinary day for him, perhaps a warm September afternoon. Maurice had gotten a letter from Rose saying that she would cross the Atlantic with the Dean of Chester Cathedral and his family for a church conference in Baltimore, and probably would not be in Denver until the end of October, a relief to Maurice since there had been a long delay in the shipment of English and Belgian-made iron rails. Putting the letter away, he wondered what his sister would make of the town. Taking a leisurely pace, Maurice rode to Colorado City on El Paso County business, then, rather than hasten back to the construction site, he rode along the northern bank of Fountain Creek, half-way back to the Springs, dismounted, and left his horse in the shade of one of the giant narrow-leaf cottonwoods so refreshingly ubiquitous along western streams.

Maurice tossed a few stones into the clear rushing water, musing on recent developments and how it happened that after all the expectations focused on London financiers, Will Palmer had been turned down—while Queen Palmer was strolling around Hyde Park—and it was the Dutch who came through. Suddenly, Maurice was startled out of his reverie by light laughter coming from the opposite bank, as though someone were reading his mind. He glanced to where the coyote willows grew thickly at the base of a majestic cottonwood, and recognized two young Utes partially hidden there. They had encamped near the town during Maurice's first winter. The Englishman gestured shyly and his greeting was returned. Uncomfortable suddenly, Maurice returned slowly to his horse, trying to recall if he'd ever heard Native people chuckle before. He felt haunted for several days. Evidently, he wasn't the only person wondering where the money was coming from for the iron rails to the new whiteman's town. Maurice couldn't brush off terrible thoughts about the Sand Creek Massacre in 1864—how some of the murderous soldiers involved had been considered heroes at the Glorieta Pass fight with the Confederates in 1862.

As time passed, Maurice's curiosity about the source of the railway money dominated, and he would find out more about it, while men in far away offices organized the reservations to which the Ute people would be confined.

The Kingsleys in their Victorian context before Colorado

There were perfectly good reasons why General William J. Palmer wanted British financing for the Denver & Río Grande Railway: Britain was probably the richest nation in the world and knew everything there was to know about railway development. The British—that is, specifically the English—were the first to address the adverse effects of the intrusive locomotive engines; city-to-city trunk and branch lines reshaped the countryside with embankments and cuttings, often carving through or near the parklands of various estates, bringing noise to quiet farmlands. Social historian F. M. L. Thompson shows that the land owners "who had been well schooled in the benefits which canals brought to their estates" through the broadening of the market for goods while lowering costs, quickly understood the advantages of railways, even though, as early as 1825, many landed aristocrats found it "natural to be apprehensive of the 'snorting steed'" of, for example, the proposed Leeds and Hull railway (Thompson, 257, 261). Scholars and historians Geoffrey Best and Richard Altick relate the railways' effects on the population in general from the disrupted agricultural landscape to the destruction of housing in established neighborhoods and the havoc of redesigning cityscapes for major rail stations. With great ease, isolated country people could now visit the city, and urban people escape to the countryside or seacoast (Best, 32-5, 68-72; Altick, 75-8).

By the autumn of 1855, when Will Palmer's family sent him to Wales to study the latest mining technology and ore transport, most any apprehension about railways had been settled in Europe. With no need to defend railway systems as such, Palmer, who already had a year or two experience in the informal college of the Hempfield Railway in Pennsylvania (Fisher, 24-5; Lohse, 12-25), could concentrate on his study of efficient ore extraction. Not quite 19 years old, Palmer soon made a brief tour of London during which his youthful admiration of English culture and society permanently lodged in his consciousness, later symbolized in the 1880s and 1890s by his rental of the medieval Ightham Mote manor near Seven Oaks and the Loseley Park estate near Guildford.

As young as Palmer was, he observed the energy of the British men whose careers advanced rapidly, while people in general were developing a sense of national interest which turned their minds to solving the seemingly intractable problems of lack of housing and sanitation, the effects of industrialization on the working class, the persistence of child labor, and careless regard for workers' health and safety—conditions which British social historians have examined. Palmer's progressive Quaker values of firm integrity and sincere goodwill were already formed, and he was ready to absorb anything of quality from the reign of Victoria. That same autumn of 1855 Palmer could not resist crossing the English Channel to visit Paris, a captivating city which inspired him later to have a railway development pamphlet translated into French and published in Paris before he opened an office there (Brayer, v. 2: 175-6). But it was England that called Palmer into his future.

While in Wales and England, Will Palmer may have heard of the Reverend Charles Kingsley whose novel *Alton Locke, Tailor and Poet* (1850) was a popular success. A narrative of ideas, *Alton Locke*, was Kingsley's response to the politically conservative tendencies in the Church of England and demonstrated his support of the demands set forth in the People's Charter. The Chartists, as the activists were known, called for fairness in electoral district representation, an expansion of voting rights without the property qualification, and a government response to workers' conditions. *Alton Locke* became at least as popular as Benjamin Disraeli's *Sybil, or the Two Nations* (1845) which narrativized the contrasting lives of the rich and the poor in an industrial town, before the author became more politically conservative and a Prime Minister. Most likely, the young Delaware-born Quaker, Palmer, was familiar with Charles Dickens's *David Copperfield* (1850), and the sentimental and wholesome portraits which Dickens produced in *A Christmas Carol* (1843), the work which would have delighted seven year-old Palmer and helped his parents forget Dickens's splenetic *American Notes* (1842), which the novelist produced after his first American tour. The interwoven social, cultural, and governmental struggles of Britain, conveyed through narrative literature, engaged Palmer's mind as he shaped his maturing vision.

With our 21st-century advantage of hindsight, we might think that Will Palmer was simply impressionable, and as an adult, easily swayed; however, like many, he looked to England for a firm stand for humanitarian values. Little did he know that even before the opening shots of the American Civil War at Fort Sumter, most of the governing class in Westminster and the economic class in London's financial district feared Washington, D.C., as a rival for international power and influence.

From the first news of the outbreak of war, all of Britain was on edge. The conflict between North and South—between two world views—reached into the depths of every Englishman's most intimate beliefs. While British opinion was by no means unified, by mid-1862, it was obvious that England and the United States of America were separated by entrenched habits that came to the surface during times of crisis. Less than a year into the war, at the beginning of this most painful national conflict, a number of high-placed British public figures had decided they could not support Washington in its struggle. The British betrayal shocked pro-Union Americans: Britain had completely forgotten its own laws abolishing the slave trade and slavery in 1807 and 1833.

The American Ambassador to Great Britain, Charles Francis Adams, knew that people disagreed on the key issues, and he understood

subtle matters such as the extent to which British people were emotionally invested in the outcome of the war. He was publicly judicious
while privately recording his experience that "The great body of the
aristocracy and the wealthy commercial classes are anxious to see the
United States go to pieces" (Cook, 18). Regarding this kind of emotional investment, Charles Kingsley shared the confused views of his
fellow Britons. Numerous recent historians including Adrian Cook,
Murney Gerlach, and Renata Eley Long have focused their study on
transatlantic relations to such an extent that we now have at least as
much and perhaps more understanding of the evolution of British
opinion of the American Civil War as anyone living at the time.

Historian of transatlantic relations, Murney Gerlach cites William Gladstone's notorious Newcastle speech of October 7, 1862,
while he was Chancellor of the Exchequer, in which he stated that
"We may have our own opinions about slavery; we may be for or
against the South; but there is no doubt that Jefferson Davis and other
leaders of the South have made an army; they are making, it appears, a
navy; and they have made, what is more difficult than either, they have
made a nation" (Gerlach, 31, n. 10; Long, 111). Gladstone restated
this position in a private letter "that Jeff. Davis & his comrades have
made a nation" but, Gerlach found that within two years, Gladstone
changed his mind and "supported the North near the end of the war
. . ." Gladstone believed the American Civil War was, in Gerlach's
words, "an issue of self-determination, not slavery which he certainly
opposed, and his pro-Southern statements were completely consistent with his calls for Greek and Italian nationalistic movements and
independence" (Gerlach, 6).

Gladstone later apologized for his "incredible grossness" in con-
fusing the issues at stake in the Civil War, and yet one suspects that
Gladstone's view in 1862 was his real opinion (Gerlach, 6-7, 9, 31).
Analyzing the same historical data, Adrian Cook found that Glad-
stone's statement that the Civil War was about Southern self-de-
termination was an incendiary comment "touching off rumors that
Great Britain would recognize the Confederacy." Prime Minister
Palmerston worsened transatlantic relations when he suggested that

the United States no longer legally existed, and that the Civil War was "merely two belligerents" not a rebel state against a legitimate government (Cook, 18-9). How British statesmen could have been confused about the principles underlying the American Civil War are beyond the scope of this study except to show that the Reverend Kingsley expressed opinions as strongly against Washington, D.C., as "middle-class and 'university' Liberals" had in favor, among them John Stuart Mill, John Bright, and Richard Cobden.

To what degree the Reverend Charles Kingsley perceived the importance of his own opinion on the American Civil War could in part be explained by his appointment to a prominent national position in 1860, Regius Professor of Modern History at Cambridge University, a title conferred by a reigning monarch, in this case Victoria, after consulting Prime Minister Palmerston (Searby, 253), and, one assumes, the Prince Consort, Albert, as Chancellor of Cambridge. Kingsley was required to give about twelve lectures each year (many later collected and published in book form).

At first, Kingsley confined his views of the United States of America to private letters, but even then his ideas are fully formed. Writing to Sir Charles Bunbury, a friend through their shared interest in botany, Kingsley is definite that the United States is an upstart nation that must learn its place in the world and is better broken up. In *The Dust of Combat*, a biography of Kingsley, literary historian Robert Bernard Martin gives a fuller quotation of Kingsley's December 31, 1861, letter to Bunbury than did Kingsley's widow Frances in 1877 (when she held back her husband's more embarrassing statements). "As for the American question" Kingsley wrote:

> . . . I have thought of nothing else for sometime; for I cannot see how I can be professor of past Modern History without the most careful study of the history which is enacting itself around me. But I can come to no conclusion save that to which all England seems to have come—that the war will be a gain to us, that the rapacity & insolence of these [American] men

must be sternly checked; that they must be taught
that there are not only laws, but courtesies, to be
observed between all nations who pretend to a voice
in the parliament of the world... So strongly do I feel
the importance of this crisis that I mean to give as my
public lectures next October term, the History of the
United States. (Martin, *Dust*, 257; Kingsley, Frances,
v. 2: 134)

Mentioning the "insolence" of Americans, the reader understands
that Kingsley was not referring to the Confederate States, but the
national government.

The Reverend Kingsley must have felt confident in writing to
Bunbury so frankly, for, in another letter to him the following year,
Kingsley expressed anger with President Lincoln's Emancipation
Proclamation of September 22, 1862, the first of Lincoln's two mani-
festos (though Martin does not specify the date of the letter itself).
Kingsley stated that the only accomplishment of an emancipation
proclamation would be to encourage further rebellion, "then a dozen
gentlemen will ride in, against 500 negroes, shoot, & hang till they
are tired; & the little sparks of rebellion will be crushed out—and the
condition of the slave worsened for 50 years" (Martin, *Dust*, 257-8).
Clearly, Kingsley, like Gladstone, did not understand the American
social, economic, and global political context.

While Gladstone's and Palmerston's words of 1862 had the color
of authority, and when stated publicly could cost lives, Charles Kingsley's views, as expressed in the above letter, remained private. And yet
he had more to say that would become public. In addition to writing
to Bunbury, while preparing for his Cambridge University lectures on
American history, Kingsley wrote to friend Thomas Hughes, author of
the influential *Tom Brown's Schooldays*, "that the Northerns [sic] had
exaggerated the case against the South infamously." Using language
that was in agreement with the opinions of other English, Kingsley
also stated that the American Civil War was "a blessing for the whole
world breaking up an insolent & aggressive republic of rogues, & a

blessing to the poor niggers, because the South once seceded, will be amenable to the public opinion of England; & also will, from very fear, be forced to treat its niggers better" (Martin, *Dust*, 258). Kingsley's derogatory statements must be quoted here in order to show how misinformed his views were and how great his reversal of opinion by 1871.

Within the year, Kingsley's early mentor, Frederick Denison Maurice—for whom he named his son—took up the cause of the Northern states. A few years later, Kingsley would lose Hughes's friendship, though not over the United States but what was called the "Eyre controversy." In July 1866, the "Jamaica Committee" was formed for the purpose of considering evidence to try Jamaica Governor Edward John Eyre for the murder of hundreds of African-Jamaicans during their October 1865 rebellion, which began in Morant Bay as a protest march of free men and former slaves who had lived in poverty for over thirty years. Governor Eyre had declared martial law and ordered villages burned. Moreover, he ordered arrested and executed two men who had the right to speak freely and live: a black Baptist preacher and a mulatto member of the Jamaican House of Assembly (Semmel, 38-41, 45-7). Thomas Hughes was on the committee to prosecute Eyre, while Charles Kingsley sat on a committee in defense of Eyre. In August of that same year, 1866, Kingsley spoke at a banquet in Southampton organized to welcome Eyre back to England—an occasion he would quickly regret.

At the Southampton banquet, Kingsley may have spoken unwittingly, not knowing all the facts of the bloody suppression of the protesters. When news of Kingsley's banquet presentation reached the British public, many felt that he had betrayed his reputation as a writer of socially relevant novels and as a Regius Professor. However, scholar Bernard Semmel believed that Kingsley had always been racially prejudiced and at Southampton had "acted in accordance with deep and long-held principles" that only certain men were fit to participate in government (Semmel, 99), suggesting that for Kingsley, Eyre was evidently fit and the mulatto and black Jamaicans were not.

Looking at Kingsley's personal context, one might believe that he supported Eyre because he was still bitter over the loss of the West Indies property that his mother had expected to inherit from her father, Nathan Lucas. Robert Bernard Martin recounts that when Kingsley was asked for a subscription to help former slaves, he refused, stating that "The negro has had all I ever possessed; for emancipation ruined me . . . I am no slave-holder at heart. But I have paid my share of the great bill, in Barbados & Demerara, with a vengeance: & don't see myself called on to pay other men's!" (Martin, *Dust*, 258). By "emancipation," Kingsley must have meant Britain's Slavery Abolition Act of 1833; however, Semmel suggests that a drop in the price of Jamaican sugar may have ruined some plantation owners, not emancipation (Semmel, 33).

The fact that Charles Kingsley's elderly mother, Mary Lucas Kingsley, was very much alive in the 1860s, and living with the family at the Eversley Rectory (Kingsley, Frances, v. 2: 318), makes one think that her daily presence was a nagging reminder to Kingsley of the loss of his grandfather Lucas's modest fortune in the West Indies and British Guiana. Writer and scholar Una Pope-Hennessy suggests that to some degree a financial insult suffered in the Kingsley family's recent past could have affected the Reverend's judgment of Lincoln's emancipation of African Americans in slavery. In a chapter on the enigma of Kingsley's personality, she describes his contradictory public behavior; one moment, he could "read patiently to a blind parishioner" and yet, express satisfaction at the legalized violence against oppressed people in Borneo and China (Pope-Hennessy, 2-3), in addition to Jamaica.

We may never know exactly what motive forces were behind Kingsley's mean remarks about President Abraham Lincoln nor the insults he leveled at African American people; however, within three years, Kingsley would reverse his viewpoint from a doubter of America to one of recognizing its economic and moral power (and, one hopes, welcoming progressive change in the West Indies). Kingsley's transformation coincided with the British government's reversal of their view of Washington, D.C., to such an extent that General and Mrs. Palmer would be the welcomed guests at the Kingsleys' Eversley,

Hampshire, home in February 1871, and that Canon Kingsley would return the visit to the Palmers in Colorado Springs in July 1874.

When ascertaining who the Kingsley was that Colorado would be receiving in 1874, we cannot stop our inquiry with Pope-Hennessy's notion that he was simply an enigma. Kingsley's life is relatively well documented, and we can make reasonable projections about why he wrote as he did. Looking into Kingsley's early life shows how his father, also named Charles, was a product of the late Georgian and Regency periods. Charles, senior, became a Church of England minister less as a spiritual path and more as a way to help stabilize the British government during times of stress which included abolition of the slave trade and a protracted war with France.

The senior Kingsley was born in 1782 at Turnford, Hertfordshire (north of London on the road to Cambridge). For the sake of easy reference, I refer to the Rector of Chelsea as the "senior" Kingsley, and his son, the Rector of Eversley as the "junior" Charles Kingsley, since the post-nominal letters Sr. and Jr. seem not to have been used in that era. Charles Kingsley, senior, started out as a traditional student at Brasenose College, Oxford, and had expected to inherit money from his father (also named Charles, the Esquire of Battramsley). From the impending loss of the discretionary income, Charles, senior, decided to train for the ministry and entered Trinity Hall, Cambridge, a very non-traditional student.

After graduation from Sidney Sussex College, nine years later—if John Archibald Venn's *Alumni Cantabrigienses* can be trusted—he was briefly curate of Swaffham Priory, then curate at the lovely village of Holne, Devon, by which time he was married to Mary, the daughter of the aforementioned Nathan Lucas. At Holne, in June 1819, Charles Kingsley, junior, was born (the same year as Victoria and Albert). During Kingsley senior's rectorship at Barnack, Northamptonshire, 1824 to 1830, two sons and a daughter were born including George, who will later write of his Estes Park, Colorado, experience. After Barnack, Charles, senior, was assigned to six years at Clovelly, again in Devon, but on the north coast. Such a scenic area may have seemed remote from major events, but when briefly at the Clifton School, twelve year-old Charles reputedly witnessed the Bristol Riots which were motivated by the failure of the Reform Act the year before it was eventually passed. Certainly, the Devonshire and Cornish seacoasts shaped the Kingsley children's love of nature. Then, in 1836, the senior Charles accepted his fateful final assignment as Rector of St. Luke's in Chelsea, when the young Charles was seventeen years old (and George about ten). Kingsley senior's lengthy rectorship in Chelsea advanced his sons' intellectual development with cosmopolitan experience.

While rector of St. Luke's, Charles, senior, was also domestic chaplain to one of the earls of Cadogan, probably his contemporary, George, the 3rd Earl, a substantial Chelsea landowner. This interdependency of pre- or early-Victorian Anglican clergy and landowners who had voting rights in Parliament was described by social historian Richard Altick, as a kind of defensive wall. Altick found that ". . . in its rocky conservatism and isolation from evolving human needs[,] the informal league of Tory landowner-Tory parson-Tory bishop constituted the most redoubtable single obstacle to political and social reform" (Altick, 205).

Scholars like Altick would surely agree that the first third of the 19th-century was a time of nation building given that the Roman Catholic Relief Act was passed in 1829, the first Reform Act or Representation of the People Act in 1832, then, various cotton mill and factory acts, and the Abolition of Slavery in 1833. Even if Charles, senior, did not experience a religious calling but decided on his career objectively, something of his authenticity came through to his son; Charles, junior, was able to choose his Anglican profession from inspiration and insight.

From his father's home in Chelsea, the young Charles had the advantage of attending King's College School in nearby Wimbledon, where he prepared to attend Cambridge University like his father. Anxious for achievement, and probably to impress his parents, Charles began at Trinity college Cambridge but migrated to Magdalene, then drove himself quite hard from 1838 to 1842, after weathering a crisis of belief in his Established Church calling during December 1838 and January 1839, that is, in the middle of his first year at Magdalene.

More specifically, what rattled 20 year-old Charles's nerves was a decade-long church controversy called the Oxford Movement—a topic I will address shortly for its significance in his 1874 American tour.

In his renewal of his Anglican faith and greater discipline in studies in 1839, Charles Kingsley was greatly aided by his future wife, Frances Eliza Grenfell, a younger daughter of wealthy tin and copper merchant, Pascoe Grenfell. Frances—or Fanny—believed in Charles, and while they were wedded in mind, he had to convince her four older brothers (their father had died in 1838) that he was on a secure path. Inspired by the stability of Frances Grenfell's outlook on life, Charles applied himself to his true focus, his pathway to ordination. He took a First in the Classics Tripos exam and graduated B.A. in Classics from Magdalene College in 1842. In quick succession, Kingsley was ordained a deacon, then a priest, then a curate. He was the Curate of Eversley for nearly two years—the fateful village on the lovely Blackwater River—before he was appointed Rector. Then, after marriage in January 1844, he took steps to publicly promote social causes, to write articles and essays encouraging working people, and to teach English composition at Queen's College London, founded by his mentor, the Reverend F. D. Maurice.

Kingsley was socially versatile, comfortable with the sons of the landed gentry and aristocrats with whom he attended college and university, yet deeply touched by the lives of the simplest rural folk. "In his long walks through the parish," scholar Robert Bernard Martin notes of him while still curate, "Kingsley got to know every farmer and labourer within miles" and in that way increased attendance at Eversley's St. Mary's church (Martin, *Dust*, 54). As Pope-Hennessy shows, clergy "acted as distributors of benefactions in kind, such as blankets, flannel, or coal" and that on occasion someone like Charles Kingsley, junior, would arise to "scandalize landlords by demanding better housing conditions and a wider ownership of property." Activist clergy seemed to come up from the "docile ranks" and like young Kingsley appeared to be a "hot-head" (Pope-Hennessy, 2).

However, Kingsley could not have been so out of place as the image of hot-head suggests. The emergence of country parsons like him, who blended parish work with supporting the causes favored by working people as a whole, could be explained in part by the differences of opinion circulating among the clergy from the High Church Anglicans who tended to be Tory to those, like Kingsley, of the liberal Broad Church persuasion, at the same time that the English traditions of social organization were transforming trade unions into international industrial labor unions.

While Kingsley conducted parish work in person-to-person interaction, he did not fear writing intimate letters, as I've quoted. Paradoxically, even in his most embarrassing correspondence—like those in which he insults Americans—his struggles seem spiritual and romantic. His love of nature in his youth called him to a liberal interpretation of Christianity characterized by a broader interpretation of Anglican theology and an understanding of the experiences of common people, a trend initiated by clergymen before him. For Kingsley, the People's Charter had been very reasonable, and he encouraged early Christian Socialism, and was zealous for sanitation science and healthcare reform. Yes, this is the same Charles Kingsley, junior, who was ignorant about the lives of enslaved African Americans, derided Lincoln's emancipation plans, and spoke favorably of Governor Eyre.

In an effort to place Charles Kingsley in his Victorian setting of such contradictions, Peter Searby, author of one of the volumes on the history of Cambridge University, explains that Kingsley, who was an eldest child, "grew up in an oppressive Evangelical rectory" and his resulting "lifelong restlessness" was a feature of his public persona (Searby, 252). One gets the impression that Kingsley was often feeling overwhelmed—when a Cambridge student or later in his public role—and from time to time worked himself to the point of nervous exhaustion. Not to excuse him, Kingsley was frequently unaware of his need for stress management, and he would respond impulsively or nonsensically to the heated issues of the day. As though to correct himself, Kingsley would turn to his true spiritual path, the two connected themes of sharing his love of the natural world, and his belief in the power of scientific inquiry to make life better for all. He was not alone in that.

In letters to friends and family, Charles Kingsley often expressed gratitude for one "S.G.O.", that is Sidney Godolphin Osborne, born into the aristocracy and married to one of Frances Grenfell's sisters, thus, the perfect choice to perform the wedding ceremony for Frances and Charles in January 1844 (Martin, *Dust*, 58). Osborne was nine years older than Charles, and a few years ahead in taking up the plight of coal miners and farm laborers. In his Dorset parish, he had initiated a campaign to replace the dirty hovels in which many farm workers lived; the enthusiasm of an aristocratic clergyman was so new that Osborne reputedly excited the suspicion of the laborers themselves. To hear Osborne rail against unsanitary housing reassured Charles Kingsley about his own efforts to improve Eversley, for the reason that—Robert Bernard Martin claims—Kingsley needed a supportive person of the aristocracy to assuage his fear of losing his place in the "Victorian social hierarchy." Be that as it may, Charles wrote of Osborne to Frances, "Heaven knows, where there are so many abuses, we ought to thank a man who will hunt them out" (Martin, *Dust*, 59).

In terms of the evolution of the clergy, Osborne was a transitional figure, since, like Charles Kingsley, senior, he did not initially find a spiritual calling in his profession. In scholar Martin's words, Osborne "... entered the clergy with neither inclination nor distaste, but simply to fulfil the duty of a younger son of a good family." It's not a paradox that before his own ordination Sidney Godolphin Osborne's true interests were "medicine, surgery, and microscopic investigation . . ." (Martin, *Dust*, 58). These areas of study gripped the minds of many youth of that day including Charles's brother, George, who would pursue advanced medical studies in Scotland. Men who chose Established Church ordination in the 1830s were able to push the previous limits of involvement in the urgent public issues of their day.

In summary, Charles Kingsley, junior, chose his Church of England profession wholeheartedly at a time when medical, scientific, and technological development in Britain was generating a rising sense of united action, a national feeling in which progressive clergy could play a role. In 1865, prominent figures like Kingsley, who had been at the forefront of English public life for twenty years, had to adjust to the fact that a reunited America would challenge British world domination. One wonders how a clergyman so convinced of English superiority could reverse his attitude to the point that he encouraged his son, Maurice, to find a home in Colorado. A close look at Washington Irving's enthralling imagery of a liberating life in the American West shows the central paradox of Kingsley's attitude toward the United States: He once wanted to be "a wild prairie hunter."

The lure of literature and Charles Kingsley's quarrel with America

By late 1871, Maurice Kingsley could safely believe that his father had given up any opposition to African American emancipation, even if not all of his English nationalist views. If he encountered Palmer's "Negro" man servant, Mr. Butler, at the livery stables or the train depot, he would not be completely embarrassed by his own father. Maurice didn't know the details of his father's conversion to respect for Washington, D.C.; it seemed that when Atlanta, Georgia, was under siege in the late summer of 1864, leading British opinion makers realized that the Union forces would triumph convincingly. However, unknown to everyone but his wife, Frances, the seed for Canon Kingsley's new understanding of the United States had been planted nearly twenty-five years earlier, during his first year at Cambridge University. In the autumn of 1838, Charles's desire for academic achievement had increased but so had his exam anxiety and his nervous hopes that his career after college would develop as he dreamed. Extracurricular reading was a way for university students to legitimately seek respite from the routine of rigorous study.

While university undergraduates did not strictly document their leisure reading, individual students recorded their preferences as did Kingsley's contemporary, William Thomson who read *Evelina*, Frances Burney's novel of 1778 (Searby, 628). But reputedly the most popular author in England in the 1830s was Washington Irving, an

American. Many young men were poring over Irving's *Astoria* of 1836 and *The Adventures of Captain Bonneville*, published to great acclaim the following year. The popularity of *Astoria* made readers look again at Irving's *A Tour on the Prairies*, published in 1834. Though the number of copies sold is difficult to trace, to be a best-seller in England, only about 1,000 copies had to be read by people whose opinion influenced others. Irving, whose reputation endured for years, was able to work his magic on the English psyche because his fourteen-year residence in England had made him thoroughly conversant with the plot and character development that British readers wanted from American writers. Moreover, fifteen years previously, James Fenimore Cooper's wilderness adventures had prepared the European reading public for Irving's tales.

Every image Irving created appealed to the upper-middle class British youth's desire for safe adventure and evening meals around a campfire: Irving's hunter-adventurers always enjoy riding long hours on the prairie, the hunting group gleefully reaches their quota during the day, every adventure concludes safely, and they have ample time for leisure in the evening. These were images comforting for brains weary of mathematics and Latin classics. As intoxicating as Irving's imagery was, no reader wanting to escape the stress of exam preparation could reasonably have expected that Western America was the innocent place that the writer illustrated. Though based on actual travels in Arkansas and Oklahoma territories, Irving wrote *A Tour on the Prairies* lyrically, with fiction-like plot development; it ought to have been considered entertainment and not a factual incitement to forsake useful studies and Britain, as it seems to have been for young Kingsley.

The fact that dramatic scenes of a carefree prairie life made Kingsley feel like shirking all his ambitions and abandoning Cambridge altogether might have been lost to literary history had he not related everything to his fiancée and soon-to-be wife, Frances Grenfell. Though we have no exact proof that Kingsley read *A Tour* and not *The Adventures of Captain Bonneville*, Frances candidly rendered her husband's early experience in the first of many editions titled *Charles Kingsley: His Letters and Memories of His Life*, first published in 1877.

When offering lengthy quotations of her husband's letters, Frances introduced each with passages of contextual exposition (including reminiscences from Rose, when the railway which carried her and her father approached the Nebraska prairie during Kingsley's 1874 lecture tour). The context that Frances Kingsley gave for her husband's need of the Western American imagery during his first undergraduate year was multifaceted, and suggests that mood transference took place among students who also shared a passion for sports and countryside rambles.

In addition to examination stress, every young man preparing for ordination was affected by the Church of England controversy called Tractarianism, more commonly known as the Oxford Movement, which developed over nine years and found expression in ninety position papers, or tracts, published from 1833 to 1841 by clergymen members of Oxford University, most notably John Henry Newman, a Doctor of Divinity there. At first an intellectual movement among the upper Anglican clergy (that is clergy of the Established Church), the Tracts were more like political position papers, systematic responses to what seemed a liberalization of voting rights after the Reform Act of 1832, which somehow threatened to loosen the standards of scriptural interpretation as well. These Oxford tracts were read and discussed by Cambridge faculty and students, and when the heated debate over the basis of the Anglican Church became known by the educated public, the entire nation seemed involved (Searby, 338-47; Altick, 208-15). In brief, the Oxford Movement tract writers went quite far in their analysis of the doctrinal basis of Anglicanism, and many later converted to the Roman Catholic Church.

At first, Charles Kingsley was too young to be involved in the discussions. In 1833, he was a 14 year-old youth at King's College School, but when at Cambridge to study for ordination, he could not ignore that certain Anglican ministers were arguing over the validity of many of the 39 Articles in the *Book of Common Prayer*, which constituted the foundation of the Church of England after the Protestant Reformation. Charles may have been reading Irving's adventure tales by 1838 to ease his mind from the religious debates.

He would soon find a way forward in the ministry through its Broad Church de-emphasis of scriptural interpretation for a focus on serving village folk and promoting medical science. Many of the most alarming criticisms aimed at the leaders of the Established Church seemed to demand that parishioners interpret scriptural revelation as though the modern developments of science had never existed.

Frances may have thought that her husband's early fascination with the Midwestern prairies—whether actually Oklahoma or Nebraska didn't matter—would come as a surprise to readers who believed he had always been a simple parish priest, a novelist, a nature writer and social reformer. In 1877, Frances offered dramatic details on Kingsley's struggle during the stress of that academic year 1838 to 1839, after he "migrated" or transferred from Trinity to Magdalene right after the Christmas break of 1838 into January 1839:

> All, however, was dark for a time, and the conflict between hopes and fears for the future, and between faith and unbelief, was so fierce and bitter, that when he returned to Cambridge [January 1839], he became reckless, and nearly gave up all for lost: he read little, went in for excitement of every kind—boating, hunting, driving, fencing, boxing, duck-shooting in the Fens,—anything to deaden the remembrance of the happy past, which just then promised no future. More than once he had nearly resolved to leave Cambridge and go out to the Far West and live as a wild prairie hunter; to this he refers when for the first time he found himself on the prairies of America in 1874. But through all, God kept him in those dark days for a work he little dreamed of. (Kingsley, Frances, v. 1: 45-6)

In summary, Frances Kingsley showed that the leadership crisis generated by the Oxford Movement tracts—which claimed that the Church of England was still Catholic—was unnerving for Charles to the point that he took up any activity that would divert his mind. Irving's seductive narratives suggested to him that dropping out of Cambridge was an option.

Even under the pressure of such a national debate as a call for the re-interpretation of the foundation of the Established Church, one can't entirely account for why Kingsley gave so much credence to Washington Irving's Western American tales of a care-free existence except that Kingsley had begun to doubt his own principles. Frances believed Charles's crisis in 1839 was significant enough to publish the details in 1877, two years after his death. By that year, her readers would have known much more about financial investment opportunities in the Western American territories, or become disabused by the bad luck stories of repatriated English emigrants. The new transcontinental rail system would have ended buffalo hunting expeditions and long prairie rides, and the sleeping cars made travel so comfortable that nights camping out had no romance, until the mid-20th-century when urbanization made summer camps popular.

The importance of this crisis in Charles Kingsley's early career, and Frances's emphasis of it, might have been underestimated by literary historians except that the compilers of the *Alumni Cantabrigienses*, John Venn (1834-1923) and his son John Archibald Venn (1883-1958) were also fascinated by Kingsley's early impulse to throw life away for a fling in the American West (though only John Archibald Venn may have compiled the data on Kingsley's life, and not his father John Venn). After listing the highlights of Kingsley's life, Venn felt the topic of the clergyman's near-abandonment of his career so important that he took exact quotations from Frances Kingsley. In the Venn compilation, digitized as *A Cambridge Alumni Database*, Venn states that "While preparing for ordination," Charles's "conflict between faith and unbelief, between his hopes and his fears, was so fierce and bitter, that when he returned to . . . Cambridge . . . in 1839, he became reckless, and nearly gave up all for lost. . . More than once he had nearly resolved to leave England and to go out to the Far West to live as a wild prairie hunter" (Venn, n. pg.). Obviously John Archibald Venn understood the significance of this rite of passage for Kingsley when he began questioning his faith at the same time that major exams loomed.

Whatever Charles Kingsley felt during that critical first year at Cambridge, he may have sensed that his parents were watching him, and he feared falling back into the desultory ways of his grandfather, Charles Kingsley, Esq., of Battramsley. Charles snapped to attention, quickly pulling himself away from distracting religious doubts, from varying definitions of masculinity, and his fear of success. He studied massively, and on May 31, 1839, wrote home from Magdalene College that he had achieved high marks in classics and mathematics exams leading up to the Classics Tripos. Certainly, the attraction of the Western American myth was only a detour, and Kingsley never doubted his love of his studies. He was remarkably diligent, and when surrounded by equally ambitious peers, he became fully engaged.

Ironically, Washington Irving was writing for an American audience and not calculating for success in England. The New York born Irving had arrived back in the United States after nearly twenty years in Europe and felt pressure to prove that he was still an American. After brief travels west of the Mississippi River acclimatizing himself to the America of the 1830s—largely the nationalism of President Andrew Jackson and his Indian Removal Act of 1832—Irving began to write dramatic narratives set in sweeping geographic spaces. Writing fictionally about an actual expedition in eastern Oklahoma, Irving blends pleasurable sport with seemingly obligatory definitions of masculinity and patriotism:

> On returning to the camp we found it a scene of the greatest hilarity. Some of the rangers were shooting at a mark, others were leaping, wrestling and playing at prison bars. They were mostly young men, on their first expedition, in high health and vigour, and buoyant with anticipations; and I can conceive nothing more likely to set the youthful blood into a flow than a wild wood life of the kind and the range of a magnificent wilderness abounding with game and fruitful of adventure. We send our youth abroad to

grow luxurious and effeminate in Europe; it appears to me that a previous tour on the prairies would be more likely to produce that manliness, simplicity and self dependence most in unison with our political institutions. (Irving, *Tour*, 44)

Writing as though consciously appealing to the brainy, room-confined university undergraduate with secret athletic ambitions and a desire to colonize paradise, Irving continues:

Our march this day was animating and delightful. We were in a region of adventure; breaking our way through a country hitherto untrodden by white men, excepting perchance by some solitary trapper. . . .

For my own part, I laid on the grass under the trees, and built castles in the clouds, and indulged in the very luxury of rural repose. Indeed I can scarcely conceive a kind of life more calculated to put both mind and body in a healthful tone. (Irving, *Tour*, 64-5)

In the face of European industrialization, Western America would have appeared to be the paradise that England could never be again:

. . . we crept feebly on until, on turning [past] a thick clump of trees a frontier farm house suddenly presented itself to view. It was a low tenement of logs overshadowed by great forest trees, but it seemed as if a very region of Cocaigne prevailed around it. Here was a stable and barn teeming with abundance, while legions of grunting swine, gobbling turkeys, cackling hens and strutting roosters swarmed about the farm yard. (Irving, *Tour*, 160)

Irving's point was clear, while giving Cockaigne a Middle-French spelling: America west of the Mississippi River was a place of luxury where the mind could expand in harmonious conditions. Compared to Irving's lush and lyrical prose, Alexis de Tocqueville's *Democracy in America*—the English translation of Volume I appeared in 1838—would have been too analytical for the undergraduate readers who wanted to know how it *felt* to be in America. Washington Irving delivered it to them.

Through his artistry in plot construction and narrative arc, Irving's adventure tales reached into the European subconscious in a way that no previous American writer had ever done on such a scale. He convinced Europe's young readers that America offered the perpetual innocence of Boy Scout activity, much like a Cambridge undergraduate outing. On the prairie, abundance is a given, Irving suggests; there are plenty of game animals, and the men seldom miss a shot. When lost, they are found; horses are never injured. The frontier is democratic; individuals stand out for their accomplishments, but everyone shares the risk and helps others. While the constant threat of encountering Pawnee warriors never materializes, the Native people's presence on the margins operates like a warning to the guilty youth that they are trespassing. But the white hunters can get away with it due to their projected aura as bringers of civilization. In effect, the West is Europe's second chance at youth.

And yet, there is something pathologically driven about this group of prairie hunters: Their male appetite for the hunt is a programmatic, scripted pursuit. In the end, university students could dismiss Irving's intoxicating prose, and resume their exam preparation. Kingsley grew forward from that critical year at Cambridge and found his footing as a clergyman dedicated to the Broad Church ideals, while the role of the Anglican Church in civil government continued to be challenged. In due course, I will review Charles Kingsley's deeply touching reaction to his first sight of the prairie landscape on his 1874 tour, which Rose witnessed as his loyal amanuensis.

In early 1870, Canon Kingsley would be in the comfort of his Eversley Rectory drawing room listening with rapt attention to William A. Bell's account of his fortuitous business partnership with a discerning Union veteran of upright Quaker background, General

William J. Palmer. Kingsley would have been effusive with gratitude that Bell's preference for the natural sciences had resulted in such satisfying work as the documentation of the floral and fauna from south-central Colorado through New Mexico and Arizona territories, while on the official survey expeditions of the Kansas Pacific Railway, work which had resulted in Bell's *New Tracks in North America*. One can imagine that as Bell turned the conversation toward Maurice Kingsley, the Canon relaxed in his high-backed chair and let his imagination roam with images of Bell's botanical adventures across prairies of waving wild grasses, long hikes up pine-covered mountain slopes, with trout in the clear rushing stream below, a safe night's sleep beneath lofty pines, after a delicious evening meal around the campfire. Kingsley absolutely understood a young man's need for adventure. He wondered why he had been so angry during the American Civil War.

While there is no written documentation specifically stating that William A. Bell visited Eversley Rectory in late February or early March of 1870, or that he visited only once, archived letters that Charles Kingsley wrote within a few weeks show that indeed Maurice was going to Colorado. Kingsley's cheerfulness in those letters was the result of the hope Bell's visit offered that Maurice would at last find a career path. The primary image Bell had emphasized was that William J. Palmer was an American of impeccable business values with whom he could link his fate—in contrast to the aggressive entrepreneurs Englishmen often heard about such as those behind the railway originating in Atchison, Kansas. In other words, the Colorado offer was authentic. In effect, Bell had answered Kingsley's most anxious question: What shall I do with my son?

What Kingsley did not know was the extent to which Bell, too, had worked through his own mistaken ideas about the United States of America.

William Abraham Bell and the rise of his Western American career

Bell's conversation with Canon Kingsley and Maurice in March 1870 was the culmination of a major stage of Bell's personal journey at the same time it illustrates how English people influenced one another's interest in the American West. Bell had no set plan for involving Canon Kingsley in Colorado, just a deep impression of the Canon's understanding of church and country and his ability to mediate cultural questions among differing people. To establish this point, I offer a narrative of two broadly interconnected areas: How Bell's visit to the Eversley rectory was a development of his genuine feeling for the Reverend Kingsley nurtured during their shared Cambridge years, and to what degree Bell had to address his own English superiority in the wake of American claims that Britain had betrayed Washington, D.C., during the Civil War. In this chapter and the next, I will reconstruct these interpersonal influences through a deductive projection, that is, a recreation from the known facts.

Departing his father's home and office on Hertford Street in Mayfair for the rail station that would take him nearest Eversley, one can imagine that like any other human being, Bell reviewed the significant themes of his life leading to the present moment, particularly how he had transitioned so quickly from his medical focus at Cambridge to joining the Kansas Pacific Railway survey expedition in June of 1867. Like the majority of English men of his class and prospects, Bell disdained the hemispheric and global ambitions of the Americans of the Northern states, but during the entire period of the American Civil War, Bell had been at Trinity Hall preparing for the Natural Sciences Tripos exam and successful completion of the *Medicinae Baccalaureus* course of study. During those student years, when anyone mentioned the American conflict it was simply to wonder which side would be militarily victorious.

It might not have occurred to British university students that Washington, D.C., had already triumphed because they had never stopped governing: In July of 1862, Congress passed the first of several Pacific Railroad Acts, authorizing taxpayer money to construct at least two transcontinental lines (all with the word "Pacific" in their corporate names). In the 1860s, young men were focusing on their studies, or rowing on the River Cam—or were taking advantage of the relaxed social standards for older students—and not thinking what the result might be if Irish emigrants joined the Union army in great numbers. If Bell had thought of the American West at all, or knew of the terrain and topography, it might have been while his fellow students in the natural sciences were casting about for a career path.

One can imagine how, under a sense of excitement over his approaching visit with the former Regius Professor, Bell's thoughts began to crystallize on that March afternoon in 1870. He didn't want to talk about Cambridge University though he and Kingsley shared that, nor did he want to discuss his role on the Kansas Pacific survey expeditions, for all that was in his *New Tracks in North America*, including his relating the unforgettable evening in August 1867 that Will Palmer rode into the camp at the base of the Ratón Mountains, nor did Bell intend to dwell on his election to the Royal Geographical Society. His thoughts were on his new business connections in America, and briefly on how the year before, his success in the American West seemed threatened by Americans themselves and their preposterous *Alabama* claims. But what would the Canon want to hear? Or, rather, what could he, Bell, say to elicit the Canon's spontaneous goodwill for Colorado? Bell's quandary was genuine.

Bell made his transformation from medical student to apprentice railway developer so quickly that he must have gotten his ability to adapt from his own father, Dr. Bell. During the years his father was simply Mr. William Bell, he had set the family fortunes on an upward course. Born in Dublin in 1804, William Bell, *père*, earned his first medical credential at the Royal College of Physicians Ireland in 1826, and had been practicing traditional medicine there when he went to Clonmel as Medical Officer for the County Tipperary Workhouse and Lunatic Asylum, according to available medical directories. While it's true that County Tipperary was beyond the English Pale, being born in rural Ireland—as was Bell, *fils*, in 1841—does not make a person Irish, particularly if one's religion is that of the Established Church and ethnically of the Protestant Ascendancy (very much like people of the Ulster provinces). Moreover, the Bells were not of the same economic and social class as the vast majority of Irish.

By 1850, Bell's father had moved the family to Norwich, England, where he worked at the Norwich Homeopathic Dispensary and Hospital, and when the senior Bell realized that his future was with homeopathy, he left Norwich to study at the University of Erlangen, Germany. The *British and Foreign Homeopathic Medical Directory*, and *The Homeopathic Medical Directory* show Bell's M.D. degree for 1858, the year the younger Bell was seventeen. Possibly, while Bell, *père*, was at the Erlangen medical school—now called the University of Erlangen-Nürnberg—Bell's wife, Margaret, and daughters Esther and Susan, may have moved to Ipswich, Suffolk, where the son he called Willie, was at the prestigious Ipswich School (founded in 1477).

Shortly after completing his M.D., by January 1859 (or taking the qualifying exam made necessary by the 1858 Medical Act), Dr. Bell founded a private homeopathic practice and residence at 18 Hertford Street, in affluent Mayfair. We can assume that Dr. William Bell's homeopathic office was also his place of residence, where the younger Bell would reside when in town. The wealth of the doctor's clients would enable the younger Bell to attend Cambridge from 1860 to 1867, and could, to some degree, finance his son's presence on the Kansas Pacific Railway survey expedition beginning in the summer of 1867. Certainly, the father enthusiastically welcomed his only son's ambition.

William Abraham Bell immediately grasped what Cambridge was all about. His name appears in Volume I of the *Alumni Cantabrigienses*, published in 1940, the first volume that John Archibald Venn prepared after his father, the mathematician, had passed away. The volume shows that the First Class finish the younger Bell earned in the Natural Sciences Tripos exam in 1863, while at Trinity Hall, was proof that his ability could match his ambition and meet the university demands during a decade when Cambridge was undergoing progressive reformation inspired by the Chancellor, H.R.H. Prince Albert. We might wonder why the Natural Sciences were considered a gateway course to medical training, but the Tripos exam was designed to endow each student "with powers of observation and reason"; and the medical student would "have the analytical acumen of the chemist and the observational powers of the botanist" (Weatherall, 107). The following year, 1864, Bell was awarded his B.A. degree, probably in the Natural Sciences as well. Three years later, in 1867, he earned the M.B. degree or *Medicinae Baccalaureus*. Many records, including Bell's, seem not to have been preserved for those years, and are to be found only in the *Alumni Cantabrigienses* or the online version, *A Cambridge Alumni Database*. However, the program of study for the M.B. included chemistry, comparative anatomy, human anatomy, and physiology.

The 1858 Medical Act had authorized the creation of a second and third M.B. degree, though the curriculum of clinical medicine and medical jurisprudence was not in place until the 1870s, as medical historian Mark Weatherall has shown in his volume on the history of medicine at Cambridge (Weatherall, 117). Further research in Cambridge archives might reveal that Bell may have signed up to "walk the wards" at Addenbrook's Hospital in 1865 or 1866 as part of his M.B. degree.

Research into the practice of medicine in England shows that the 1858 Medical Act would have permitted Bell, *fils*, to practice medicine with one M.B. degree because the "courses of study and examinations for the MB were changed to ensure that holders of the degree possessed sufficient knowledge to practise medicine" (Weatherall, 117), but none of the 19th-century medical directories currently accessible show that Bell, *fils*, was licensed to practice, in contrast to his father, Dr. William Bell, who appears in all medical registries and directories available on internet archives. Also important to note, it's possible that the Medical Act may have permitted Bell to be addressed as "doctor" with only one M.B. degree (depending on the interpretation of clauses in the 1858 Act). However, in the United States, the title "Dr." or being called "doctor" signifies the M.D. degree. And, as though to point out that Americans assume being called "doctor" means an M.D., the *Colorado Springs Directory* for 1879 shows "Wm. A. Bell, M.D." on the Board of Trustees for Colorado College, when, in fact, Bell did not earn an M.D. degree at Cambridge or elsewhere. It seems that Bell could not stop Americans from giving him a title, if they insisted that all their Englishmen have titles.

Evidence shows that Bell had no time for further medical study. First of all, he did not wait to pick up his *Medicinae Baccalaureus* diploma at the Trinity Hall ceremony in July 1867; by then, he had already thrown aside any thought of a medical career and sailed for Philadelphia. In his introduction to *New Tracks*, Bell doesn't state why such a sudden departure from England, but given the swiftness of his decision and his subsequent actions, he was self-fashioning a career based on his natural sciences preference and a strategic use of his medical training. Bell's purpose in Philadelphia was to call on an American geologist and entomologist acquaintance, Dr. John Lawrence LeConte (often spelled with a space as Le Conte). LeConte was based in Philadelphia, a center for the arts and sciences, and home of the Pennsylvania Railway whose J. Edgar Thomson had fostered Palmer's career. It's possible that Bell met LeConte earlier at Cambridge University where the American had contacts, as suggested by a letter to him (LeConte) from Benjamin Dann Walsh, a Trinity Fellow, who had emigrated to Illinois and become an entomologist there (Searby, 466). In short, Bell knew of John LeConte before departing England. Moreover, Bell's Trinity Hall college credentials could open doors in any scientific community.

The first topic LeConte would have raised with his guest, Bell, was the Kansas Pacific survey expeditions planned through the Territories of New Mexico and Arizona, into the state of California to the Pacific Coast, which—as noted earlier—would take place during a Kansas Pacific construction slowdown between Salina and Phil Sheridan, Kansas, the work camp near Fort Wallace. The KP expeditions were on LeConte's mind quite simply because he had accepted the position of official geologist. In his impressive Philadelphia office, LeConte must have spoken enthusiastically to Bell, for the younger man had a flash of insight about what the American West could be for him. The KP expeditions were then in the final stages of preparation. Only one position remained unfilled—photographer—and LeConte hastily finessed this spot for Bell, who completed a crash course in the art. They quickly headed west for the survey expedition organizational meeting at the KP headquarters in St. Louis, Missouri; then, with the one-hundred or so members of the survey divisions, continued on to Salina. Based on the timing of events and Bell's movements, he had no time to study medicine further, let alone "practice" at St. George's Hospital in London as some accounts of Bell's movements have claimed.

Prior to the expedition launch in Salina, Bell may have thought he would write an account of his Western experience, but the idea of a two-volume production did not crystallize in his mind until he found an inspired listener in William J. Palmer. Bell recounts with a sense of awe how Palmer and his personal assistant Captain Colton rode into the surveyors' camp on August 7, 1867, the encampment of the division to which Bell was temporarily assigned, at the base of the Ratón Mountains, east of the village of Trinidad just within the Colorado Territory line. Bell knew enough about botany and geology, and about narrative style, to write a travel account, however, Palmer's leadership showed Bell how his life could evolve after the expedition's conclusion. Palmer was actually timing his cross-country ride to reach Santa Fé in mid-September to give an "Address" to the citizens of New Mexico on the desirability of bringing the railway there.

With visions of a brilliant future guiding him, Bell wrote an account that still stands as perhaps the most comprehensive narrative ever produced on the southwestern territories of New Mexico and Arizona, the full title of which is *New Tracks in North America: A Journal of Travel and Adventure whilst Engaged in the Survey for a Southern Railroad to the Pacific Ocean During 1867-8*. Unfortunately, from time to time Bell lowers the heroic tone of his natural sciences saga to the baseness of his negativity toward the Native people who are resisting the aggressive encroachment of the railway and the death sentence it represents.

Bell's commentary on the Native threat is precise and, as a result, strangely informative, since he reveals the prevalent business ideology in the contact zone of the rapidly moving frontier. In his disgust, one can see the degree to which middle-men like him believed that the Apache and Navajo-Diné, or Kiowa and Arapaho were blocking access to the riches the investors desired. Perhaps as early as St. Louis, or at least Salina, Bell had fully grasped the broader political and financial implications of such a knowledge-gathering expedition as the Kansas Pacific surveys, namely, that every living thing must be examined for its value to those profiting from the iron rail technology. In addition to derogatory remarks on American Indian self-defense, Bell did not hesitate to exercise his Anglican superiority when describing the earliest *nuevoméxicano* villages of the arid uplands, collections of mud huts or *jacales* which did not resemble the finest dwellings of East Coast Anglo-Americans. While New Mexicans were not blocking access to resources as American Indians were perceived to do, they were not bringing the ores to mass market—another observation Bell intended to use to motivate the European investor.

When reading *New Tracks*, one feels sure that Bell's buoyant attitude was not just his natural disposition but because he and the survey engineers were heavily armed, as depicted in one of the Vincent Brooks, Day & Son lithograph illustrations titled "Surveyors at Work" showing rifle-carrying men posted as lookouts while the surveyors take measurements. As one can gather from *New Tracks*, the American West was already militarized, and the railway survey route was intended to run as closely as practicable to the numerous forts and encampments which lined the route to California. Free from fear, and assured of success, Bell and the survey divisions traveled from the adobe village of Santa Fé and its Fort Marcy on the bluff above, southward along the Río Grande to Fort Craig, then westward through Arizona. Bell recorded flora and fauna, probable coal and mineral deposits, in addition to noting the earliest layers of Anglo-American attempts at settlement. His travels generated more ideas than he could understand at the time. Within five years, Bell would take action on several business ventures based upon what he saw during the expedition, including gaining a clear title to one or both of the Pedro Armendaris Land Grants which seemed to languish untouched from the days of Spanish rule, near the village of San Marcíal on the Río Grande, which Bell saw first hand as the survey divisions arrived at Fort Craig.

William A. Bell's assignment as expedition photographer was brief; he was soon reassigned as physician, and able to move from one of the five survey divisions to another, seemingly to accommodate the expedition needs but also with the liberty of pursuing his own ambition. In southeastern Arizona, Bell and a single companion—probably a Mexican citizen guide for hire—departed Camp Grant to explore a route across Sonoran Mexico to Hermosillo then to Guaymas on the Gulf of California Coast. However, Bell did not return to Arizona, but sailed from Guaymas to La Paz, then around Baja California to San Francisco, the agreed upon rendezvous of the cross-country divisions including Palmer's. In February 1868, Bell, Palmer, and Colton returned eastward over the Sierra Nevada in its winter conditions. They traveled only 92 miles on the Central Pacific Railroad (since it was not nearly finished to Promontory Summit, Utah), then by stagecoach to Salt Lake City, and over eight hundred miles by "mud-wagon," a type of heavily-built coach, through Wyoming to Denver, and by stage to the expedition origination point near Fort Wallace (Bell, *New Tracks*, 1870, 466-9). With energy to spare, Bell was back in New York within a few weeks to embark on the eleven-day crossing to London, to his parents' home in Mayfair where a quiet room and writing desk awaited him.

As for John LeConte, his publications included *Notes on the Geology of the Survey for the Extension of the Union Pacific Railway, E.D.*, as well as reports for the American Entomological Society. By the end of September 1868, William J. Palmer had gathered all of the scientific data collected by the survey crews, and narrativized the whole for his *Report of Surveys Across the Continent*, a somewhat grandiose title since the State of Kansas was already in the middle of the country. Palmer finished the *Report* in December and submitted it to John D. Perry, the President of the Kansas Pacific Railway Company (still officially called the Union Pacific Eastern Division), who then handed it to the January 1869 session of Congress to strengthen the bid for funding.

While Palmer's document was finished, Bell's journey was just beginning with a few unexpected turns on the road to publication.

Bell's reaction to the *Alabama* claims as the threatened ruin of British investment in Colorado

B ell had hardly written a chapter of *New Tracks* when he attracted a publisher, Chapman and Hall, experts in transatlantic travel accounts. In June of 1868, Bell was still working on a first draft when— as noted earlier—the gentlemen of the Royal Geographical Society elected him a Fellow. In April of 1869, he was putting the finishing touches on the final draft of *New Tracks*, when a United States Senator from Massachusetts, Charles Sumner, made a speech in an executive session of the Senate that increased American Anglophobia to an incredible level, which the Senator had not intended but came as a natural result of the facts he had of England's conduct during the American Civil War. The topic of discussion had been whether or not the Johnson-Clarendon Convention should be ratified by the Senate when it was actually the weakest legislation possible on British and American relations.

Named for the U.S. Ambassador to Britain Reverdy Johnson and the British Foreign Secretary Lord Clarendon, the convention was to settle any and all claims that the two nations had against each other during the Civil War. However, the substance of Senator Sumner's speech was that the British government had not yet acknowledged the damages caused by the Confederate States Ship *Alabama*, which had been built in England, armed for war, and had sailed around the world for nearly two years destroying American merchant vessels.

Sumner said that the Convention document was not worth signing. His colleagues agreed.

In Sumner's speech, April 13, 1869, published as "Claims on England—Individual and National," the senator called out the British subterfuge with facts. He showed that the British government's Neutrality Proclamation of May 1861, made a month after the Confederate States opening attack on Fort Sumter, was, in effect, concocted for the sole purpose of giving aid to the South, allowing them to use British ports for cotton shipments, while concealing their joint activities of constructing warships. The reaction in London was instant denial. In their preoccupation with financial gain, British businessmen—that is English men specifically—did not realize that Sumner had proof of British Foreign Office incompetence; they just wanted to get on with making money in America through Reconstruction contracts and westward expansion.

Sitting at his desk in his father's Mayfair home, Bell probably maintained an even temper as befitting a gentleman with expectations. He had already been recognized by an élite group, the R.G.S., and, moreover, the nearly-completed manuscript of *New Tracks* was in front of him. And he trusted in his new business partnership with a war veteran of steady nerves, General William J. Palmer, an Anglophile who knew the power of British investment. The bitter reaction to Sumner's speech was shared by businessmen on both sides of the Atlantic, though Palmer seems to have remained silent, while Bell could safely respond to Sumner. At present, my purpose is to show how Sumner's speech affected Bell as he was finishing a publishable draft of *New Tracks in North America*, while I will gradually offer relevant details on British Foreign Office negligence in what came to be known as the "*Alabama* claims."

With the furor continuing in England over Sumner's demand that England pay reparations for the damage caused by the CSS *Alabama*, Bell suddenly realized how connected he was to the terrain of the southwestern U.S. and to the book he was preparing for publication, and how much Palmer appeared as his guiding light. Bell looked forward to the days of August 1870 when the wild grasses of the plains east of Denver would crackle with excitement over the completion of the Kansas Pacific, when he and Palmer could work full time on the Denver & Río Grande plans, and yet, Bell hadn't—until Sumner's speech—put into words how much his experience in the Southwestern American territories had meant to him. He couldn't explain the hypnotic feel of the long rides across rolling hills of native brome grass, the sight of a distant line of lofty peaks promising sublimity, the surveyors taking measurements while he noted the texture of the pink-red of the sandstone formations. Of course, a group of native tribesmen in the distance could be ominous, but now Sumner's speech about British betrayal was the real threat to ruin Bell's future because the Massachusetts Senator made enemies of the most intelligent British people, even though the newly reunited United States needed more than ever (Bell believed) the law-abiding sort of English, Welsh, and Scots to provide a model for emigrants from non-English speaking countries.

With only a few weeks to review his final draft of *New Tracks*, Bell decided to revise the last chapter, giving his ideas of the idiocy of the *Alabama* claims and arguing for the necessity of controlling the emigrant Irish. Titled "Emigration," this final chapter was meant to be similar to the standard material in numerous previous travel accounts written by English men, and though Bell does recommend the creation of information bureaus to assist people intending to emigrate, Bell addressed the American government's failure to deal with Irish American activists and for continuing with the preposterous *Alabama* claims, largely because it was a protracted drama bearing on the economic development of America, while Irish emigration affected the labor force for such development.

In the following passage, Bell argues that if the number of antagonistic Irishmen entering the United States increases and becomes powerful in the government, peaceful relations with England will be impossible, and thus add to the transatlantic animosity already generated by what the English see as the ludicrous demands for reparations:

> It is . . . our desire, and also greatly to our [England's] advantage, to remain on the best terms with our American neighbours. With one section of them—

the emigrant Irish—this is at present impossible. They hate us so intensely that, were it possible for them to gain the ascendancy [in America], war would surely follow. It should therefore be our aim to maintain the ascendancy of the Saxon and Teutonic elements in [the] States. (Bell, *New Tracks*, 1870, 513)

Bell was a bit worked up in his fear that the United States would make war with England over Irish American dreams of an independent Ireland. However, his reference to Irish American hatred of England was similar to the opinion of the majority of native-born Anglo Americans who feared that a massive immigration of Irish would overwhelm the institutions which were intended to aid new citizens to assimilate to American laws and ways. Members of the Fenian Brotherhood had crossed into Canada several times in 1866, the year after the end of the American Civil War, and felt they could violate international law to gain attention for their cause—a topic I will return to shortly.

After his paragraphs on Irish activism in the "Emigration" chapter, Bell shifts his argument to the maritime damage claims, stating that the most desirable emigrants will cease to flow to America if Washington, D.C., continues its unreasonable pursuit of compensation for damages supposedly inflicted by the Confederate-manned ships:

The Americans complain of our gross ignorance as re-gards their politics, institutions, and social life; . . . If the North was not unanimous in its views as to the desirability of carrying on war with the South, how could they expect us all to be of one mind? Yet most Northerners believe that we sided altogether with the South, and they look upon us as enemies in conse-quence.

. . . This drifting of the majority of Englishmen towards acquiescence in the unity and prosperity of the States will receive a severe check if the American

Government perseveres in its most unjust treatment
of the Alabama question; for it will convert many
to the opinion that perhaps, after all, we should
have done ourselves and the world generally a great
service by assisting in the partition of the Union
instead of remaining strictly neutral in the quarrel. If
the Americans insist upon keeping up ill-feeling by
refusing to settle amicably these outstanding claims;
if they continue to make mountains of molehills, and
think it worth while to risk a war [with England],
which would be thrice as expensive as that which they
have just waged, for the sake of gratifying a vague
feeling of jealously which has no real foundation, they
will receive from us very few emigrants and very little
capital. (Bell, *New Tracks*, 1870, 513-4)

These paragraphs of Bell's are so packed with faulty cause-effect
reasoning that it's difficult to choose which statement to address first.
He refers to American demands as making "mountains of molehills"
and "keeping up ill-feeling" when, in fact, the evidence was clear that
the English-built CSS *Alabama*—and in part her sister ships the
Florida and the *Shenandoah*—had harassed and destroyed over sixty
American merchant vessels during a two year period beginning in
1862. Then, Bell's phrase that Americans "think it worth while to risk
a war" is rather extreme, and his notion that Americans have a "feeling
of jealousy" toward England adds too personal a cast to transatlantic
policy.

In general, Bell's grating tone in the *New Tracks* final chapter
"Emigration" is so factually inaccurate, and contrary to his railway engineering and natural sciences emphasis, that the reader is puzzled
until concluding that Bell did indeed write this chapter or revise it
within a few weeks after Senator Sumner's searing address unmask-
ing the London government's incompetence in failing to stop the
Alabama from being launched out of the Mersey River, across from
Liverpool. It is certainly no coincidence that Bell's final chapter ap-

pears to be his response to Sumner and the other senators who scoffed at the Johnson-Clarendon convention. Bell's stridency is understandable given that Sumner's "Claims on England" threatened England's global position.

Looking at the *Alabama* claims controversy today, it seems impossible that English investors didn't know of any actions that their government had taken to aid the Confederate States of America. The American delegation to Britain, headed by Charles Francis Adams, was sure that the British foreign minister, Lord John Russell, knew that Britain's Neutrality Proclamation in May 1861 would allow Southern ships to shelter in British ports worldwide. After the war, Sumner built a case showing that British ministers tried to hide their conscious deceit by pretending the damage to American shipping was financially inconsequential (Sumner, v. 13: 58, 66-8). William A. Bell seems not to have heard any of this.

Also, in the above quoted passage, Bell exhibits his arrogance in his statement that the U.S. will "receive from us very few emigrants and very little capital"—a strange conclusion since economic historians have shown that neither emigrants nor money ever ceased flowing from Britain to the United States. One can say that Bell's lack of knowledge about the effects of British subterfuge was hardly becoming to a man who aspired to partnership with an American Civil War general on the side of the Union. However, had Palmer read these last pages of Bell's *New Tracks*, he more than likely ignored them as transitory comments, and considered that Bell was only twenty-eight years old, and that his national feelings were hurt and he wrote in haste.

Of course, Bell had every intention of persuading well-to-do compatriots to invest in Colorado. His Cambridge and R.G.S. networks, as well as his father's homeopathic medical connections, may have learned of Bell's interest in supporting Palmer's railway-to-town projects, his insider information on the natural resources along the route, and where British emigrants were needed. When finished with the final chapter of *New Tracks*, Bell must have believed he'd written with accuracy and conviction, ideas with which General Palmer would agree. Ultimately, what held Bell and Palmer together during this international argument over Civil War reparations was the entrepreneurial spirit of Victorianism, their common belief in economic development.

The next day Bell wrote the *New Tracks* Preface, signing off with his father's Mayfair address, then he wrote the dedication page to William J. Palmer of the Kansas Pacific at St. Louis, and to his father, Dr. Bell. Fully confident of himself in the eyes of the Royal Geographical Society, Bell sent the draft to his London publisher. The "Emigration" chapter which concludes volume two of the 1869 1st edition of *New Tracks in North America* was retained as the concluding chapter to the handy one-volume 1870 American edition published the following year by Chapman and Hall in partnership with Scribner, Welford & Company of New York.

This overview of the historical context in which William A. Bell inspired the Kingsleys to visit Colorado, and in which Bell struggled with his own desire for adventure and investment in the American West, would not be complete without offering further details on the *Alabama* claims to show how news reports mislead the British public and circulated fear among English men with financial plans similar to Bell's. In that speech of April 1869, Senator Sumner quoted an official Report to the Secretary of the Treasury that if one totals up the value of the merchant ships destroyed by the CSS *Alabama* and her sister ships the *Florida* and the *Shenandoah*, plus the damage to the merchant marine's profitability during the years the *Alabama* was in action, the "national loss" would be $110,000,000—an incredible figure in 1869 dollars. But one must recall that Sumner did *not* invent this figure, and he didn't say that Britain would have to pay $110 million: He was quoting the Treasury Report which calculated the damages. However, a rumor rapidly circulated in Britain that this sum was the American demand (Cook, 75; Sumner, v. 13: 83). Unfortunately, the anger generated from the rumor took attention away from the key issue which was the British betrayal of United States's national interests. The greatest shock for many American statesmen was the appalling fact that Britain consorted with the Confederate States. For the United States government, any figure that they would eventually demand in reparation would symbolize the hurt the British perpetrated during the struggle to build a solid democracy.

Perhaps the rumored sum of one hundred ten million dollars did serve to make a point: The London government would have to take seriously American accusations of criminal negligence. Near the end of his speech, Sumner rephrased a point that he had begun earlier, namely, that for future transatlantic relations to exist at all America must have a reckoning with England: "If the case against England is strong, and if our claims are unprecedented in magnitude, it is only because the conduct of this power [England] at a trying period was most unfriendly, . . . Life and property were both swallowed up, leaving behind a deep-seated sense of enormous wrong, as yet unatoned and even unacknowledged . . ." That day in the Senate, April 13, 1869, Sumner concluded his speech, stating that the proposed Johnson-Clarendon Convention was an "attempt to close this great international debate without a complete settlement"; such weak legislation would be "puerile" (Sumner, v. 13: 90).

Important to note, Charles Sumner softened his tone as much as possible: "The truth must be told,—not in anger, but in sadness," the Senator stated, "England has done to the United States an injury most difficult to measure" (Sumner, v. 13: 93). In that way, the Senator effectively pointed out that no further agreements of any kind could be made with Britain until the truth about their covert actions were fully revealed, and a process begun to demand restitution—the entire set of international relations covered in the appellation "*Alabama* claims." Only with a thorough examination of the documented facts could integrity be reestablished in British and American relations. While numerous businessmen on both sides of the Atlantic feared a long grievance process, they understood the necessity of regularizing government-to-government relations. Moreover, European investors wanted their American property protected with goodwill, not just a signed contract.

While the *Alabama* depredations were well known during the Civil War (and evidently needed Sumner's speech to precipitate a solution), the Fenian Brotherhood agitation grabbed headlines faster. Before the Civil War, many Irish Americans in the major cities of the United States had organized into Fenian Circles intending to raise money and take action to win Irish independence from English rule. The war between the Union and the Confederate States had not been an interruption; many naturalized Irish Americans learned military skills that they would use later to further their goals. After the end of the war, the Fenians tightened their organizational structure and their ability to raise money for actions they believed necessary to make the Irish cause felt. While it's a fact that the majority of Irish Americans settled peacefully, especially those employed in the expanding West, the numbers of Irish immigrants and the nearness to Britain made Fenian actions on the East Coast more likely.

In March 1866, Fenians exploited insecure and uncertain international boundaries at Eastport, Maine, near the New Brunswick border across from Campobello Island, where a number of the Fenians gathered, their numbers increasing in April. On the 14th, a group of Fenians sailed to Indian Island off Campobello and seized the British flag, then returned to Maine, an amateurish fiasco which the American military sternly but peacefully rebuked. But matters intensified when the Fenians caused alarm in riverside and seacoast villages such as Calais and St. Stephen, and St. George and St. Andrews (Neidhardt, 44-54; Jenkins, 135-41). Scholars such as Brian Jenkins and W. S. Neidhardt tell essentially the same story of the Fenians in North America but with differing degrees of emphasis and detail. Bell's sense of urgency at the end of *New Tracks* is two-fold: An exhortation directed at Americans who should dismiss the *Alabama* claims as political theatre while demanding that American congressmen who fear the Irish vote must consider trade relations with Britain first.

Early on June 1, 1866, hundreds of Fenians crossed the Niagara River from north of Buffalo, New York, into Canada intending to march on Ft. Erie but rerouted to Ridgeway, where they killed seven Canadians, the Fenians also taking losses. Almost at the same time, Fenians gathered near St. Albans, Vermont—certainly an unlucky village—where in October 1864 three banks had been robbed by Confederate States soldiers hiding in Canada. This particular occasion in June 1866, the Fenians crossed from Vermont into Canada and occupied villages or wrecked property at Pigeon Hill, Frelighsburg, St. Armand, and Stanbridge (Neidhardt, 59-63, 76-81). These and other attempts to get at England through British North America were indicative of a border security problem, and Canadian people (technically British North Americans) began to demand stricter control at a time when Britain had hesitated to spend money on border defense. The Canadians continued the proceedings that would conclude in the Confederation of the Dominion of Canada on July 1, 1867. Creation of a national militia was a priority.

To further complicate matters, Secretary of State William Henry Seward may have believed the United States could gain a strategic position by allowing the British to fear that the Fenians would attack Canada again, and many Fenians believed that Seward encouraged them though there is some debate as to Seward's actual intentions (Jenkins, 67, 158; Neidhardt, 30, 44). Whatever the case, the United States government had to determine what action to take to prevent naturalized Irish Americans from harassing British North America that would be both mindful of the Irish American vote but also observe international law.

The British government seemed less eager to solve the problem of naturalized Irish American Fenians who returned to England to cause trouble there, and had suspended habeas corpus; moreover, they believed that once born in Britain a person could never become the citizen of another nation, called the doctrine of inalienable allegiance. In an effort to solve the question of citizenship for all Americans living abroad—and eventually to clear up the *Alabama* claims and border disputes between British Columbia and the State of Washington—Britain and America agreed to a Naturalization Treaty in July 1870, a treaty which was the London government's admission that American citizenship was a legally defensible status, and Irish Americans had to be released from British prisons. A result that the Fenian Brotherhood had not anticipated was that their raids provided Britain and the United States with a reason to settle the matter of expatriation, while stronger border defenses meant they could no longer pester Canada (Jenkins, 11, 22, 248-81). Though further details on the Fenian Brotherhood's actions is beyond the scope of this study on how the Kingsleys arrived in Colorado, one can see that American businessmen wanted to attract European investment, but not to areas where emigrant labor might cause civil disturbances.

The British Foreign Office and the American Secretary of State were attempting to resolve the Fenian Raids by addressing naturalization when Senator Charles Sumner spoke against the Johnson-Clarendon Convention in April 1869. Another two years would pass before sound legislation was crafted and put into final form as the Treaty of Washington, and ratified by the United States Senate on May 8, 1871 (though other proceedings may have continued to June 17). Under the mandate of the Treaty of Washington, the *Alabama* claims would be settled on September 2, 1872, in Geneva, Switzerland, for a mere $15,500,000. I shall return to this topic since these maritime crimes played like subtle but discordant music behind nearly every international business transaction until settled that September, as well as directly affecting Canon Charles Kingsley's involvement in Colorado.

Looking at Bell's *New Tracks in North America* overall, the Chapman and Hall publishers may have perceived it as not so much a travel adventure as an investment prospectus intended to ease apprehension about sinking money into American mines and railways at a time when emigrant labor was necessary yet fraught with potential problems. It's too easy to fault William A. Bell for his Anglocentrism, and maybe we could forgive him for his fear of a minority of Irish Americans, but his views are impossible to ignore. Moreover, when we consider the factual accuracy of Senator Sumner's speech on perfidious Albion, we can interpret Bell's strident antipathy to Sumner's courage as that of a businessman who was being deprived of his treasured dream of profitable investment.

On further investigation, one finds that there are more ways to interpret Bell's reaction to Sumner, as suggested by social historian Geoffrey Best. In 1850, Lord Palmerston—as Foreign Secretary—spoke of the men of talent, ambition, and good manners in Britain who, though without land, wealth, or title, should be allowed to rise in the "social scale," if the "removable inequalities" of a lack of hereditary title could be handled properly, and if the man in question exercised his entrepreneurial intellect for the good of Britain (Best, 233-6, 251). Success came so early in Bell's life in this new atmosphere in which men of merit were welcomed into the upper levels of the British social hierarchy that Bell could not conceive how he could fail, unless his plans were blocked by forces (like the Fenian Raids and the *Alabama* claims) over which the working aristocracy had little control. Bell's reaction to Sumner's pointed speech on England's subterfuge also suggests that Sumner threatened the socio-economic system in which Bell had entrusted his identity. In that light, the subtext of *New Tracks in North America* is that Bell was writing to men of his own achievement level for whom obstacles to rising should be removed. From 1868 on, during the time of his election to the Royal Geographical Society, Bell rose in this social scale.

Twenty-first century readers attuned to the excesses of the imperialistic attitude might perceive that for his personal success Bell didn't really need to make it in America; his father, Dr. Bell, was becoming wealthy from his medical practice and had earned prestige from it (as one of the three ancient professions including the church and canon or civil law), and Bell had been a star scholar at Cambridge and welcomed by the R.G.S. In short, Bell's pursuit of financial riches in America was his choice. In his view, his ability to detect any risks to his advancement was a key to his success. In future, he would find every legitimate pathway forward.

In summary, Bell's engagingly written adventure presented the resources of the American Southwest as delectable offerings for the investor, a complete menu of every resource or landscape view Europeans could desire from profitable coal mines awaiting rail transportation to stream-fed mountain valleys awaiting the best breed of English cattle. Bell let the *Alabama* and Fenian Raid conflicts distract him from writing an appropriate conclusion to *New Tracks*, that is, a final chapter summarizing the land itself. During the months that the transatlantic disputes dragged on, ordinary working-class settlers moved forward with their lives and did not wait for governments to come to terms. The census-takers of 1870 recorded the names of many Scottish, Welsh, Irish, and English settlers who, without care for the *Alabama* controversy or concern for the Fenian Brotherhood, emigrated or migrated to the new western territories of Colorado, New Mexico, and Arizona.

In whatever way we explain Bell's nationalistic faults, *New Tracks* has proven to be more complex than on first reading. In addition to the topographical and natural sciences information, Bell's travel account is a record of the camaraderie that one Englishman experienced with individuals from a meritorious class of Americans, represented by General Palmer and Captain Colton. While Bell clearly stated his hatred of Native Americans, he also described that first layer of Anglo-American settlement—mostly trappers and traders who had become ranchers—whose modest establishments along the river banks would also be forever altered by the iron rails.

William A. Bell could never have dreamed that one day he—and English men like him—would be singled out for the fault of being too wealthy.

The unpredictable fate of an English investor in America

If we put ourselves back in the Eversley Rectory drawing room with Bell and Canon Kingsley and Maurice in March 1870, we can understand more clearly Bell's initial indecision as to what to say to the people he wanted to succeed with the most. Bell could not calculate how much the Canon and Maurice would absorb of the grand opportunities he had just begun to enjoy. Certainly, Bell wasn't going to ask the eminent Church of England clergyman to invest in anything, for to do so would be highly improper; however, Bell felt he'd been drawn to Eversley as though to request a blessing on his business projects in Colorado, the only future he could conceive of for himself. He envisioned that his fortune would be made in the American West, and this was what he hoped to convey to the Kingsleys.

Bell had to admit that his anger over Senator Sumner's speech had subsided, as had his severe doubts about Irish Americans. After *New Tracks* came off the printing press in the summer of 1869 in London, and Bell had gotten back to Palmer's trackside office in western Kansas, the American showed that the *Alabama* controversy and the conduct of Irish Americans hadn't bothered him at all with regard to seeking British financing for his own railway. In all truth, Bell agreed that any squabbles between the United States and Britain were only a distraction from the real business at hand: the economic development of the Western American territories.

For Bell to say much about these large scale plans to the Canon and Maurice could potentially overwhelm them, Bell thought, so he simply mentioned that Palmer had telegraphed him in early March stating that he and Alexander C. Hunt had taken the first modest step toward his railway-to-town development project and purchased the 6,000 acres near Colorado City, which he, Hunt and Bell with Meeker had looked at the previous autumn (Brayer, v. 2: 80). Maurice Kingsley was not one to drop his jaw, but six thousand acres was a much larger estate than the majority of English gentry could expect at home; his father was sure to allow him to try Colorado. When Mrs. Kingsley, and their daughter, Rose, joined in the conversation, Bell felt sure that all he dared hope for would come to be and that all the Kingsleys would warm to his own inner fire.

At an appropriate point, for the sake of manners, Bell turned the conversation away from business toward the interests he shared with the former Regius Professor, that is, on botany and geology. Bell told him of the incredible species of plants he had seen in southwestern America like the yucca, or Spanish bayonet—a prickly nuisance—but also the astounding ocean of grass across Kansas and eastern Colorado into New Mexico. In fact, while financial success was crucial to Bell, nothing could replace his original experience of the American West: the aroma of the piñón and juniper pines, the crunch of the Ponderosa needles beneath one's boot heel, and the tenderness of the infant wild flowers protected by the leafing out of the mountain mahogany and squawberry bush. For sheer geological wonder, nothing surpassed the shiny basaltic rim rocks on bluffs and canyon ledges, the results of recent volcanic activity. In that dramatic landscape setting, the studied concentration of the surveyors at work—Americans like Holbrook, Eicholtz, Miller, Runk, Greenwood, and Schuyler—made the entire enterprise heroic.

Of course, there were physical challenges in surveying across central New Mexico and southern Arizona, but the embers crackling in the evening campfire, and the magnificence of the royal blue sky after sundown arching overhead like a vaulted cathedral ceiling gave the beauty of religion to all they did. In a sudden awareness of interpersonal influence, Bell paused when the Canon gazed away for a while as though his imagination had taken wing. On taking his leave of Eversley, Bell was sure that Canon Kingsley would write an essay or a letter that would function as an informal sanction from the Church of England, thus encouraging more fine settlers to gravitate to central Colorado, away from other English towns forming in Iowa and Kansas. Something in the Canon's manner made Bell feel that he had truly succeeded with him; it gave him a touching sense of his former professor's sensitivity. Bell had hoped to persuade Maurice to go with him, but he would follow when he was ready—as I've shown earlier in this study.

William A. Bell stepped into the horse-drawn gig that would take him back to the rail station for London, and as he passed the line of trees above which the four spires of St. Mary's church stood out, Bell's thoughts refocused on the beauty of England. There was nothing more to be done to make the English landscape perfect. Even the new railway cuttings did not touch the most beautiful places. In London, Bell packed for the Atlantic crossing, and to learn more about railway finance and the purchase of land out of the public domain. He would bring about his own fabulous career out of the abundant materials of the American West.

The irony is that Irish Americans did, to some extent, catch up to any English landowner who, like Bell, had no intention of becoming a naturalized American. In the 1880s, an anti-alien agrarian movement caught on when farmers seeking to move further west from the settled Midwestern states, perceived that non-resident British subjects as well as English and Scottish syndicates owned an outrageous number of acres. While Bell was far from being such a large land owner, the anti-alien, or specifically the anti-English fury was aimed at men who had acquired a great deal of profitable agricultural land which native-born and naturalized Americans felt was their right. Joseph Nimmo, Jr., the head of the Bureau of Statistics in the U.S. Treasury Department, with the staff of congressional representatives, had collected information on the acreage owned by non-resident British individuals, and foreign corporations (including Dutch and German), and

Nimmo compiled the figures in a *Report* on the range cattle industry submitted to the Secretary of the Treasury on May 16, 1885, many years after the last time the Kingsleys visited, but within the years Bell was making a profit from his partnerships in Western enterprises.

The data of another *Report* was used by the Committee on Public Lands and presented to the 49th Congress as Report No. 3455, "Ownership of Real Estate in the Territories" on July 31, 1886 (U. S. *House* of *Representatives*). This Report No. 3455 was used to generate legislation that would bar non-resident aliens with no intention of becoming citizens from owning or controlling any land in any territory of the United States, though by 1886, most western territories with arable land had been made states, such as Colorado in 1876. Though the *Report* titled the "Range and Ranch Cattle Business" seems to have exaggerated the numbers of acres in alien hands (Nimmo, 45), and many owners were not practicing "landlordism" as claimed—that is, demanding exorbitant rent payments—the native-born Americans, and those naturalized who intended to settle on land they hoped to own, made the injustice known by speaking out. The result of the 1885 submission of the Nimmo *Report* to the Committee on Public Lands was the federal government's March 3, 1887, Statute.

For British investors, the Statute was unclear in its application—but clear in its intention—as historian Roger Clements shows. To clarify the application of the law, legislators of Nebraska, Kansas, and Colorado allowed local modifications and amendments to the Act to guide the role of foreign investment. For example, Colorado and Nebraska passed laws to "prevent non-resident aliens from gaining title to real estate" though mining was exempted. Even with these allowances, "New ventures in absentee ownership were now more difficult . . . ." and "Consequently these laws sometimes accomplished their object indirectly by persuading Englishmen to assume American citizenship" (Clements, 216-7, 222-5). Scholar Douglas Nelson noticed that in addition to exceptions for mining operations, the Congressionally-subsidized railways, even the Kansas Pacific, were allowed to sell land to alien corporations. Irish Americans and their native-born children agitated for the passage and enforcement of these anti-alien land laws

(Nelson, 47, 49-50, 57). The land sales that the law sought to end were those to wealthy individuals like John Adair, the Anglo-Irish creator of the JA Ranch in the Texas Panhandle; in 1875, William A. Bell had contacted him to (unsuccessfully) solicit his investment in the Denver & Río Grande Railway (Scamehorn, 14).

Economic historian Mira Wilkins places the 1887 Act in context when she explains that this Act ". . . to restrict the ownership of real estate in the Territories to American citizens" was "enacted barely a month after the Interstate Commerce Commission Act and three years before the Sherman Antitrust Act" and "reflected the same populist viewpoint" (Wilkins, 581). Even with allowances to mining operations, the federal act was generally interpreted as severe, as William J. Palmer expressed in a letter to Bell dated February 19, 1891, in which Palmer wrote that he was ". . . hampered in his business dealings with British investors by the Colorado statute, which he [Palmer] described as 'conclusive and prohibitory'" (Clements, 224-5; Scamehorn, 29).

By then, 1891, Bell was living mostly in England, though staying in Colorado for much of every year, and still gaining financially from his investments in mines in Utah and western Colorado. In 1893, Bell purchased Pendell Court, an old manor-style house in the Surrey village of Bletchingley (in ancient times spelled without the 't'). It had never occurred to Bell to become an American citizen. Even though Bell's English style never wore off in frontier conditions, his fiancée might have doubted his promise that their children's future would be in England; in May 1872, he had wed Cara Georgina Whitmore Scovell while in Britain on business.

As it turned out for the Bells, they were right that England's proven social connections would benefit their descendents, but that is not the whole picture: William and Cara Bell were successful in transmitting to their children a love of family, and a supportive atmosphere in which their grandchildren could flourish in turn. The Bell's oldest child, Cara Rowena Bell, born in England, 1874, married Harold Vyvyan Pearce, a Vice-Consul in Denver, whose father had been a mineralogist as well as previous Vice-Consul. Margaret Angela Bell, born in 1875 also in England, married Sir Montagu Frederick Montagu-Pollock, the 3rd Baronet, a Cambridge University graduate.

The Bell's third child, daughter Hyacinthe Mary, born at the Briarhurst house in Manitou Springs in 1881, married Captain Patrick James Boyle, the 8th Viscount Kelburn, who on December 13, 1915, inherited his father's title and responsibilities as the Earl of Glasgow. The Bell's youngest child and only son, Archie, that is William Archibald Juxon Bell, England-born in 1883, married Isabel Maude Ottley, the daughter of the Reverend Edward Ottley of Bletchingly. In 1921, at his father's death, Archie inherited the Pendell Court manor house and eventually had no ties to Colorado.

In the next chapter, continuing with the historical context of British financial investment in Colorado—before turning to the topic of Rose Kingsley's lyrical sojourn—I'll investigate further the role of independent financier William Henry Blackmore. In the Blackmore story, we get deeper into the entanglement of financial and emotional investment in Colorado. As an independent, Blackmore had the freedom to engage in any enterprise that suited his desires, however, he was as a result more vulnerable to failure. Within seven years of his historic deal with the Dutch purchase of the Costilla Estate (the southern half of the Sangre de Cristo Land Grant) and their financing of the Denver & Río Grande Railway, Blackmore's missteps and failures began to tell on him.

After his successful marketing of the Costilla Estate, Blackmore over-extended his New Mexico land grant holdings to include the substantial Cañón de Chama Grant, even when the Panic of 1873 seized American markets after the Vienna stock market collapse had spread to Germany, a market for American railroad securities (Wilkins, 121). Blackmore was so enthralled with the American Southwest that he assumed his fascination with the land—and the ease with which he wrested enormous acreages from the original *nuevoméxicano* heirs—would attract investment even when there was no hope that a railway would be constructed in the area. Or, maybe Blackmore was heady with the "champagne air" many Europeans noted in Colorado, and the absence of any of the diseases that occasionally swept through England's major cities.

In addition to overestimating his potential, Blackmore seems not to have given himself enough time to mourn the loss of his wife, Mary Sidford, who died far from home, in Bozeman, Montana, probably from peritonitis, while she and Blackmore (and his nephew Sidford Frederick Hamp) were on the August 1872 Hayden expedition to the Yellowstone country. These personal and business missteps became embarrassing in 1878 when Blackmore couldn't even scrape together the cash to visit his New Mexico land holdings.

As one can imagine, his career had begun with such promise.

British financier William Blackmore's pivotal role in Colorado development

As soon as William J. Palmer's work for the Kansas Pacific was complete, he opened an office in Denver—as noted earlier in this study—and incorporated the Denver & Río Grande Railway Company on October 27, 1870, then, departed for Europe with Queen Palmer after their November wedding in New York, and on arrival in London, commenced searching for railway financing. When archivist Herbert Brayer sorted and analyzed the D&RG business papers in the 1940s, there was no clear evidence that Bell and Palmer immediately contacted William Blackmore or if they first met with other financiers; however, other documents suggest that Bell first solicited minor investments from individual Englishmen, perhaps, during the winter of 1869 to 1870. It's possible Bell had already met Blackmore in England during the previous winter of 1868 to 1869, when he (Bell) was learning as much as possible about the bond market for the Union Pacific Eastern Division (Brayer, v. 2: 38-43), and, I might add, while writing *New Tracks*. Since Palmer needed major backing for the D&RG, he and Bell sought out the independent financier, a move which suggests that Bell's fears that the CSS *Alabama* dispute would impede transatlantic investment were unfounded.

By the end of October 1870, Blackmore had become a celebrity in the financial world due to his much publicized success persuading Wertheim & Gompertz of Amsterdam to enter into a contract to purchase a million dollars of bonds from the United States Freehold Land & Emigration Company, the corporate owners of the Costilla Estate, a land development contract that Blackmore had worked for since early 1869. By the time that Palmer and Bell met with Blackmore in his Belgrave Mansions office December 29 (1870), the English financier was experienced enough about the operation of the global railway financial markets to effectively advise them (Brayer, v. 2: 41-4). Blackmore's eagerness to advise Palmer was due to his need for a railway route to enter the San Luís Valley to ensure the value of the Costilla Estate for the Amsterdam investors, even though Palmer himself didn't know when he could build a branch line into the Valley, a challenge he would be forced to address while sitting in Blackmore's Belgrave office.

Some knowledge of how Blackmore got this far in his career is crucial to understanding how the D&RG financing came about. Economic historian Brayer worked to get Blackmore's papers from his heirs in England and create an archive in Santa Fé (where Blackmore's sister had resided). While cataloguing the extant records, Brayer established the fact that the Wertheim & Gompertz financing of the First Division of the Denver & Río Grande Railway Company was directly connected to their purchase of the Costilla Estate (which, as noted, was mostly in south-central Colorado with one degree of latitude in New Mexico). After cataloguing Blackmore's papers, Brayer began to construct the story of the Englishman's career; due to the great number of documents and the necessity of giving narrative coherence to the story of the financing of the railway and Blackmore's land grant deals, Brayer decided to write of Blackmore's land transactions as a volume 1 of *William Blackmore*, and the development of the Denver & Río Grande as volume 2. I offer the reader a sketch—a necessarily brief one—that will show, through Brayer, how the business interests of Blackmore and the Dutch company and the distinguished American Civil War veteran coincided in those autumn days of 1870; in addition, the successful conclusion of these business meetings in Amsterdam and London was celebrated by General and Mrs. Palmer in a five-day visit to the Kingsleys in Eversley, Hampshire.

Given Blackmore's rise to fame in the European financial world, and his connection to the Costilla Estate in south-central Colorado, it was inevitable that Palmer contact him (since Palmer's associates had already agreed to avoid congressional financing). And, given that Blackmore was highly professional and appeared competent, Palmer could not have been aware of the financier's personal faults nor suspected how his tragedy would unfold, even if Palmer was the most perceptive person. Going back to the year of William Henry Blackmore's birth, 1827, one can get an idea of the mid-Victorian setting in which Blackmore would rise in social and financial status. His father was a very successful woolen draper and cloth merchant in Salisbury; his mother, Eliza Shorto, was the daughter of a jeweler and cutlery merchant who influenced his grandson's interests in geology, botany, and archeology.

As described by biographer Anthony Hamber, young Blackmore's energy and aptitude were recognized by his accomplished and supportive family. After attendance at King's College in Bruton, Somerset, Blackmore became an apprentice solicitor at his uncle John Lambert's firm in Salisbury before moving to Liverpool in 1849 to join solicitors Duncan, Squarey and Duncan, at a time when the Liverpool port was expanding (Hamber, 11-14). In short, it would be reasonable to say that Blackmore's early success was shaped by the network of maritime merchants, bankers, and law firms which were entangled with the American system of enslaved labor because with profits and prestige, they could rise in the British social and economic system of the 1840s.

Many of the complexities of English investment in the United States in those years—before, during, and immediately after the Civil War—were witnessed by William Brown, whose nephew John Crosby Brown wrote of them in his *A Hundred Years of Merchant Banking*, a history of the two investment firms mentioned earlier as working with Blackmore in various transactions, namely, Brown, Shipley & Company and Brown Brothers & Company. In his tome on transatlantic banking, Brown demonstrates, through extensive quotations from business correspondence, that the habit of granting credit to Southern businesses was directly related to the expectation of profits mostly from enslaved labor. One of the Brown Brothers associates mentioned that greater profits were expected after the war from the labor of free men, but that observation may have been made (or put into print) only after the Civil War began—obviously, another subject suggesting research possibilities beyond this study on English travelers to Colorado.

When Blackmore and the Brown Brothers reduced their connections to Liverpool and trade with the Southern states, it may have been for strategic business reasons and not moral ones. Though Blackmore and the Brown brothers could see from the beginning that the Southern cause was hopeless due to the economic power of the North, that didn't mean they wanted to withdraw all their financial ties from the South. But the salient point about Liverpool by April 1861 was that more cotton than ever before was being shipped through to the Lancashire textile mills where—it should be noted—varying degrees of low-wage labor and unhealthy working conditions had been the norm.

In 1862, the international business lawyers Blackmore worked with might have known nothing of the construction of the CSS *Alabama* across the Mersey from Liverpool in the Birkenhead docks; however, Hamber points out that Blackmore's law partner, Andrew Tucker Squarey, was an advisor to the Thames and Mersey Marine Insurance Company and by 1857 was solicitor to the Mersey Dock and Harbour Board (Hamber, 43), proof enough that Squarey knew that in 1861 ships were under construction for the Confederate States. Maritime historian Renata Eley Long's detailed account shows that Squarey was not only well-informed by intelligence agents but was admirably diligent in preparing evidence that the *Alabama* should be immediately seized for violation of the Foreign Enlistment Act (Long, 90-3, 96-8).

In 1865, Blackmore purchased Shepley House south of London that would become his showcase home, having moved his primary business office to the same Founders Court, Lothbury, London, building as Brown, Shipley and Company, with whom Blackmore remained closely associated. While in Liverpool, Blackmore had become a "significantly wealthy man" and would maintain a small office there since Americans on Atlantic crossings used the port (Hamber, 36-7, 39, 43). Entrepreneurs like Blackmore believed that, in Hamber's words, "America held the possibility of even greater opportunities" after the war, and that new wealth could be made in America by "a new type of British private middle class investor" (Hamber, 42-3), meaning, one assumes, that the industrial North would be victorious. Blackmore's plan was to represent those new types of British—specifically, English—investors in the American West, as though investing in America with money first made from Southern contracts was an act of benevolence.

Blackmore's transition from maritime commerce to a focus on Western American railways, mining, and real estate is easy to understand given that London financiers had long invested in American railways, as economic historian Mira Wilkins shows. From about 1853 to 1860, U.S. railways "added 16,786 miles of railroad track" during a time that British banking institutions were in the business of attracting other European investors to the American railways in which they owned interests (Wilkins, 96). Though Wilkins's narrative is not easy to follow for readers unused to financial data, she explains the entry of German and Dutch investment into American railways as a result of competition with British firms.

As it happened, the "Illinois Central was the pioneer American railroad on the Amsterdam exchange in 1856" partly because "British ironmasters, who received railroad securities in exchange for iron rails, would . . . sell their securities on the Continent" and, as a result, "German investors in Frankfurt became greatly interested in U.S. railroad issues" (Wilkins, 97-8; cf. Brayer, v. 2: 61, n. 56). By 1858, an estimated "two-thirds of the shareholders in the Illinois Central were English" (Wilkins, 96). Just before the Civil War, seven American railways in addition to the Illinois Central—all in the Northern States—were listed on the London Exchange; moreover, the investment of London bankers in the Philadelphia & Reading was so great that they "installed the president of that railroad" (Wilkins, 97). One can be sure that William J. Palmer would not allow bankers so much power that he could lose control of his own railway. "Overall," Wilkins states, "the inflow of foreign capital into America between 1854 and 1860 appears to have been large, the 1857 Panic a mere blip in the growth of American prosperity" (Wilkins, 101).

In 1863, during his first visit to the United States, Blackmore may have noted—as Wilkins's research suggests—that for many British investors only clear Union military victories could guarantee a safe environment for investments. After key victories such as Gettysburg and Vicksburg, railroad securities once again became popular on the market, and by 1865, "U.S. railway securities issued in London represented roughly one-third of all railway securities issued in that market that year . . ." (Wilkins, 105). Though this percentage seems substantial, much of the post-Civil War investment in the reunited States was made by ever-vigilant German financiers. Indeed "London and Frankfurt houses bought [bonds] and would make 'vast fortunes' when bond prices rose" after the war, Wilkins points out, quoting Paul H. Emden, an earlier scholar on the power of 19th-century European capital (Wilkins, 102).

Financiers representing Dutch interests entered the post-war American railway market when the British investors who owned a majority of the securities of the Atlantic & Great Western Railroad found, while touring the United States in late 1866, that the A&GW was not in prime financial condition. The British investors formed an investigating committee, and among the independent observers was Frederik Willem Oewel of Wertheim & Gompertz. The British investigators put the Atlantic & Great Western in receivership in early 1867 (Wilkins, 114; Veenendaal, 70-5). Such a fate as that of the A&GW may have added to British investors' caution with American railways; but even when the British hesitated only briefly, the Dutch found an opportunity. The outcome of the investigation of the Atlantic & Great Western that pertains to the financial history of the Denver & Río Grande was that, as Veenendaal shows, F. W. Oewel became very familiar with the profitability of other American railways, and would pursue investment in Colorado and New Mexico when a railway there made access to resources feasible. Oewel became so knowledgeable about American railway investment that he thought of them as "his" railroads (Veenendaal, 74).

While the A&GW Railway was in receivership, Blackmore cultivated his American and Dutch connections (which would eventually result in the January 27, 1871, meeting between Palmer and the Dutch). In August 1868, while at his London office, Blackmore received an invitation from several Union Pacific railway officials to accompany them on an inspection tour of as much of the line as had been completed into Utah (toward the final link to the Central Pacific at Promontory Summit, which would not happen until May 1869). While Blackmore was in London packing for this extended sojourn, his second in the States, Charles A. Lambard, a financier for the Union Pacific (and secretary-treasurer for the U.P.E.D. land agency) was in London on business and called on Blackmore, whose previous legal and financial advice had been helpful to him (Brayer, v. 2: 43). While they discussed railway financing, Lambard (not to be confused with Charles B. Lamborn, the Secretary of the Kansas Pacific) mentioned that a friend of his in Denver, Morton Coates Fisher, was attempting to market the 1,000,000 acre Sangre de Cristo Land Grant of which he was co-owner with a former governor of Colorado Territory, none other than William Gilpin (Brayer, v. 1: 72-3), who had acquired the tract in 1864 from Charles Beaubien and his heirs.

Blackmore easily admitted he had never heard of any such million acres granted to individuals by the former Mexico government, and he knew absolutely nothing about the part of Colorado which Lambard described. Lambard explained to Blackmore that nearly the entire Sangre de Cristo grant was in Colorado Territory, with just one degree of latitude in New Mexico Territory; and though there were no railways anywhere near such a remote area as the interior valley of San Luís, Denver would soon have a connection to meet the Union Pacific at Cheyenne, Wyoming, then, surely soon someone would think of building south of Denver. Both Lambard and Blackmore assumed at the time (mid-1868) that the U.P.E.D. (Kansas Pacific) which had just surveyed a route—supervised by Palmer—over the

Tamara M. Teale

Ratón Mountains to the coast near Los Angeles, would get the funding to complete that plan. Despite the unlikelihood that a railway would be built anywhere near south-central Colorado in the next two years, Blackmore felt a sense of opportunity and assured Lambard that on his arrival in New York he would enquire into the feasibility of placing such a huge acreage on the European market.

It's essential to note that long before Blackmore's 1868 investment tour in the United States, and before his first visit in 1863, Blackmore spontaneously took up every opportunity to combine business and social interests. Early on, in the mid-1850s, Blackmore had become a member of the Historic Society of Lancashire and Cheshire and of the Liverpool branch of the National Society for the Promotion of Social Science. He was active in artifact collecting, and was an avid photograph and art collector, and founded a museum in Salisbury, as scholar Hamber shows throughout the early chapters of his book *Collecting the American West: The Rise and Fall of William Blackmore.* When the 21st-century reader glances over the albumen prints of American Indians collected by William Blackmore (assembled in Hamber's book), and the photograph taken of Blackmore in American Indian regalia, one can't help feeling that in collecting so-called artifacts, a fascination with destruction was in play since the men and women of Native Tribes and Nations of the American West were very much alive. Moreover, the collecting interests Blackmore pursued were those of other tradesmen's sons and characterized the rising professional class, the men of merit Geoffrey Best described for whom the lack of gentry status was not considered an obstacle to advancement. Blackmore enthusiastically shaped his life to fit into the British social order. His ability to socialize would pay off in America.

On his arrival in New York in 1868, Blackmore utilized the network he had cultivated from his 1863 visit, and made new contacts among the railway executives, military authorities, financiers, and men of science invited on the Union Pacific inspection tour, one of whom was Ferdinand V. Hayden, the celebrated geologist (Brayer, v. 1: 48, 73). Blackmore told Hayden what Lambard had said about the Sangre de Cristo Grant in the remote San Luís Valley over two

100

hundred and fifty miles from the nearest railway transport, and requested that Hayden do a detailed inspection of the presence of mineral resources (Brayer, v. 1: 48-9). Hayden agreed and accompanied Blackmore at least to Cheyenne (or, perhaps, they met while in the West); then Hayden headed southward, possibly via Colorado City and Pueblo and the road over La Veta Pass, to the military post of Fort Garland on the northern edge of the grant (in the portion that would become the Trinchera Estate). In the meantime, Blackmore had continued on the Union Pacific, and after the end of the line at Green River, Wyoming, traveled by stage to Salt Lake City. After a lengthy visit there, with business meetings and tours in the area, he returned eastward, nearly three months having passed in the bracing Western altitudes.

After a brief pause in Omaha, Blackmore stopped in St. Louis to visit the headquarters of the U.P.E.D. (KP) to confer with President John D. Perry regarding the marketing of the bonds in England (while William J. Palmer was in a nearby office assembling the expedition surveyors' reports for presentation to Congress at the January 1869 session). Somewhat audaciously for a non-American, Blackmore might have mentioned to Perry his hope that the U.P.E.D. could be routed from Kit Carson, Colorado, to the Arkansas River (near La Junta and Bent's Fort) then over La Veta Pass to Fort Garland and through the Sangre de Cristo Grant (though a route from the Arkansas River to Fort Garland had not been in the KP survey plans). The Englishman continued on to Washington, D.C., and New York City, where he conferred again with Charles A. Lambard, who was home from London. At that time, Blackmore had probably received at least a brief report from Hayden, dated December 5, 1868, since he (Blackmore) decided to sign that contract with Lambard and Morton C. Fisher to be the European marketing agent for the Sangre de Cristo Land Grant (Brayer, v. 1: 73-5).

This second, long sojourn, shows how Blackmore's combination of business and sociability was a winning formula. Around the time he had conferred with Lambard in New York City, in December 1868, Blackmore was a guest at a dinner given by the New York Bar

Association in honor of United States Attorney General William M. Evarts and was a guest at the American Ethnological Society in New York City because of their interest in Blackmore's growing collection of American Indian artifacts (Brayer, v. 1: 56-7). All this time, Blackmore had not even seen the land which he had agreed to market in Europe, but he believed, in Brayer's words, that "There were vast unsettled lands which could be readily and cheaply purchased, . . ." and that "the undeveloped resources of these lands offered an almost insatiable market for surplus British investment and speculative money"—and Dutch money, as we will see. Blackmore's vision (or greed, one might say) expanded as an "outgrowth of his contacts with the officers and directors of the Union Pacific and the renamed Kansas Pacific" (Brayer, v. 1: 57-8).

After a month or two back in England, Blackmore was unsuccessful in marketing the development rights to the Sangre de Cristo Grant; it suddenly dawned on him and the owners (Gilpin, Morton Fisher, and others) that potential investors could not comprehend what to do with a million-plus acres. As a solution, Blackmore divided the grant into two manageable sections; the northern half, called the Trinchera Estate, would be marketed by the Colorado Freehold Land and Emigration Company, newly incorporated for the purpose, and the southern portion, the Costilla Estate, bounded by the Culébra Creek with nearly one degree into New Mexico Territory, would be marketed by the United States Freehold Land and Emigration Company, another corporation created specifically to market the land and development rights (Brayer, v. 1: 76-9).

While Blackmore was preparing promotional material, he received Ferdinand Hayden's full report. Hayden wrote many passages with exaggerated claims, which he later regretted and would never do again. For example, he claimed that the land grant area ". . . could not have been more perfectly adapted to the wants of an agricultural region if it had been arranged by the hand of art" and it was "by far the finest agricultural district I have seen west of the Missouri River . . ." (Blackmore, 197; Brayer, v. 1: 73), statements which were hardly accurate given the aridity of the land. Blackmore would include

Hayden's report in his marketing documents to the Dutch, which I will describe shortly.

Meanwhile, in January 1869, Congress had been looking at William J. Palmer's *Report of Surveys Across the Continent*, written in an engaging style, as noted earlier, to persuade Congress to appropriate funding to build the Kansas Pacific to the Pacific Coast. However, Palmer's *Report* did not have the planned effect. Palmer had included an official military committee statement stressing the "military necessity" that the KP extend into Southern California (Palmer, *Report*, 237-41), and still Congress did not vote for it. In March, Congress formally renamed the U.P.E.D. the Kansas Pacific, and ordered it to resume construction to Denver and terminate there. Blackmore had wanted the KP to be routed toward the San Luís Valley, and he may have hinted to a few of his congressmen friends that having the KP do so would encourage the Dutch to invest with him, however, Congress was not accustomed to financing a railway based on how an Englishman hoped to make money (Brayer, v. 1: 73, 76).

Without hesitation, William J. Palmer resumed his work as Supervisor of Construction and saw the Kansas Pacific through its completion to Denver in August 1870, while Alexander Hunt and Palmer's other associates worked at purchasing the right of way for their own project south of Denver. As noted, Palmer had incorporated the Río Grande Rail Road & Telegraph Company in the city of Santa Fé on February 1, 1870, as an initial step to warn off competition, the same reason for incorporating the Fountain Farms Trust (near Colorado City) to protect the land at the base of Pike's Peak for future town sites. After Congress declined further funding to the Kansas Pacific, Blackmore still had to market the Costilla Estate, while Lambard and Fisher focused on the Trinchera Estate. One can safely assume that by late 1869, Blackmore had heard that Palmer had plans to build a railway south from Denver.

Essential to a full understanding of the impact of international land sales on Colorado is that the Sangre de Cristo Land Grant was not without official heirs, settlers who had been invited by Charles "Carlos" Beaubien to live permanently along the tributaries of the left bank of the Río Grande. In the 1840s, possibly earlier, these families Beaubien welcomed had walked and driven wagons north from Taos to found villages such as Amalia, Costilla, San Luís de la Culébra, San Pablo, San Pedro, Chama, and San Francisco at the western base of the Sangre de Cristo mountain range. Perhaps as early as 1763, a fortified *placita* had been located at the San Luís or Costilla sites; Gilpin's acquaintance, metallurgist Nathaniel P. Hill, recorded that he had stayed at the home of a man named Amidor Sanchez (Hill, 267).

The villages mentioned were the well-established results of slow settlement. The Hispano and *nuevoméxicano* settlers raised their sheep, worked their *acequias*, and were grateful for every harvest. In the late winter and early spring, when the snow-covered summits of the Sangre de Cristos glowed red from the setting sun, the Hispano settlers saw reflected in them the blood of Christ and were inspired. Visually, the blend of irrigated meadows, cottonwood-lined streams, and cobalt blue sky over lofty mountain summits suggests that the early *nuevoméxicano* settlers were indeed infused by religious feeling. Even today, a mystical aura surrounds each summit; a haunted feeling radiates from every austere volcanic bluff.

For European entrepreneurs in the post-Civil War era, hearing of cheap land in Western America seemed a release from the angry nations of Europe. The success of the Hispano settlers had already proven the worth of the land. Though much of the San Luís Valley resisted cultivation—particularly the area near the massive sand dunes—something approaching an obsession made Blackmore go full speed with the marketing of the Costilla Estate. Blackmore went forward not knowing or not caring about the well-established settlers to whom Charles Beaubien had promised that the land grant would be their home in perpetuity (of which promise there was written proof). William Gilpin seems to have ignored the original settlers; however, to his profound regret later, he had underestimated the extent of Blackmore's land grabbing hunger.

In the village of Costilla near the 37-degree New Mexico Territory line, a citizen's committee formed to establish their prior rights and resist potential quit claims. The local leaders included Jésus Maria

Barilla, Noberto Marquez, Faustin Medina, and Juan de Jésus Bernal, who elected local merchant Ferdinand Meyer as chairman to defend them from Blackmore's and Gilpin's plans to market the development rights in Europe (Brayer, v. 1: 106-13), thus establishing a land and water rights legacy that has lasted into the 21st-century.

Blackmore's publication *Colorado* and the way to London

While the track-laying crews of the Kansas Pacific crossed the eastern Colorado prairie, and Palmer's as yet unnamed railway was taking shape on paper, Blackmore used his editorial skills to keep Colorado on the minds of the European businessmen he wished to attract. In August 1869, two months before Wertheim & Gompertz's agent, F. W. Oewel, agreed to plan an investment strategy for the Costilla Estate, Blackmore published a sizeable book of testimonials covering every investment-worthy aspect of Colorado. The full title was *Colorado: Its Resources, Parks, and Prospects as a New Field for Emigration with an Account of the Trenchara* [sic] *and Costilla Estates in the San Luis Park*, a title chosen by Blackmore that was almost identical to that of an article on Arizona Territory published in 1865. Blackmore's *Colorado* was a sophisticated production published by the well-known Sampson Low, Son, and Marston of Fleet Street, London, which he dedicated to his friend (at the time), William Gilpin, the first governor of the territory, as noted, from March 1861 to March 1862, who stood as a symbol of Colorado's increasing transatlantic renown.

At two hundred pages, *Colorado* was—and *is* still—a compendium comprised of public letters, book excerpts, scientific reports, and newspaper articles. Blackmore included previously published material from novelist Bayard Taylor, and from Samuel Bowles, newspaperman and author of *Summer Vacation in the Parks and Mountains of*

Colorado, and from Methodist Episcopal Bishop Calvin Kingsley (no relation to Canon Charles Kingsley) who stopped in Colorado when commencing an international tour. Blackmore quoted passages praising Colorado from the report Ferdinand V. Hayden had prepared for him, as well as paragraphs from an earlier pamphlet edited by Albinus Z. Shelden, the official U.S. Surveyor residing in Colorado City, and Edward Bliss, author of many pamphlets such as *The New Gold Fields*. Also in *Colorado*, Blackmore employed passages from William Gilpin's English acquaintances Charles Wentworth Dilke, Cambridge graduate (Trinity Hall, of course), and William Hepworth Dixon, writer and Dilke's British travel companion when in America. Investors could glance over the table of contents of *Colorado* and know that though Englishman Dilke's writing might be bloated with adjectives and over-written passages gushing about Colorado—similar to Gilpin's prose—the *Mining Journal* would not be wrong nor would Professor Hayden fabricate the presence of mineral resources. Samuel Bowles was certainly justified in calling Colorado the "Switzerland of America," and Bishop Kingsley wouldn't lie about the health and beauty of the travel experience. Blackmore intended *Colorado* to have coffee-table appeal and to sit prominently on the reference shelves of the most knowledgeable and well-connected financial advisors in Europe.

William Blackmore's book production had the polish and style—and length—that previous literary attempts did not, but *Colorado* would not have taken its final form if others before Blackmore had not attempted similar promotional efforts. Like many Englishmen, Blackmore had originally heard of Colorado gold mines from—of course, William Gilpin, the premier visionary gentleman pioneer. Gilpin's early birth year of 1813 enabled him to participate in the age of exploration (as noted earlier, as an expedition companion of John C. Frémont) and play a foundational role in the settlement era as well. Gilpin's pamphlet *The Central Gold Region* (1860) had been circulated in Europe, but Gilpin's lyrical sentences owed more to fiction than to science. Nonetheless, Gilpin's views carried weight. Among the first Anglo-Americans to be smitten with the San Luís Valley, Gilpin had made many friends there (at first). He had acquired most of the Sangre de Cristo Land Grant by 1864 largely because Charles Beaubien had an affinity with Gilpin as a fellow entrepreneur. After Beaubien's death, his widow followed through on her husband's wish to ensure that Gilpin would control the land grant (Karnes, 304-5). Then, Gilpin formed the aforementioned partnership with Charles Lambard and Morton C. Fisher to place the grant on the international land market, probably because taxes would be due.

Every quality Gilpin extolled about Colorado in 1860 caught on after the civil conflict concluded. Gilpin might have been the motivating force behind the pamphlet edited by the Colorado City resident mentioned, El Paso County Surveyor Albinus Z. Shelden. Shelden's *Statement, Reports and Examination of the St. Luis Park Grant, in Colorado Territory*, of 1865, was strengthened by his authority as a land surveyor, though to liven up his account, he quoted Bishop Matthew Simpson (1811-1884) of the Methodist Episcopal Church, and from Gilpin, of course.

In 1867, Samuel Bowles & Company published Ovando J. Hollister's *The Mines of Colorado*, an exhaustive history of those who first developed the mining region to the west of Denver, their interconnectedness, and their relationships to the land and its development. In March 1868, Ned Farrell published *Colorado, The Rocky Mountain Gem, as it is in 1868*, claiming in a subtitle to provide "Information for the farmer, mechanic, miner, laborer, capitalist or tourist." For Farrell, Colorado City was not the gambling and drinking den that Rose Kingsley would find in 1871, but a place with "two good flouring mills, good schools, several protestant church organizations and good society" (Farrell, 43). Given the limited number of full-time residents, Farrell's claim lacks credibility, but it's very possible since population could fluctuate suddenly.

Another precursor to William Blackmore's *Colorado* was published by Robert O. Old only five months before Blackmore's tome. Signing as R. O. Old, in April 1869, while Senator Charles Sumner was delivering his speech against the ill-conceived Johnson-Clarendon Convention, Old's booklet was titled, *Colorado: United States, America;*

its History, Geography, and Mining. His *Colorado* included a "Comprehensive catalogue of nearly six hundred samples of ores" and was published by Old's British and Colorado Mining Bureau, Ltd., which he operated with William Cope out of their Bartholomew House office, a building that housed the Bank of England. In the Preface to this 60-plus page work, a statement Old makes constitutes proof that mining interests were developing at the same time as tourism. "Should a study and an analysis of the statements herein made induce any agent of capital," Old wrote, "or capitalists themselves to visit Colorado with the ulterior view of investing in her Mines, . . . the object of the writer will be attained." And in the very next sentence, "Further—addressing myself now to that large class whose object is recreation, and travelling for pleasure only, denominated 'tourists'—it should be said that certainly in no other country in the world, . . . is there such an extent of plains and mountains . . ." which would make Colorado "the Switzerland of America" to repeat Samuel Bowles's phrase (Old, 3-4). Despite Blackmore's emphasis on ore extraction and railway transport in *Colorado*, he took note of Old's mentioning tourism and included articles emphasizing health such as one by Bayard Taylor titled "Salubrity of Climate."

While numerous pamphlets provided information to emigrants and were serviceable, Blackmore's book-length *Colorado* had the scope and polish that got it noticed by major financiers. Economic historian, Augustus Veenendaal, Jr., notes that English and French travel books on the United States were quickly translated into Dutch and available in Amsterdam. Blackmore's *Colorado* had been reviewed by a Leiden University professor of history (Veenendaal, 40). With these laudatory publications on Colorado Territory circulating in Europe, one can see that Will Palmer and his English contingent could reasonably expect a readership in London and Amsterdam to be well informed about the scenic Rocky Mountains.

By October 1869, Dutch bankers Abraham Wertheim and Leon Gompertz may have read Blackmore's chapter on the Costilla Estate in *Colorado*, and were willing to make some form of proposal to acquire it through their representative Frederik W. Oewel, introduced earlier.

Blackmore found that the Amsterdam executives were very educated as to the legalities of purchasing land in other countries and wanted the strongest possible assurance that the land grant was the acreage that Blackmore claimed and that the title to the Sangre de Cristo Grant was authentic. Above all, the Dutch wanted the corporation owning the Costilla Estate, that is the United States Freehold Land and Emigration Company, to be validated by the United States Congress—not by a territorial government.

As a British citizen, Blackmore could not initiate an Act of Congress, but he knew a Senator who would be willing to do that for him, a result of his declaration in 1863 that he was pro-Washington. In addition, Wertheim & Gompertz placed the condition on Blackmore that their own representatives must check the presence of the natural resources which Hayden had assured Blackmore were there (Brayer, v. 1: 79-81). In December 1869, Blackmore wrote to Hayden to the effect that he had an informal agreement with the financiers in Amsterdam but they wanted their own people to see the land themselves. With strict conditions such as these, Blackmore probably did not immediately celebrate his first contract with Wertheim & Gompertz.

From January to October 1870, Blackmore and his business partner, James Parrish, had a series of meetings with F. W. Oewel, representing Wertheim & Gompertz, probably communicating via telegraph or cablegram. On January 25, 1870, Wertheim & Gompertz made a second informal agreement (the date uncertain), reaffirming their earlier commitment to purchase the mortgage bonds of the United States Freehold Land and Emigration Company which owned the Costilla Estate, but not until February 14 was the Company incorporated in Denver, and only as a first step since the Dutch company believed— with reason—that territorial governments were not as authoritative as congressional guarantees (Brayer, v. 1: 81). Understandably, Wertheim & Gompertz wanted their investment protected.

On March 8, Senator Henry B. Anthony of Rhode Island introduced a bill to incorporate the United States Freehold Land and Emigration Company. Senator Anthony was inspired to do so partly by the persuasion skills of former Colorado Territory governor William

Gilpin; however, it must be said that during the time Gilpin and Morton Fisher attempted to market the entire Sangre de Cristo grant in New York (before Lambard contacted Blackmore), Gilpin had found men willing to buy a portion of the grant—men whose names carried weight in Congress. One in particular was Governor of Rhode Island, Civil War veteran Major General Ambrose E. Burnside, who became a co-owner of the Costilla Estate, and another powerful name was General Robert C. Schenck of the Ways and Means Committee, who was elected a Director of the new Company (Brayer, v. 1: 76-7; 82-5). Without the influence of Burnside and Schenck, it's unlikely that Gilpin alone could have swayed Senator Anthony.

On July 8, after four months of discussion and revisions to the bill, the Company was incorporated by Act of Congress, a phenomenal feat since Section 5 of the Act stated that "the general objects of such corporation are . . . to promote and encourage emigration to and establish settlements on the lands of said company . . . to purchase, hold, lease, sell, and mortgage any real estate situate in the San Louis [sic] Park . . ." (Brayer, v. 1: 342), even though the land, i.e., the Costilla Estate had *not* yet been surveyed for an exact acreage. With the United States Freehold Land and Emigration Company incorporated by Act of Congress—though the Act did not confirm the title to the Costilla Estate—the next step taken was on July 14 when Morton Fisher, acting for the trustees Gilpin and Charles Lambard and others, deeded the Costilla Estate to the Company, and executed "a mortgage deed covering the entire estate in favor of the trustees for the bondholders . . ." (Brayer, v. 1: 84-8, 343).

All through this 4-month congressional process, Blackmore knew that for the Dutch to finalize a deal with him, he had to respond to their requirement that railway transport for natural resources and emigrants must be routed close enough to the Costilla Estate to make the venture profitable. A solution to the lack of railway was offered to Blackmore through his friend, William Gilpin, who, though not a businessman by profession, had kept himself aware of all business enterprises in or approaching Colorado; it was public knowledge that the Kansas Pacific had launched their final construction effort to Denver, and would reach that city not long after the U.S.F.L. & Emigration Company was incorporated by Congress. Even without being informed by Gilpin, Blackmore had probably already heard that Palmer would be seeking funding for his own north-south line running along the eastern base of the Rocky Mountains, near enough to warrant at least a branch line from the location of Walsenburg over La Véta Pass. On July 19, 1870, five days after Morton Fisher and the Estate owners (including Gilpin and Ambrose Burnside) transferred the Estate to the congressionally-recognized Company, France declared war on Prussia. The financial markets were temporarily unsettled but Blackmore remained calm.

All pathways to railway financing were leading to Europe, and Gilpin prepared to go to England. He arrived in Liverpool to address the British Association of Science on September 26, 1870, arranged by William Blackmore—of course—at the request of the Royal Geographical Society (Brayer, v. 1: 90). The former governor's presentation was titled *Notes on Colorado*, an impassioned argument that the Rocky Mountain's San Juan Range (the western boundary of the San Luís Valley) was the backbone of the North American continent—not entirely unjustified since several rivers originate there.

While *Notes on Colorado* was well received in Liverpool, six months later, in February, Frances Kingsley would have in hand a printed copy, probably given to the Kingsleys by Will Palmer when he and Queen visited. Such a typeset copy, which can be studied at leisure, might well have made a very discerning woman pause while reading. Archivist Herbert Brayer discovered a rare letter (or copy of it) from Frances to a friend—"Mrs. William H. Callcott," that is, Maria Callcott, wife of the religious music composer—in which Frances summarizes *Notes on Colorado*. While Gilpin's earliest biographer Hubert Hugh Bancroft "called the speech 'one of Mr. Gilpin's ablest efforts,'" Brayer continues, "Mrs. Charles Kingsley . . . took a slightly different view." Frances Kingsley's letter to Mrs. Callcott, dated March 9 (1871) states:

> We sometimes talk of all going off to Colorado in
> the Rocky Mountains, where our darling boy Mau-

rice is, [to get] a rest from civilization, Polemics, &c!!
It may amuse you to look at some pamphlets on the
said Colorado, written in that strange exaggerated
style, which, alas! Yankees indulge in—'tall talk' as it
has well been called.

Governor Gilpin is, I believe, a very remarkable
man, but his writing is simply absurd. The charm of
the country cannot be too highly praised, I believe,
but how could the British Association have stood
such ridiculous language? (Brayer, v. 1: 90)

It's easy to agree with Frances Kingsley about Gilpin's high-flown
rhetoric when we read such sentences as these from *Notes on Colorado*:

Where Colorado embraces and arches over the extreme salient corner of the Cordillera, is found the
stupendous culmination in bulk and altitude of the
mountains, of the valleys, of the running waters, and
of the climatology of the whole continent. To this su-
preme apex the whole continent ascends, by easy gra-
dations, from the trough of the Mississippi . . . Here
is the summit altitude of a stupendous cone of elevation, whose diameter has a foundation of 2000 miles"
(Gilpin, 15).

Perhaps Mrs. Kingsley believed that Gilpin leaned too heavily on
"stupendous" though it was a favorite adjective in that era. Certainly,
she hoped that something about Colorado was genuine. It would have
pained her if her son were chasing after exaggerated opportunities.

Making his way toward London, Gilpin met old friends and
maintained ties with his mother's family, the Dilworths of Lancaster.
It's possible that Gilpin traveled with Morton Coates Fisher since they
were related by more than Denver enterprises. Fisher's grandfather,
Jabez Maud Fisher was one of the younger brothers of Lydia Fisher,
William Gilpin's Quaker grandmother who married Thomas Gilpin.

Morton Fisher would marry an English woman in 1876, as recorded in *Genealogy of the Fisher Family 1682 to 1896*, by Anna Wharton Smith, privately printed in Philadelphia in 1896.

On October 4, Fisher and Gilpin were in London for a meeting with Blackmore during which the two Americans agreed that since Blackmore was the moving force in all the arrangements with Amsterdam, and had brought about the Act of Congress, that he should be allowed to have five thousand acres from the Trinchera Estate as additional payment for his expertise, a promise that Gilpin would avoid fulfilling (until Blackmore threatened him with a lawsuit) (Brayer, v. 1: 91, 116-8).

While Gilpin and Fisher were enjoying a splendid October in London, Palmer was in Denver attempting to finalize his railway plans while attending to his private life, a scenario I've referred to earlier. He had chosen the name the Denver & Río Grande Railway Company but it was not official. Miraculously, he was able to incorporate the D&RG in the office of the Territorial Secretary of State on October 27, 1870, only ten days before he was due to be in Flushing, New York, simply because on the 24th, Wilson Waddingham, an Anglo-Canadian, had walked into Palmer's office and given him $50,000, a phenomenal sum. Waddingham was the kind of adventure-seeking entrepreneur who shows up in Western American history from time to time though Palmer was acquainted with him through the Maxwell Land Grant, near which the D&RG was supposed to run on its way to Santa Fé and Albuquerque (after crossing the Ratón Mountains). That same day, Palmer received another wedding present: Samuel E. Brown, president of the Denver & New Mexico Southern Railway Company—Palmer's only competitor for a north-south rail route—went to the office of the Colorado Territory Secretary of State to dissolve his corporation (Brayer, v. 2: 27-30), thus leaving Palmer's D&RG as the sole railway company planning to build south of Denver. Also on October 27, or the next day, Palmer dashed off the telegram to Queen Mellen stating that Bell would meet "Mr. M. Kingsley" at Teachout's near Monument. Palmer sped to the East Coast.

In various archives, historian Brayer found drafts of plans Palmer wrote for creating a railway construction company and plans to market the first mortgage bonds dated November 5 (Brayer, v. 2: 31, n. 53), suggesting that Palmer took an executive express train departing Denver or Cheyenne, Wyoming, on October 30, arriving in Philadelphia first on November 4 for the business meeting the next day, and perhaps an overnight stop, then on to Flushing on the 6th where Queen was awaiting the appearance of her fiancé, while also packing for the crossing to London. There would be no let up in the pace of Palmer's life.

The telegram that William A. Bell received from Palmer to meet Maurice Kingsley at Lydia Teachout's country inn suggests that Bell had time to get Maurice set up at the Monument Farms, then ride forty miles back to Denver (an overnight trip with a change of horses or mules) to catch a train to attend Palmer's wedding (though his attendance is not a sure fact). From New York, Bell may have sailed with the newlywed Palmers, arriving in London in mid-November.

With a new but solid reputation as Will Palmer's second in command, it was critical that Bell prepare promotional materials. In the standard practice of combining literary and informational features, Bell gathered letters and newspaper articles for *Latest News from Colorado*, a 35-page pamphlet printed in London in January 1871 by Witherby & Company. Brayer suggests that William Blackmore, not Bell, may have created this brochure (Brayer, v. 1: 95); however, the brochure reflects Bell's future style. Moreover, while the only signed articles were by Dr. H. Latham and Nathan Meeker, an archived copy in Colorado Springs shows a handwritten signature "W. A. Bell" at the end of an article on the Kansas Pacific construction to Denver. Bell had enough knowledge about the colony style of town development to have written the articles on Greeley and Longmont. *Latest News* included the usual categories of "Farming in Colorado" and "Crop Results" but also a public address given by Edward McCook, fifth governor of Colorado Territory, "before the Colorado Agricultural Society" as reported in the *Daily Rocky Mountain News* in October 1870. McCook reported that eastern Colorado would one day be "recognized as the best stock-growing country of the West . . ."

(Bell, *Latest*, 5). This prediction would indeed become true in the late 1870s, when many British invested in stock-raising at massive ranches across five states, but until then investment was largely in mining and railways.

In addition to compiling, editing, and printing *Latest News from Colorado*, Bell was contacting wealthy individuals to persuade them to invest in the Denver & Río Grande. His limited success in this may have, as noted, precipitated the rendezvous with the celebrated independent financier. When Palmer and Bell made arrangements to meet William Blackmore in his Belgrave Mansions suite, they might not have known exactly how far advanced Blackmore's negotiations were with Wertheim & Gompertz for the Costilla Estate (after the Act of Congress in July). A clear understanding of the role that the sale of the Costilla Estate played in financing the Denver & Río Grande Railway Company is easy to overlook since the documents are usually separated in Brayer's two volumes: the business meetings and agreements to market the land grant both precede and follow the dates of meetings to finance the D&RG. While Queen and Will Palmer enjoy their honeymoon in London, he and Bell finalize a meeting with Blackmore for late December.

With the foregoing details on the career of William Henry Blackmore, the path to Amsterdam is clearer. In the next chapter, I conclude this narration of the international intrigue behind the financing of the Denver & Río Grande and set the final stage for the appearance of Rose Kingsley in Colorado Springs and her witnessing of the early days. For the present, I return to the scene of December 1870 of Palmer and Bell in Blackmore's office where Will Palmer must confront the realities of the railway finance world.

Blackmore takes Bell and Palmer on the path to Amsterdam

On December 29, 1870, with promotional materials and numbers in hand, Palmer and Bell called on Blackmore and James C. Parrish, a Philadelphian residing in London, to discuss their recent adventures in the wilderness of investment options. Palmer and Bell had determined that British financial houses were reluctant to invest in Western American railways for various unstated reasons. Since businessmen, like people in general, can't write down everything, it's impossible to know conclusively why the British had hesitated with certain railway investments.

Historian Herbert Brayer never states that the still unsettled CSS *Alabama* grievances hindered transactions; fallout from the British support of the Confederate States was a government-to-government matter, and investments were determined only by estimates of the profit potential and long-term risk. London bankers wanted to know why building the D&RG was cost-effective. "To the ambitious railroad promoter, cognizant of financial obstructions," Brayer writes of Palmer, "the most seductive argument [to encourage investment] was the assertion that the cost of constructing a narrow gauge railway would be thirty-seven percent less than a broad gauge line over the same territory." Brayer continues, "Here was an answer to the chief complaint of British investments: that the initial cost of railroads, especially in America, so raised fixed charges that dividends on stock issue were small and frequently non-existent." In a footnote, Brayer points out that complaints about the cost of building railways in America "is a strange argument" because British railways had much higher construction costs (Brayer, v. 2: 38). It would seem that even though the British had every financial instrument possible—especially limited liability fine-tuned by numerous Acts of Parliament— they still feared the failure of a railway in isolated Colorado Territory. Brayer relates that Blackmore had found London financial houses "temporarily suspicious of Rocky Mountain ventures, because of losses in the Colorado gold boom (especially those in which American investors themselves appeared reluctant or hesitant to join)" (Brayer, v. 1: 6-7).

When discussing his London experience with Blackmore and Parrish, Palmer might have expressed deep disappointment since he still admired English culture. He may have been sentimental about his 1855 experience in Wales and his observations of narrow gauge railways there. However, in London in December 1870 even Bell— the supposedly well-connected Englishman—recorded his regret that his investment friends were "cool toward the projected pool" of risk capital, as noted by Brayer (v. 2: 38). In sum, London financial houses had no motivation whatsoever for financing a railway south of Denver in a territory where the total population in an area nearly the size of Great Britain was only 40,000 (Schulze, n. pag.). Nor did the British financial houses show an interest in the Costilla Estate in the San Luís Valley. In contrast, the Dutch had the true motive to finance the railway.

At the fateful December 29 meeting in Blackmore's Belgrave Mansions office, the English financier told Palmer and Bell that he was near a final agreement with the Dutch to purchase the Costilla Estate, however, some promise as to rail transport was a necessity. One can imagine Palmer looking squarely at Blackmore and, without hesitation, stating that he intended the D&RG to be routed into the San Luís Valley. Blackmore took Palmer at his word, and crafted a proposal for Wertheim & Gompertz to develop the Costilla Estate and suggested that they also fund the D&RG.

This proposal was quickly drawn up but revised over several days, and on January 6, Blackmore contacted F. W. Oewel with Will Palmer's plans in which he, Palmer, stated that he expected to have the First Division of his D&RG finished to the Colorado Springs townsite by June (1871) (Brayer, v. 2: 43-8), a somewhat astonishing statement considering that the iron rails had not arrived from England and Belgium (and probably had not even been ordered from the manufacturer). Herbert Brayer did indeed find Palmer's claim in a document dated January 5, 1871, now in the Blackmore archives in Santa Fé. The connection between the Dutch purchase of the Costilla Estate and their funding of the First Division of the Denver & Río Grande Railway is unmistakable.

Knowing that he should immediately act on the promise he made, Palmer telegraphed to the Denver office that the project must go forward, though the Dutch had not presented a final agreement. Chief Engineer James Mersereau and Consulting Engineer William Greenwood, and the officers of the North and South Construction Company arranged with labor contractors Thomas M. Field and Moore & Carlisle of Denver to put crews to work grading the route which they had recently surveyed from the downtown Denver depot to Summit Lake and on to the future site of the log cabin depot below the Colorado Springs townsite (Brayer, v. 2: 53-4).

On receiving Blackmore's proposal, January 6, Frederik W. Oewel found that Palmer's promised rail transport warranted taking another move toward a final contract; Blackmore sent Parrish to Amsterdam to meet with Oewel, the watchful representative of Wertheim & Gompertz already well acquainted with the assets of Colorado Territory. Once in Amsterdam, Parrish telegraphed to Blackmore that two meetings were set: one for January 20 to make the preliminary steps to develop the Costilla Estate (as earlier agreed to by the Dutch) (Brayer, v. 1: 96), and a second meeting on January 22 with Palmer and Bell to discuss funding for the Denver & Río Grande (provided that it would run near the Estate as Palmer promised Blackmore). Blackmore then accompanied Bell and Palmer to Amsterdam—with Queen Palmer—and Gilpin and Fisher and other trustees of the United States Freehold Land and Emigration Company, who would manage the Estate for the Dutch.

In narrating these events, the researcher faces an interpretational quandary, since Brayer doesn't give an exact date for the conclusion of the sale of the Costilla Estate to the Dutch company. Brayer states that "After some months of negotiation, renegotiations, and investigation, Wertheim and Gompertz purchased $1,000,000 in bonds of the United States Freehold Land and Emigration Company for the sum of $500,000" (Brayer, v. 1: 91). However, this sum due the United States Freehold Land and Emigration Company was not "safely deposited in England" until February 17, 1871. Brayer's "some months" must refer to the lapse of time from October 1870 to February 1871.

Further complicating the lack of an exact date for the Costilla Estate transaction, Thomas Karnes, the only detailed biographer of Governor Gilpin, states that the Wertheim & Gompertz agreement was completed on January 17 (Karnes, 322), which it could not have been if archives show the Amsterdam meeting was indeed January 20. Also, Brayer claims that Gilpin had written from London to Richard E. Whitsett in Denver that the Dutch payment of half a-million dollars had been concluded on January 14 (Brayer, v. 1: 95, n. 1); Gilpin could have been off by several days, or "17" had been transcribed as 14. In any case, scholar Karnes's main concern was narrating the role Gilpin played in bringing about the marketing of the Estate in which he was co-owner. More likely, Gilpin's biographer meant February 17, when, as noted earlier, Brayer found that "the Dutch bankers had paid the half million dollars due the [U.S. Freehold] land company and the funds were safely deposited in England" (Brayer, v. 1: 95).

At the January 22 meeting, the discussions began between Palmer, Bell, and Blackmore, and Oewel and Abraham Wertheim and their New York representative, Louis H. Meyer. Oewel and Blackmore agreed that a financial instrument like a first mortgage loan would be the best approach to pay for the construction of the railway to the Colorado Springs townsite. Some few days after January 22, Blackmore had to return to London but authorized Parrish to act for him, leaving Palmer (and probably Bell) to finalize details. These meetings reached a major event on January 27 with Wertheim &

Gompertz agreeing to finance the railway and "to market $480,000 worth of first mortgage 7% interest bearing bonds, with an additional $240,000 optional for three months from February 10..." (Brayer, v. 2: 46-52; 49, n. 29). Much discussion was still necessary at least through the early days of February, but the key to Wertheim & Gompertz's agreement was the assurance from Palmer and Blackmore that the Denver & Río Grande Railway Company would complete a line into the San Luís Valley (which it did though several years later than hoped). Blackmore played the key role in finding major financing for Palmer's railway while ensuring that Wertheim & Gompertz and Louis H. Meyer would be satisfied that the Costilla Estate would have rail transport for mineral resources and emigrants.

On a daily basis, Palmer may have been telegraphing the Denver office of the D&RG keeping his associates up to date on developments, for on February 6, Alexander Hunt, William Greenwood, and Edward H. Johnson (perhaps an attorney) incorporated the Poncha Pass Wagon Road Company in the Denver Office of the Territorial Secretary of State (Brayer v. 2: 93, n. 50, 299) intending it to enter the San Luís Valley (from the Arkansas River near present-day Salida) and over Poncha Pass, thus ensuring that Palmer's promise to Wertheim & Gompertz could be fulfilled with more than just the La Veta Pass route as an *entrada* into the Valley.

Since Palmer was so taken with English culture, and he wanted to attract as many well-to-do English tourists and settlers as possible, his disappointment at not finding London financing may have been keen. Yet, the scholar Augustus Veenendaal found that "Palmer had become a great admirer of the Dutch and their heroic revolt against Spain in the sixteenth century through Palmer's reading of John Lothrop Motley's account of the birth of the Dutch Republic." For that reason, "Dutch financial help for his railroad must have appealed to him" (Veenendaal, 63-4). Practically speaking, Palmer and his associates could not wait for England to come around to Colorado investment; they had to accept the Dutch offer, for the reason stated, namely that the Dutch had the greatest need for rail transport of resources out of the Costilla Estate to the nearest market.

While the Palmers would leave Amsterdam to make a five-day visit to the Kingsleys at Eversley in early February, for the sake of narration of the overlapping business meetings, it's best to note first that after the Palmers left Eversley, they returned to London where William A. Bell had by this time opened an office, and the Palmers remained in London at least to the first week in March. Recalling that February 17 is the date for the Dutch bankers depositing half a million dollars in an English bank, again, the exact dates of financial transactions seem tangled, or there was more than one agreement, or an unforeseen delay, and yet a February 27 communication shows that Parrish telegraphed Blackmore that Wertheim & Gompertz were ready to "carry out the agreement made exactly one month earlier" (January 27) to "market $480,000 worth of first mortgage 7% interest bearing bonds." On March 2, Palmer (who was still in London) notified Blackmore that he had received a certain amount of "money" or probably stocks and bonds from Wertheim & Gompertz in fulfillment of the agreement; Palmer attended another meeting in London on March 6 with Bell, Parrish, and Blackmore (according to the Blackmore archive documents). Meanwhile, in the Philadelphia office, on March 8, three trustees of the D&RG, William Mellen, Thomas Wood, and Robert H. Lamborn, confirmed the arrangement with Wertheim & Gompertz, and as a result, on April 13, "[a] first mortgage deed of trust in the amount of $14,000,000, or approximately $16,000 per mile from Denver to El Paso [Texas], drawn in favor of the trustees, was authorized . . ." (Brayer, v. 2: 51-3). It was this finalization on April 13—by chance the second anniversary of Senator Sumner's speech accusing London of betraying American interests during the Civil War—that Brayer notes was the conclusion of all agreements with the Dutch, truly an event to celebrate.

The Denver & Río Grande railway was no longer merely a dream which Palmer had while gazing over the prairie from a Kansas Pacific car window. All through January, February, and March, the executive engineers Mersereau, Greenwood, and Schuyler had been directing the route grading (which they had surveyed the year before). Track laying and ballasting would begin after the driving of the first stake of the D&RG at the Denver depot on July 29, 1871 (two days before the placement of the first stake at the Colorado Springs townsite, near present North Cascade and Pike's Peak avenues). Within a few weeks, William Sharpless Jackson and construction superintendent, William H. Greenwood, were leading Sunday excursions for $2.50 round trip to the end of the track at the Littleton station (Brayer, v. 2: 63). In August, one of the excursionists was William Blackmore.

Regardless of how excited people were at the arrival of rail service, the celebration was not to last for everyone. The terms of the agreement with Wertheim & Gompertz had to be altered at some point when it became obvious that the D&RG could not build anywhere near the Costilla Estate for another six or seven years (Brayer, v. 2: 173-4). The Panic of 1873 caused much delay in construction; then the extension to Trinidad became more urgent than building into the San Luís Valley, in order to head off the Atchison, Topeka & Santa Fé.

The task I've taken up in this chapter—of simplifying Brayer's documentation for the reader—has been necessary if we are to understand how the Wertheim & Gompertz agreement to finance the D&RG took place two days after their purchase of the development rights to a half-million acres in Colorado. Clearly, railway and land development in Colorado involved international capital. Until economic historians like Brayer, Veenendaal, and Wilkins focused on the European financing of Colorado railways, it was possible to avoid mentioning the Dutch, as evident in George L. Anderson's book of 1936, *General William J. Palmer: A Decade of Colorado Railroad Building, 1870-1880*, in which there is never a word about Wertheim & Gompertz. Admittedly, the trustees of the Denver & Río Grande Western probably did not give Anderson access to their archives, and research conditions were very different in 1935 as compared to ten years later, but it's difficult to imagine how it could be forgotten that Wertheim & Gompertz enabled Palmer's railway to become a reality.

Of course, if George L. Anderson had wanted to research further, he would have been unable to do so since in 1945 he left Colorado for Lawrence, Kansas, to begin a distinguished teaching career. In any case, Anderson's brief book on Palmer is interesting for other reasons, namely, that even the Dutch as well as the small British investors Bell solicited, could not finance everything. In March 1871, Anderson explains, just before Palmer's return to the Pike's Peak region from his financing tour and honeymoon, citizens' meetings were held in El Paso County (that is Colorado City), Pueblo County, and Frémont County (Cañon City) to consider floating bond issues to build train depots, even when no one knew precisely where the railway would be located, though a preliminary route had been surveyed. In 1870, the official U.S. census shows that the population of these three counties was 4,314 (Schulze, n. pag.).

Overall, the Dutch had been persuaded not so much by Palmer and his crack railway team, as they were convinced of their own reasons for investing. Wertheim & Gompertz took appropriate actions, and sent Frederik W. Oewel, J. S. Smithers, and R. M. Krapp to verify the natural resources of the Costilla Estate; they would visit Colorado Springs in July 1872. Accompanying the visitors on their tour were Palmer's friends and colleagues including Colonel Charles B. Lamborn, former secretary of the Kansas Pacific Railway, and William P. Mellen, in his role as president of the Central Colorado Improvement Company and as a Director of the D&RG. Unlucky for us, travel writer Rose Kingsley was on her return to England or she would have given us a delightful description of the Dutch financiers.

On the Palmers' combination honeymoon and railway financing adventure, Will and Queen had sought time to relax, but railway promotion could never be far from Palmer's mind. Perhaps while ferrying across the North Sea from Holland, he thought of his affinity for England and Wales; Queen had already decided she loved England. One wonders about the timing of events, for on February 1, the news was broadcast that after six years of evasion, England had admitted its fault in allowing the *Alabama* to be fitted out for war and launched to destroy American merchant shipping. The United States and Britain announced the formation of two Joint High Commissions with the intention of reaching an agreement to be called the Treaty of Washington, after which the sum that Britain must pay in reparations would be determined in Geneva without animosity on either side of the Atlantic.

After a day or two of rest in London, the Palmers took a local train on February 7 into the Hampshire countryside and arrived
as scheduled at the Eversley Rectory, where Charles Kingsley himself met them at the door. Awaiting the Palmers in the next room
were his wife, Frances Eliza, and his eldest daughter, Rose Georgina, at twenty-six years old already a distinguished civic-minded
woman. At last the Palmers met the Kingsleys about whom they'd
heard so much from William A. Bell. In her journal of the honeymoon, Queen Palmer doesn't mention the presence of the youngest
Kingsley daughter, Mary St. Leger Kingsley, who would have been
18—only three years younger than Queen Palmer herself, nor the
youngest child, Grenville Arthur Kingsley, who at thirteen may have
been away in boarding school. Of course, Maurice was not there but
in Colorado expanding his agricultural and stock raising skills, awaiting the foundation of Colorado Springs. But the "expected delightful
visit we anticipated with the Kingsleys" began, Queen Palmer wrote.
The Palmers settled into their private rooms, then changed clothes
for dinner. "Mr. Kingsley took me in [to the dining room] and we
had a most interesting conversation," Queen wrote, "and I went to
bed feeling sure that I would *love* all of the charming family,—and
wishing that we were to spend weeks instead of days with our new
friends" (Palmer, *Honeymoon*, n. pag.; Baker, 188).

The next day, February 8, "After breakfast Rose, Mr. Kingsley
& Will & I took a long walk through Bramshill Park to Bramshill
House" the old mansion of the Cope family nearby, financial sponsors
of Eversley Rectory. Additional meetings in London called "Will"
away, that is General Palmer: "After lunch," Queen relates, "Will
went to the city and Rose, Mrs. Kingsley [and I] took a walk to their
pond." Thirty-six years later, Rose Kingsley describes how the house
and pond appeared then:

> When my father settled at Eversley Rectory in 1844,
> most of the garden consisted in a line of fish ponds,
> running from those in the glebe field, past the house,
> and joining the large pond belonging to the Church

Farm, behind the church [St. Mary's]. He at once became his own engineer and gardener. The ponds, except three in the glebe field which in course of time were stocked with trout, were drained. What had been a wretched chicken-yard outside the brick-floored room which my father took for his study, was laid down in turf, with a wide border on each side . . . (Kingsley, Rose, *Eversley*, 256)

When *Eversley Gardens and Others* was published in 1907, General Palmer had only two years to live. Only Rose remained to write of the site of the Palmers' visit.

Queen ends her *Honeymoon Journal*, as it's titled by the Colorado Springs Pioneers Museum. Mysteriously, words written by Queen at the bottom of the page are "Maurice the Idol" and then the entire next page has been ripped out, with a thin strip of the missing page still attached in the upper binding, as though a single motion of the right hand grabbed the page on the lower left and pulled upward to the right. The Pioneers Museum archive had received the Palmers' *Honeymoon Journal* in that condition. Certain mysteries such as a ripped out page cannot be solved, but one wonders if one evening at Eversley, while Queen Palmer sat next to the Canon Charles Kingsley, he might have talked too much about his son, building him up to the point where, years later, Queen regretted that she had written something negative about Maurice, then tore the page to get rid of her intemperate words.

The Palmers return to London—and Will to his meetings—before setting sail for Philadelphia in March, while Rose plots how she'll get to Colorado within the year.

Fate was not so kind to William and Mary Blackmore. While strolling around the grounds of his Shepley House in Carshalton after the end of various London meetings for the numerous enterprises in which he was involved, Blackmore might have mused about his rise in the social and business hierarchy of England. Though little evidence has come to light that titled aristocrats and landed gentry had entrusted their investments to him, he was well respected by the wealthy tradesmen and manufacturers who sought him out like John Horatio Lloyd, Gerald Potter, and Henry Hodding—men to whom he did not have to prove his social status or that he was a gentleman. Persuaded by him, they too, would invest in Colorado. Before long, Blackmore purchased land in the Red Rock Cañon area less than a mile west of Colorado City (and hired Ike Yoho, who might have owned land there himself). An ambitious and sociable man, Blackmore planned for himself and his wife, Mary Sidford, to join Hayden on his 1872 expedition to the Yellowstone country.

Looking at the narrative that historian Herbert Brayer crafted based on archived memoranda and draft copies of contracts, Blackmore took on business deals as though international gambling were his reason to exist. He'd like to own the entire Mora Land Grant through which the Atchison, Topeka & Santa Fé will plan a route, along the east base of the Rockies, and he makes a deal with Thomas Benton Catron, who had served in the Confederate States army. Blackmore will try to acquire the Chama and Conejos land grants, and he looks at one of the Gervacío Nolán grants for his grand scheme, the New Mexico Trust Lands program. He will inspect gold and silver mines in Utah and Arizona, a sulfur mine in Texas. Businessmen from around the world arrive at his Founder's Court or Belgrave office seeking further aid to Tunisia, hoping to attract his interest in India and South American enterprises, a diamond mine in Africa, and prospects closer to home, in Wales (Brayer v. 2: 42).

It's as though Blackmore had no *arriére pensée*, a point at which he could pause to reconsider the path he was on. He can be said to have a kind of addiction, but an abstract concept such as obsession cannot explain why he expanded his financial interests into four continents, and could not keep away from land grants in parts of New Mexico so remote that no railway could possibly approach the area. The only way to account for his obliviousness to the Hispano land grant protesters in Costilla is that Blackmore's early environment in Liverpool proved that textile workers and enslaved African Americans could be ignored. Moreover, the phenomenal success of some areas of the British economy created an illusion that he and the United States could avoid the Panic of 1873, and other economic downturns, crises, and defaults.

For Blackmore, business difficulties will exacerbate personal weaknesses. He doesn't seem to take a break to mourn his wife's death at Bozeman on the Hayden expedition. The albumen print visiting card of Mary Sidford Blackmore in *Collecting the American West* shows her as a refined and intelligent lady, her absence a personal disaster. Perhaps, Blackmore drinks a little too much, and then in the summer of 1877 he suffers a sunstroke, and before he's recovered he gets word from the Surveyor General of New Mexico that land grants must be officially surveyed and accurate boundaries determined *before* an Act of Congress can confirm a change in land title. Blackmore did not see that difficulty coming: He had promised investors that the grants were far larger than what the U.S. government will allow. It may have become obvious to Blackmore that he couldn't be sensible like his brother Henry or his cousin, George Lear Blackmore, both of whom had no problem giving up the English social hierarchy to settle into country life in the San Luís Valley villages of Costilla and Monte Vista.

By the autumn of 1877, Blackmore's "congestion of the liver" returns, while his investments in the Chicago and Rock Island Railroad and the West Shore Hudson fall through. Then the Denver & Rio Grande Railway defaults, and is blocked from the Ratón Pass by the Atchison, Topeka & Santa Fé, a mammoth railway enterprise with financing from Kidder, Peabody of Boston and Baring Brothers in London. By February 1878, Blackmore realizes that he can't get enough ready cash together to go to New Mexico for the month of May to accompany the official surveyors of the Cañón de Chama Land Grant; it would be surveyed at about 184,000 acres, not the 710,000 on which he had marketed the grant in Europe (Brayer, v. 1: 313-5, 338; v. 2: 279-80).

In March, distracted and lacking caution, Blackmore falls from an omnibus in London and suffers a concussion. His head wound is slow to heal, but driven forward by the business daemon, he goes to his office to complete pressing paperwork. Gloom descends on him, and he can't see his way forward. It's a simple achievement to attract easy-going Americans, but he will not be able to save face in front of his compatriots whose acceptance of him is conditioned on his remaining very rich.

On April 12, 1878, Blackmore commits suicide by gunshot while at his desk. His brother, Humphrey Purnell Blackmore will be his heir and executor though unused to the business world.

Rose Georgina Kingsley: "Mustang fever . . ."

In late-October 1871, the train which carried Rose Kingsley and her churchman escort departed Kansas City and moved slowly through the night, stopping at every town that had sprung up along the tracks. At daybreak the Kansas Pacific stopped at Salina, which, Rose knew from reading Bell's *New Tracks*, had been the terminus in the summer of 1867 where all goods were loaded onto wagons and passengers into stagecoaches for the long trek to Denver. Now, near the top speed of about twenty-five miles an hour, Rose was crossing the prairies where the tufted grass was "rolling away wave upon wave, like some great ocean turned into land in the midst of a heavy ground swell after a storm." Isolated ranch houses would appear from time to time. "It is a lonely life, that of a rancheman," Rose mused, ". . . . the only human beings whom he sees are the passengers on the daily train, or some passing emigrants, wearily crawling over the plains with their white-covered ox-waggons" (*South by West*, 32-5), in the customary spelling with two 'g' letters. With long hours on the train, gazing out her window when not writing in her journal, Rose was mesmerized by the breeze-tossed prairie grass.

One wonders who was the Rose Kingsley that the infant Colorado Springs would be receiving, and she might have wondered herself as the train brought her closer to the base of the Rocky Mountains. Rose had begun her public life as her father's secretary, accompanying him as he led the residents of Chester on seashore walks identifying shells and plants. In December 1869, she had sailed with him to the West Indies for a three month sojourn where they were the guests of Governor Arthur Hamilton-Gordon, only three years after the brutal putdown of the Morant Bay Rebellion. Canon Kingsley produced the book *At Last: A Christmas in the West Indies* (1871); however, he didn't know how to weave his daughter into his travel narrative, and, as a result, the tale reads at though he had traveled alone. For Rose, being her father's amanuensis was enough. At almost 27 years old, she was a true Anglican pastor's daughter—genteel and generous, actively concerned for all types of people—and in the American West was finally on the way to shaping her independence. She carefully observed the various American types as the train took on passengers at every farming community.

While crossing the night prairie, Rose might have, in fact, thought her father quite liberal in allowing her to leave England. Just the year before, her life course faced Continental Europe. The Franco-Prussian War had begun in July 1870, just a few months after she and her father returned from the West Indies. Rose completed nurse's training in Chester, intending to serve near the war front. She perfected her French, while her father was fulfilling his term as a Canon of Chester Cathedral. His letter of recommendation for her—addressee uncertain—shows how much he tried to shape her future, while writing a somewhat grating summation of her character, which he thought would help her. He wrote as follows:

> My eldest daughter wishes to know if—& how—she can be of use in the hospitals for the wounded on the Rhine, & especially at Bingen. She has, at the Chester Infirmary, thoroughly qualified herself for a hospital-nurse, & has received a certificate to that effect . . . . She is perfectly free from vanity, envy, superstition, & all those little vices & weaknesses which make so many lady-nurses troublesome . . . She (& I) object to her belonging to any Protestant sisterhood, or

engaging herself to 'obedience' to any Englishwoman, or English society of ladies. But she is most ready to give hearty obedience to any medical man—a class for whom she has learned thorough respect. (Martin, *Dust*, 275-6)

The person who received this letter from Canon Kingsley was probably deeply troubled by it. Thankfully for Colorado, Rose never embarked for the Continent, for the French nurses were meeting the military needs and did not ask Rose to join them. Within a few months, the Canon's duty at Chester was at an end for the year— Maurice having departed for Colorado much earlier—and the Kingsleys were back in Eversley where the newlywed Palmers would visit in February 1871, as described. The Franco-Prussian hostilities ended for the most part by May, and Rose was packing for the Atlantic crossing by the end of September.

In the early pages of her book *South by West*—the first hundred of which are her Colorado Springs sojourn—Rose does not drop the reader right down into Colorado, but sketches the context for her arrival. After a smooth Atlantic crossing to New York City, Rose and her escort, the Dean of Chester Cathedral, John Saul Howson, and his colleagues arrive about two weeks before the opening session of the Episcopal Church Convention in Baltimore, Maryland. Still, their time is tightly scheduled; Rose and her companions visit Niagara Falls. By October 10, they find it difficult to pull themselves away from the soothing atmosphere there, but they must continue on to Toronto. By the 13th, while on a tour of the north shore of Lake Ontario, everyone recognizes the rank odor of smoke as from burning wood; the dark ash obscures the lake view. Continuing on the way to Montreal, via Kingston, Rose learns that the smoke is from a massive Chicago fire and burning forests in Wisconsin (*South by West*, 16-8).

Heading southward from Montreal, the Howson party stops at West Point, the Academy nestled perfectly among wooded hills in autumn color. Everyone attends a church service at the cadet chapel. Rose notes that this is her third Sunday "in America." Already, she has met many church dignitaries; she and the Dean of Chester are magnets for any England-born visitors and residents. With a brief stop in New York City—to meet up with the Bishop of New York and his daughter and several churchmen who attach themselves to the Howson group—Rose and her new friends continue on to Baltimore where they arrive after dark. The next day the convention begins, and Rose is introduced to "Mr. S." who will escort her westward, apparently a clergyman from one of the Episcopal or Methodist churches of Denver, though his full name has not been discovered. During the convention, Rose notes the ability of each speaker; by the age of twenty-six, she has heard quite a few and is capable of judging. Her account is telegraphic—short sentences relaying only facts and recording only the initials of the people she meets. Rarely does she identify anyone, and when she does, her criteria for doing so is not specific. "Bishop Wilmer" of Louisiana, and his cousin Bishop Wilmer of Albany ask her about her approaching Colorado adventure, curious themselves about the new West. While in Baltimore, she sends a telegram to her brother that her arrival time in Denver is fixed.

Rose's Baltimore host, "Mr. B.", takes her to the train depot at about 10:00 p.m. at which time she rejoins "Mr. S." as arranged (*South by West*, 28), for no lady travels alone, especially the daughter of a churchman. Rose had been charmed by Mr. B., "who is a good botanist"—Rose being quite a good judge of botany as well. "Mr. B. . . . helped us out of some of our puzzles about the new trees and flowers we saw at every step," she recalls. "I got to know locust beans, buttonwood nuts, a kind of plane, black walnuts—and learnt to my cost the difference between hickory and bitter hickory nuts, which look just alike, till you unwarily try, and tasting the wrong one seem to be eating a mixture of sloe-juice and tannin" (*South by West*, 14). In her train berth, Rose falls asleep quite easily, perhaps even before the train pulls out of Baltimore for the westward journey, approximately five days to Denver. As the train continues through western Pennsylvania, Rose might have awoken suddenly recalling how the sound of the rushing and plunging water at Niagara Falls had made sleep all but impossible, while the Virginia creepers and golden-red maples were lit by the early sun shining through the mist (*South by West*, 12).

Though early in her travels, Rose Kingsley is already planning to write a book, but wonders how much of her thoughts to convey to the reader, being keenly aware of her parents' high-profile social and cultural position in English life. Neither of her parents were emotionally repressed, contrary to the stereotyped image of the Victorian household; however, Rose decided that, for her, personal admissions were not suitable in public writing. Her audience should expect plain and sensible prose. Rose decides on a moderation of emotion: "It was hard, after three days of such perfect enjoyment, to tear ourselves away from Niagara. Each hour that we stayed only brought out some fresh beauty, and made us long to spend weeks there instead of days. Were any one to take the whole journey from England and back again, and see nothing in America but Niagara, it would, I think, be well worth the trouble" (*South by West*, 16). When writing up her journal notes, Rose might have wondered if anything new could be said about the falls that had not already been written in the long record of Niagara tourism, but the falls lives up to its old reputation: Her nerves trembled at the power of nature. She need not have worried; when everything is new, one day's adventure is replaced by the next.

As the train heads toward Altoona, Pennsylvania, Rose heard that during the night the airbrakes had been used to avoid a collision with another train—one type of fearful experience on American railways. With the pine forests of the Allegheny Mountains on either hand, she notes "some black from recent fires, others with a brilliant undergrowth of sumac and dogwood." And, then the famed horseshoe bend was unlike anything she had seen. After Johnstown and the Connemaugh River and through the Packsaddle Gap, everyone changes trains in "the Wolverhampton of the States"—that is, Pittsburgh—for the run westward. As night descends again Rose sees a stern-wheel steamer on the Ohio River (*South by West*, 29-30).

At St. Louis's Missouri Pacific depot, Rose and her escort, Mr. S., have a break of a few hours to stroll around the central downtown, where she discovers an "Arctic Soda" flavored with strawberry for ten cents. We are reminded that Rose is English and writing for a European audience for whom a "drugstore" is a novelty. These "soda fountains are found at every 'Drugstore' in the large cities, with taps of different flavours, and generally one marked 'Tonic,' which produces something considerably stronger than the innocent raspberry and pineapple syrups." Rose explains that "Chemists are not allowed to sell spirituous liquors, except for medicinal purposes; and the police are supposed to search their stores at intervals," but any officer who asks "is occasionally silenced by a glass of 'Tonic and Soda'" gratis and "leaves the chemist alone till the next time he feels thirsty" (*South by West*, 31-2).

Rose and her escort resume their westward journey. As the railway runs near the Mississippi River, she feels herself to be on "enchanted ground," she writes, "to which if you have once set foot upon it, you must sooner or later return." Her words suggest that she was caught in a pleasant snare:

> 'Mustang Fever' is the name which Westerners give to that wholly inexplicable feeling, which is said to allure people back into the wilderness, almost against their own wills, when they try to cure themselves of their roving tastes, by living in the cities of the Eastern States, or even in Europe. Ere I went thither it was easy enough for me in my ignorance to laugh at this theory: but now I am not quite sure that I have wholly escaped the contagion. (*South by West*, 32)

Here, Rose has felt the force that could make her brother leave the gentle green hills of cultured and cultivated England, remove himself from hearth and home for extended periods, perhaps in imitation of their uncle, George Henry Kingsley, M.D., and his long voyages. In her reference to the hypnotic feeling of travel on the prairie as "Mustang Fever," Rose might have meant "prairie fever," a term used as early as 1851 by novelist Captain Mayne Reid in *The Scalp Hunters*, to show that thoughts of home were easily replaced by pleasure in action and indulgence in illusory ambitions. A wild horse fever or not Rose describes the power of the gently rolling landscape to call forth feelings which overpower reason.

"The moon was so bright," she continues, "that I was tempted to sit up looking at the country till nearly every one else had gone to bed." This "enchantment," which she first experienced at Niagara Falls, has come back stronger, this insidious necessity—which lasts longer than a mere "thrill"—that makes one stare into the night. With passages such as this, and throughout the Colorado portion of *South by West*, the reader can't help wishing that Rose had explained in more sensory detail the enchanting wonders. But had she expanded her metaphors and written a passage that the "mustang fever" coursed through her every fiber or that the moon was liquid, it would not have been Rose Georgina Kingsley. Within a few years, in comparison, Isabella Bird will give sensory detail; but Bird would be forty-two years old by the time she reached the Rocky Mountains: Sensual writing was allowed her. Even so, with Rose Kingsley the reader gets the sense that this 26-year-old woman was a very sensible person concerned with concepts of rationality, with no intention of gushing over the sight in front of her. Writing in simple imagery was more accurate.

As the train moves across the Kansas prairie past Salina, the mystery of the landscape galvanizes Canon Kingsley's daughter into getting up early:

> Now began great excitement in our car, which was the last on the train; and some of us went out on the back platform to watch for the appearance of the buffalo. This is not a very safe proceeding, as there is only a rail just across the end [of the platform], and the sides are open. Still there is something pleasantly exciting in sitting there as one whirls along the single track, over dry water-courses on fragile-looking trestle bridges; or between sandy banks, with high snow-fences to keep the snow in the winter from drifting and filling up the cuts; . . . (*South by West*, 38)

Rose wouldn't relinquish her spot on the platform, so entranced was she by the sight of the iron rails receding into the distance.

Continuing on its marvelous way across the prairie, the train halts at Topeka, then Manhattan and Fort Riley and other military settlements including Fort Harker and Fort Hays, passing many long stretches of blackened prairie where a spark from the train's "smoke stack" had set the buffalo grass on fire during the recent dry summer. And sadly, Rose confirmed what so many other travelers had seen: The train passed many dead buffalo in "various stages of decomposition" from the "cruel and foolish fashion . . . of shooting the poor animals from the cars as they go along, for the mere pleasure of killing" (*South by West*, 39). Thankfully, no such shooting was done on the train which carried Rose to Denver, but it seemed a fact that the buffalo were doomed. Rose noticed something peculiar about the telegraph poles; large nails had been driven into them in a futile attempt to stop the buffalo from using them as backscratchers. Instead, the nails acted as combs and provided the buffalo with a pleasurable sensation they were sure to repeat, until the poles fell down (or the bison were killed).

Arriving in "Ellice"—or, rather, Ellis—west of Fort Hays, the Kansas Pacific Railway stops long enough for passengers to get dinner and to exercise. Rose sees this as her chance to walk on the prairie. Sensitive to all plant life, Rose comes back into the train cars "with a handful of common weeds which were all new to me," she wrote. "Most of them were in seed, as the season for flowers, alas! was over; and some of my fellow-travellers were not a little puzzled at any one taking an interest in such rubbish" (*South by West*, 40). Rose's extreme botanizing flummoxed the American passengers, but she had collected plants since childhood on long walks with her father and the numerous people who accompanied him. Fresh on Rose's mind would have been the fact that just before she left England, her father had formally organized his natural history club into the Natural Science Society of Chester.

As the Kansas Pacific approaches the station nearest Fort Wallace, Rose is gratified to know that this stretch to Denver was the one for which General William J. Palmer had been construction supervisor.

Rose describes Fort Wallace as one of the "little centers of civilization with their neat white quarters, and the welcome Stars and Stripes waving from the tall flagstaff, as guarantees of order and protection out on the desolate prairie" (*South by West*, 42). This sea of grass near the boundary line between the State of Kansas and Colorado Territory had recently been the scene of American Indian self-defense measures as the iron rails and noisy locomotive engine encroached on their hunting grounds. It could be that Rose had also heard of the Beecher Island battle in September 1868 that took place just a bit further to the north near the Nebraska stateline or the battle of Summit Springs in July 1869, northeast near the South Platte River.

While Rose was comfortable with all social and economic classes, the American West in the 1870s made her face cultural tensions for which she was unprepared. Even though she knew that various Christian denominations had created missions and schools in an attempt to soften the blow of the new world order, for Rose, American Indians were simply primitive and hopeless. This is Rose Kingsley's one blindness. And it's painful to read about as detailed by scholar Karin Morin who finds that her transitory sightings of American Indians brought out the British imperialist in her (Morin, 322-3). It's no accident that Rose had quoted extensively from William A. Bell's racially-charged scenes in *New Tracks in North America*, and perhaps, for that reason, Rose tells her readers that the "name of Fort Wallace is associated with such horrors" as attacks by "Redskins" (or, in another point of view, their ability to lay down their lives for their native nations). Such views as Rose's foretell how she will be too willing to criticize the behavior of the Ute who camp outside Colorado City along Fountain Creek (*South by West*, 104, 134-5), who, in their viewpoint, might simply have wanted to satisfy their curiosity about the activity at the white people's new town—or possibly to act out in front of an English lady.

Putting her hasty observations in context as a newcomer, Rose was capable of some humorous self-reflection. Though she states she could not "divest" her mind of Plains Indians attacking, ". . . we met with no worse a misfortune than a very bad supper; and sped on towards

Denver" (*South by West*, 41-2). Not to excuse Rose's inability to understand racially imbalanced frontier conditions, it must be said that what comes through in her writing is her naïve authenticity, the same genuineness with which she writes everything. She had no educational background that would enable her to understand Native Tribes and Nations as Helen Hunt Jackson would before the decade was out. And Rose didn't know how to interact productively with indigenous tribal people as would her cousin Mary Henrietta Kingsley in Africa in the 1890s. While Rose Kingsley pondered the development of the American West, the Kansas Pacific reached the depot at Kit Carson, Colorado, which only fourteen months earlier had been the terminus of the line. With understandable pride in modern technology, and gratitude to General Palmer, Rose notes that the rail line had been completed to Denver in a one-hundred day burst of construction in the prairie heat from June to August 1870.

On the morning of October 30, Rose was up before dawn. From the prairie just east of Denver, the rising sun cast pink light over the mountains, the Front Range of the Rockies. Rose states that her train pulled into Denver at 6:00 a.m., with this mountain view she just described. One never doubts Rose's sincerity, and yet, the reader questions her, since such an hour in late October is quite dark—with or without Daylight Savings Time. However, we can trust that on her arrival, there on the platform stood her brother, Maurice. Throughout *South by West*, she will refer to him only by his first initial "M" as she will with others, out of a sense of discretion and to avoid possible false attributions. Rose admits to the reader that she was so glad to see him, that she said goodbye to "Mr. S." her generous East Coast escort almost as an afterthought.

She and Maurice take breakfast in the dining room at Charpiot's Hotel, the Parisian quality establishment which counted Grand Dukes, Earls, and rich cattle and sheep ranchers among its clients. The transcontinental rail link enabled well-to-do travelers and prominent East Coast businessmen to arrive at Charpiot's within about four days, weather allowing. Larimer Street would have been a bustling scene despite Denver having hardly over 5,000 in population. To Maurice, the town had grown tremendously in the twelve months since he first arrived. Later on October 30, Rose and her brother have lunch with "Colonel and Mrs. G." that is Mrs. Greenwood and the Chief Engineer of the Denver & Río Grande Railroad, after which they tour Denver—by horse-drawn carriage, of course—more than likely reaching the eastern edge of town in less than thirty minutes.

Early the next morning, November 1, sister and brother board the Denver & Río Grande for the trip to the Colorado Springs terminus, accompanied by the Greenwoods and "Mr. N.," Rose's discreet reference to Edwin S. Nettleton, the lead city engineer of the Fountain Colony at Colorado Springs. Nettleton had educated himself to this point in life when he could truly appreciate Rose Kingsley, not simply that she was the eldest child of an Anglican clergyman, but that she carried with her a certain cultural atmosphere. Ever since Maurice had told Nettleton that his sister would be coming to Colorado, Nettleton had been alert. Then, being in her company on the narrow gauge for the four-hour run to the Springs, Nettleton knew Rose would be the guiding light of the new town. More than General Palmer or even Queen, Nettleton saw that Rose Kingsley could set down the cultural structure in the same way that the streets are platted at specific angles. She would give the technological enterprise a justification; she would start the town toward having a soul.

Within an hour after the D&RG departs from the Denver depot, they pause at the village of Littleton, and soon the narrow gauge negotiates riverbanks and sharp corners which a standard gauge could not. They continue past the Plum Creek station, and the Douglas station (present-day Castle Rock), and the narrow gauge climbs to Larkspur, passing a large steam saw-mill "in full work" fueled from the trees available in "the pineries." Reaching the meadows where Maurice first tended livestock the year before, Summit Lake, what Rose calls the Divide, the train stops to allow businessmen to use the telegraph service. Winding along Monument Creek, the narrow gauge passes the Husted's ranch (*South by West*, 46), now mostly encompassed by the property of the United States Air Force Academy. The train slows along the Monument just north of town, the bare branches of the cottonwoods along the river banks dignified in their late-autumn forms. Rose has already written much in her journal for what will become her book, the full title of which is *South by West: Winter in the Rocky Mountains and Spring in Mexico* (1874).

The train reaches the Colorado Springs station close to 12 noon. Rose steps down, and glances around: the log cabin depot is the only building in the immediate area, and the only signs of activity are men loading wagons with the construction material the train has delivered. Maurice suggests to Rose that she wait inside the log cabin station with the others while he gets the luggage and ensures it's placed on a small wagon for the upslope trek to the town site. Rose and the Greenwoods and E. S. Nettleton all step into an adjoining room, and to Rose's complete "amazement" it is an elegant dining room as though in a very sophisticated city: "I was in a state of complete bewilderment." Maurice and Rose and their friends began to eat oyster-soup and roast antelope "when in came General and Mrs. P." Rose writes, "It was pleasant to find well-known faces among so many new ones" (*South by West*, 47), a hint so vague that no reader would guess that the Palmers had been guests at the Eversley Rectory eight months earlier.

As the Palmers join Rose's table, one imagines that she and Queen Palmer clasp hands briefly. Mrs. Palmer—so thrilled to have an English friend—explains that she herself had arrived only the day before on one of the first trains. Rose gazes at Queen with concern, gauging the young American's physical strength for mountain hiking, such a delicate woman—born 1850 in Prestonburg, Kentucky. Rose could not know—could not have imagined—that in five months, in mid-March 1872, she and the Palmers will leave the Pike's Peak region for Mexico, via Denver and San Francisco, and then by sea to Manzanillo, in the company of 4th Territorial Governor Alexander C. Hunt, for a route reconnaissance expedition to assist the Mexico National Railway, a tale of travel and adventure which is two-thirds of *South by West*—and beyond the scope of this study.

A Colorado colony: "of strictly temperate habits and good moral character . . . "

After luncheon at the log cabin depot, and the departure of the Palmers and the Greenwoods, and Nettleton to resume the business day, Maurice guides Rose up to the town site. "You may imagine Colorado Springs, as I did, to be a sequestered valley, with bubbling fountains, green grass, and shady trees" she writes, "but not a bit of it." Rather the reality is a "level elevated plateau of greenish-brown, without a single tree or plant larger than a Spanish bayonet . . ." Rose's description is unadorned prose, too. Maurice guides her to the office of the Denver & Río Grande Railway Company, a temporary building of only three small rooms "in which all the colony work is done till the new office is finished." The one-room wooden shanty with the tent in which Maurice had been working is sixteen feet by twelve—Rose is exact about this—and, still used by Maurice. It is "perfectly wind-proof, and really quite comfortable, though it was ordered on Thursday and finished on Saturday." The tent over the front door of the shanty will serve as a "sitting-room by day and his bedroom at night; so we can warm both tent and room with a stove in the former . . ." In one corner is a large pail of water and over it hangs "an invaluable tin dipper, which serves for saucepan, glass, jug, cup, and every use imaginable" (*South by West*, 48-9). That night, Rose's first in Colorado Springs, she sleeps on her camp bed, warm under buffalo robes; the next morning the water bucket has a quarter-inch thickness of ice.

She might have wondered what she'd gotten herself into, but she's got pluck and is familiar with travel hardships.

The very next morning at 9:00 a.m., Rose sweeps out the shanty and completes other household duties which enable her to settle into the new environment assisting Maurice in his work at the Fountain Colony office of "writing out agreements for lots and memberships" (*South by West*, 50), that is, responding to the mail addressed to the Fountain Colony. Rose doesn't give details on the cost of land or memberships in the Fountain Colony to avoid appearing a booster rather than a traveling writer. If her readers had ever gone to an emigration information store front such as the Labour News Office in the West End of London to pick up a pamphlet there, they would understand the pricing system for a Colorado colony. Scholars Willard and Goodykoontz show that in the 1870s the term 'colony' referred to towns platted quickly for new emigrants or Americans who weren't settlers, but wanted to leave the Midwest and East Coast and were willing to tolerate the early stages of town development, if a corporation would manage the details for them.

The Chicago-Colorado Colony which became Longmont, Colorado, had been advertised as being formed with a now-familiar corporate structure including an auditing committee, an agent in Chicago, a president and executive council. The constitution and by-laws of the Chicago-Colorado Colony clearly stated that the purpose was to attract people of "strictly temperate habits and good moral character," men with families who will "assent to this plan of organization" and pay "an initiation fee of five dollars ($5) on enrolling his name, to be used in defraying the expenses of the preliminary organization . . ." An additional payment of $150 would entitle the new settler to "all the rights and privileges of membership" in the colony at Longmont (Willard, 138-9), and not only for people from Chicago.

The Longmont Colony organizers further educated their readers that "The advantage of the colonization system for the West, consists in simultaneous occupancy of the land, and by co-operation of labor and mutual help, each makes a permanent, comfortable home on his own tract" (Willard, 143). At the time that the Longmont Colony was founded, the Great Fire of Chicago had not yet occurred, and when it did, in early October 1871 (as Rose noted while in Canada), people quitting the Chicago area could find homes in a number of Colorado towns including the Fountain Colony at Colorado Springs.

When Rose Kingsley refers to assisting her brother to write agreements for colony memberships, it was the colony corporation practice to call the town lot purchases "members' certificates." Archivist Herbert Brayer located the first "prospectus" of the Fountain Colony that was "issued and widely distributed throughout the United States and in Great Britain" in the Everett D. Graff collection at the Newberry Library. The prospectus, also called a broadside, was titled, "Our New Saratoga: Colorado Springs and La Font" and "Villa La Font: the Fountain Colony—A mammoth enterprise—Colorado Springs Purchase and a city to be laid out . . . ." The latter document was issued in October 1871, and because of its broad distribution, mail poured into the Fountain Colony office—and to Maurice Kingsley's desk. Brayer points out that "The Fountain Colony was not designed for the poor or dispossessed of either Europe or the United States" and was "based upon attracting persons of means" (Brayer, v. 2: 82-4). Of course, Palmer and his associates knew that well-to-do people in a health resort setting could not function without a broader community of laboring people to fill every type of need especially road and building construction and repair, wagon and harness repair, livestock tending, farming and food marketing.

Bell understood the entrepreneurial spirit required of the working families who would settle in Colorado Springs to engage in occupations which required physical labor and could provide an income for more than mere survival. Details from Bell's pamphlet *The Colonies of Colorado*, printed in April 1874, suggest what the earliest Fountain Colony advertising was like. Copies of the 16-page pamphlet were available at the Labour News Office located on Long Acre near Covent Garden and Charing Cross as though to be nearest the type of people Bell wanted as newcomers to Colorado. Early in the pamphlet, Bell states that he and Palmer actively encourage "middle-class emigration to Colorado" (Bell, *Colonies*, 4), which, in England, would signal to urban tradesmen that if they are unable to improve their status, they should try Colorado. Bell described the various acreages available in the Fountain Colony lands adjoining the platted downtown Colorado Springs, stating that town lots were £10, £15, £30 and that a 40-acre tract is worth £160 (Bell, *Colonies*, 7).

These prices might also have applied to other "Colony towns" including Longmont, Evans, Ft. Collins, Manitou, and South Pueblo (platted on the mesa above the new D&RG railway depot at the southern edge of the older Pueblo town). No doubt appealing to the mid-Victorian tradesman's desire for stability and honesty, Bell assures his readers that the trustees of the Fountain Colony at Colorado Springs are "men of the very highest standing, and that the Denver and Río Grande Railway Company is also directly associated with the colony organization" (Bell, *Colonies*, 14). Rose knew that Palmer and his American associates wanted to create a city of knowledgeable, community-minded people, of all types of occupation, who sought educational entertainment and restful leisure—features not really so different from an English country town.

As though illustrating the good attitude necessary in central Colorado's frontier conditions, Rose wrote of the Palmers' own situation. On November 2, the second full day Rose was in the new town, General Palmer and "Mrs. P" wanted to show her their home under construction in a secluded valley about four miles northwest of the Springs at the base of steep terrain—later called Queen's Canyon. The Palmers take Rose out to Glen Eyrie for afternoon tea while Maurice follows in a light wagon or carriage in order to return Rose to the Springs later, actually well after dark at about 9:00 p.m., by Rose's report—late indeed for a Colorado winter.

The original Glen Eyrie house that Rose saw under construction was of wood, though designed to provide every comfort. But until the house is finished, Rose writes, the Palmers "live in a sort of picnic way, in rooms 10 x 10, partitioned off from the loft over the stable!" In other words, the urbanized Queen Palmer was willing to endure almost any inconvenience for her husband's dream city. "There was just room for us all four to sit at tea, and we had great fun," Rose recounts. "There were four cups, but no saucers; and we had borrowed two forks from the [railway depot] restaurant, so that we each had one." Their 'tea' served by the Palmers' "coloured servant" consisted of "venison and 'flapjacks' . . . California honey, blackberry preserve, first-rate coffee, and baked potatoes" (*South by West*, 51). These urban pioneers insist on maintaining custom in the face of the impossibility of arranging all the domestic details.

The next English style event which Rose relates is her 27th birthday, November 7, the day which—by one of those fateful coincidences—happens to be the Palmers' first wedding anniversary. General and Mrs. Palmer celebrate in Denver, then, graciously return to the Springs and head straight to Maurice's shanty-tent bringing Rose a "silver-back bear robe." In the following passage, Rose Kingsley recounts her birthday celebration. She refers to William A. Bell, then an unmarried gentleman though affianced to Cara Scovell, as "Dr. B." out of respect for his Cambridge accomplishments. Rose refers to her brother as "M." as mentioned, but notes the attendance of an unnamed Englishman she refers to as "Mr. — " perhaps a man who worked with Bell and the civil engineer John Collinson at the Maxwell Land Grant headquarters in Cimarrón, New Mexico. While Rose was writing letters home and keeping a journal for what she envisioned would be her British readership, she wrote with attention to detail in an almost sociological exactness:

> We invited Dr. B. and Mr.—to tea in honour of my birthday, and M. and I had great fun preparing for our house-warming. He went out and got a white teapot and milk-jug, six tin mugs, six forks, knives, tea-spoons, and plates: a tin basin for washing the dishes, a packet of tea and sugar, a bag of crackers (biscuits), and two boxes of sardines. We laid the table in English style, and felt quite 'high-toned'—to use a Westernism— when our guests came in. We had previously insisted on Dr. B. going down to the restaurant and eating a large supper, for fear of making too large an inroad

on our tea, which was exactly like boiled hay. We thoroughly enjoyed being four Britishers together so far away from the old country; and, after our sumptuous tea, sat chatting and singing songs round the stove till eight, when our party dispersed, as the haunting demon of America—business—called for their services again, and M. got out his office books, and I answered home-letters. (*South by West*, 53-4)

The sentimentality of this episode must not be overlooked. Scholars of British habits have noted that English women were leaders in domesticating almost any place they visited; we can read in these details Rose's role in attracting British settlers, or we can interpret them as a relatively simple expression of homesickness.

The "haunting demon" of business Rose refers to at the conclusion of her birthday party meant that Bell returned to his desk to finalize the paperwork which Palmer and William P. Mellen required for the creation of the Central Colorado Improvement Company four days later and the filing of the papers in Denver (Brayer, v. 2: 94-5), a real estate and mining development company which William Blackmore had agreed to earlier in the summer. In the history of Colorado Springs, this particular evening of Rose Kingsley's birthday, the 7th, turned out to be significant also for Bell because he cherished this domestic image of an English birthday tea party for a genuine English Rose, and maintained customs like these after establishing his own socially high-profile home in Manitou Springs. Even so, Rose's English domesticity should not be suspected as an act of colonization for England's informal empire, but as a beginning effort to give the Springs a foundation in classical art, music, and literature while the town was under construction physically and philosophically.

Perhaps, Rose Kingsley did symbolize an empire of the English senses. By about 1890, Colorado Springs would be commonly referred to as "Little London"; and, though no one knows who first used the nickname, the carefree tone of an article "Was a Day of Contests" in Denver's *Rocky Mountain News* for June 18, 1896, suggests the name

Little London was a kind of Chamber of Commerce invention to create a marketable identity distinct from Denver and Pueblo, when, in fact, none—or very few—of the settlers or businessmen in central Colorado were actually from London. At times, the appellation seems derogatory or sarcastic, as though there were so many English in the Springs, it's really a 'Little London.' However, having said that, Americans at the time genuinely felt that all English people—no matter how far from London their place of origin—believed that Buckingham Palace in London was the home of their hearts. Queen Victoria had proven that a conservative monarchy could inspire progressive political change, and that an elegant and gracious female monarch was the guiding light.

Rose gave us another scene of English country domesticity one evening when she was feeling "in a very energetic frame of mind." She and Maurice had moved into the top floor of Field and Hill's store, and though reluctant to leave the shanty, she was relieved to have a well-plastered room to herself. Rose put all her "small amount of furniture into the middle of the room, covered the floor with tea-leaves, which I had saved from our last tea-party, and swept out my room on the most approved English method" (*South by West*, 80). In these scenes of English housekeeping, one might imagine that Rose was attempting to slow the pace of the railway-to-town development boom by creating a space she could call her own.

Whatever social situation Rose found herself in, she called upon her true self, that of a minister's daughter. As noted earlier, Rose was as socially comfortable with bishops as she was with settlers and working people. Rose mentions stopping in Mrs. Giltner's Boot and Shoe store on Tejon Street: "It looks resplendent . . . one of the best buildings we have got in the town" (*South by West*, 80)—which shows Rose's good intentions even if there were only twenty buildings. She recounts her numerous visits to "Mrs. C's" (whose identity remains unknown) to do "a quantity of washing. . . ." Rose recalls, ". . . it was hard work; and I am to iron the things to-morrow" (*South by West*, 65). On the theme of the Anglican clergyman's role in society—and including that of his children—writer Una Pope-Hennessy elaborated that the cadre of rectors and canons and curates were "[b]uffers between the owning class and the landless class" and, like their clergymen fathers, the daughters "set an example of friendliness that was recognized by those among whom they moved"; moreover, these Anglican ministers had a "stabilising influence" (Pope-Hennessy, 2-3). Rose Kingsley was such a model.

Formal education was uppermost in Rose's mind, though she assures us that she did not organize the first school in Colorado Springs, nor was she the first teacher: The honor goes to Queen Palmer. On November 13, Rose visits the "pretty three-roomed house," which "Mrs. P." had rented until a more suitable building could be constructed, and saw seven children there. The next day Rose writes out numerous copies of the school circular which Maurice distributes to outlying settlers, riding as far in all directions as practicable, though probably not as far as Templeton Gap and Austin's Bluffs. A week later, when Maurice and "Dr. B." go to Denver on business, Rose visits Mrs. Palmer at the school and witnesses a "spelling-match," which Rose tells her British readership can be described in "that most remarkable book, *The Hoosier Schoolmaster*" (*South by West*, 79).

Almost a month later, December 20, Mrs. Palmer had to remain in Denver, and telegraphed to the Springs that she could not make it back the next morning. Rose walks up to the school room building to post a notice, but finds twenty young people eager and waiting in front of the locked door, instead of the mere seven she recalled a month earlier; likely, none of them were the Mellen children, Queen's half-brothers and sisters from her father's second marriage who when in the region had a private tutor at Glen Eyrie. Rose assists two of the smaller boys to get in through a window and unlock the door; she lights the stove and they begin their school work. The next day isn't so easy since "some of the boys were evidently determined to try how naughty they could be" (*South by West*, 91).

Rose mentions that the children were between five and fifteen years old. The U.S. Census for Colorado City in 1870 gives us a fair picture of the children of the region who might have been at the Colorado Springs schoolhouse late in 1871. George Brown was ten years old, born in Ohio, his 32 year-old mother a single parent; Milton Ayers was eight, born in Nebraska, his father worked on the stage coach line between Denver and Santa Fé; Clement Kinsman was eleven years old, his father a blacksmith from Massachusetts. Jamie Rose was age 15, and his father a farmer born in Virginia. Mary Swisher, six years old, was born in Colorado, her mother from Kentucky, and her father also a Virginia farmer, probably partner in Swisher & Holmes Stables, which had relocated to Tejon Street from Colorado City or opened a second location. Ten-year-old John T. Stone, was born in Missouri, his father a stock raiser, and could have been the little boy who pulled the little girl's pigtails that started them all crying. This frontier experience may have shown Rose Georgina Kingsley that boys and girls should not attend school together. Years later, Rose became a "passionate advocate for girls' education," and in 1884, co-founded, with Dr. Joseph Wood, the "Leamington High School for Girls" (Lundberg, 33), in Leamington Spa, Warwickshire, now called the Kingsley School.

In Colorado, Rose began to follow her own path.

ILLUSTRATIONS AND PHOTOGRAPHS

Moore of La Font

W.E. Pabor where Mrs. Palmer had school. Owned later by Channing Sweet

Acacia Park

B I J O U   S T

COLORADO SPRINGS 1871

C A S C A D E   A V E

N E V A D A   A V E

Here was a well

K I O W A   S T

T E J O N   S T

Cola Springs Co

1st unfurled here

John Potter's Cabin
later Wanless Block

Doc SMITH'S General Store

Wm B Young's House

Old Log Cabin

P I K E S   P E A K   A V E N U E

C.S. Hotel   La Font   Photo
1st stake here   Livery   Gallery
Thornburg's Store
Field and Hills   Shop
Alva Adams' Lumber and Hardware
Barton and Hageman's Furniture
Matt France and   Dr. Gatchell
Nye Restaurant   Pase House
Becker's Harness
Warner's House   Freeman's Meat Market
Dithridge's Tobacco   Goodrich and True later
Jerry Little's   J.P. True's
Boot and Shoe Shop

Wheel of fortune

Swisher and Holme's Livery

First Gazette Building

H U E R F A N O   S T.

Dr. Clutter's Office   Foote Building
on 1st floor
Barrett's Drug Shop

Mrs. Cultver's Boot and Shoe

Gen Palmer's and R-R Offices

Dr Bell's Tent used by Rose Kingsly

M.E. Church

Chicago Houses is here

Grant's paint Shop

Fountain Restaurant

GOV. HUNT BUILT THIS

Mansion House
Rayner's Place   Best well in town
Reat and Allen Meat Market

C U C H A R R A S   S T

Hanley's Newspaper Place

T E J O N   S T

Thorn House used by Matt France

V E R M I J O   S T

COLORADO SPRINGS IN 1871 AND '72

156

Northwest corner of Tejon and Huerfano 1871 with Goodrich and True on the right, Foote's Hall on the left in the distance (looking west along Huerfano St., renamed Colorado Avenue). Colorado College Special Collections. Colorado Springs Area Early Views D4.

Opposite: **Map of Colorado Springs in 1871 and '72, The Book of Colorado Springs by Manly and Eleanor Ormes.** Pike's Peak Library District Special Collections.

Colorado Springs in 1874, (looking west from hilltop above Shook's Run). Margaretta M. Boas Photograph Collection. Pike's Peak Library District Special Collections, 001-626.

Opposite top: **Early Colorado Springs, looking north along Cascade Avenue with the Colorado Springs Hotel far left, Foote's Hall with downstairs Pharmacy on the right, c. 1875.** Abby Kernochan Collection. Pike's Peak Library District Special Collections, 103-4095.

Opposite bottom: **House where Rose Kingsley stayed on way to Manitou Park, January 1872, (called Bergun's Park until 1875).** Colorado College Special Collections. Colorado Springs Area Early Views A20.

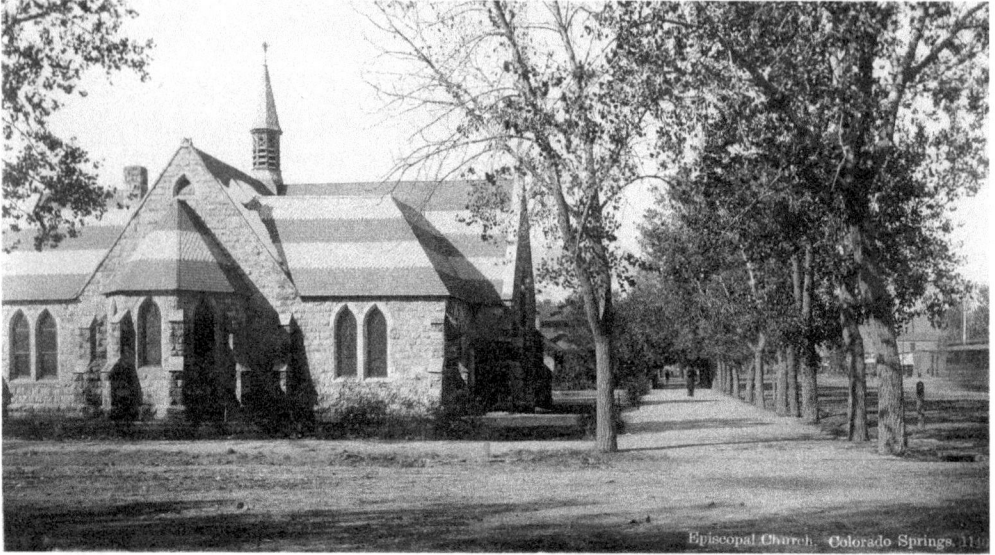

Episcopal Church, Colorado Springs, on Pike's Peak Avenue looking west. Canon Charles Kingsley gave a sermon here, July 1874. Margaretta M. Boas Collection. Pike's Peak Library District Special Collections, 001-4935.

Glen Eyrie, Residence of General William J. Palmer, as it appeared in 1874. Stereographic Image Collection, Pike's Peak Library District Special Collections, 175-3872.

Gateway at the Garden of the Gods, 1874. Stereographic Image Collection, Pike's Peak Library District Special Collections, 175-3647.

Mr. William A. Bell, Palmer's English business partner, c. 1910. Rhoda Wilcox Collection, Pike's Peak Library District Special Collections, 214-355.

Mr. William Blackmore, the London-based independent financier, who assisted General Palmer, c. 1868. Photo from the frontispiece of volume 1 of Herbert Brayer's book, *William Blackmore* (1949).

Dr. George H. Kingsley, M.D., C. 1865. Photo from the frontispiece, *Notes on Sport and Travel* (1900), edited by his daughter, Mary H. Kingsley.

Rose G. Kingsley in Eversley about to go riding, c. 1865. From the Kingsley Family Archive. Peter Covey-Crump, curator.

Canon Charles Kingsley and Mrs. Frances Kingsley, St. Mary's Rectory, Eversley, c. 1870. From the Kingsley Family Archive. Peter Covey-Crump, curator.

Maurice Kingsley at a photographer's studio in Mexico City 1872 during the route survey. From the Kingsley Family Archive. Peter Covey-Crump, curator.

The cultural pioneering of an English Rose

When looking at Rose Kingsley's four months in Colorado Springs, it's difficult to decide which of her activities to describe first. There are four interrelated areas in which Rose shaped the early town: her prairie walking excursions, her foothills hiking adventures, her promotion of the first public reading room which would host the Fountain Society of Natural Science, and her planning of the first classical and popular music benefit concert; these latter two cultural events are best treated last (and in chronological order) due to the number of townspeople involved.

Regarding the serious pursuit of outdoor activity, Rose Kingsley was right in step with new Western European practices of healthful habits that began much earlier than the mid-Victorian years, but had become an identifying factor of the rising middle-class by the 1870s. Historian Bruce Haley found that *mens sana in corpore sano* "was a dominant concept for the Victorians," that is, mental health is part and parcel of physical health. Moreover, Victorian thought leaders embraced "the mind-body harmony as their model for spiritual health" (Haley, 4). Because Rose was a clergyman's daughter, she would have been aware early in life of the notion of spiritual health as part of the mind-body dynamic.

In Colorado Springs, Rose took this idea of mind-body and spiritual health even further. She intended to do some extreme hiking in her quest to experience the westside foothills and the prairie to the east of town. Her pursuit of the picturesque was unstoppable. And, because she was the first to write of it, all her area hikes and walks stand out as exceptional and historic. One walking adventure that is impossible today due to urban development is Rose's and Maurice's hike from the town center to a knoll two miles southeast, grandly called Mt. Washington, at the southwestern edge of today's Evergreen Cemetery. Walking with two dogs—probably English hounds that William A. Bell had brought over with him—Maurice and Rose scramble through the dry gulch of Shook's Run, climb up through sandy soil, cross broad expanses of gramma and buffalo grass, passing the bones of cattle and antelope. They notice the seed-pods and dead stalks of "fifty varieties of flowers" (*South by West*, 60). Rose recounts that from the top of Mt. Washington one could see far to the south, attesting to quality air. When standing at the edge of the cemetery today, we can imagine this walk from the center of town before it was paved with roadways and filled in with housing; the contours of the earth remain immutable.

About a week later, "fortified by a good English dinner," Rose and Bell explore a canyon which commences at the end of present-day Cañon Avenue in Manitou Springs, later named Williams Cañon. For a quarter-mile, the walk is through an ordinary "wooded mountain gorge" until one reaches "a narrow gateway of rocks, a hundred feet high or more," the rocks "worn into the most fantastic shapes, battlements, castles and pillars, hundreds of feet high, sometimes almost closing in the path ..." Rose tells of a "sudden twist" in the path where "the rocks almost met over our heads, sandstone on one side, limestone on the other; and I touched both sides of the cañon at once, without stretching my arms to full length." We must allow Rose this slight exaggeration, regarding the width of the passage between the rocks, but she is most certainly describing a spot called The Narrows, one of the most photographed in the area, as numerous antique postcards attest. "It was the wildest scene—the towering rocks, black pines, and white snow," Rose recalls. She "had never heard such stillness before; it was quite oppressive; not a breath of wind, not a leaf stirring" (*South by West*, 77-8). The contemporary hiker can still witness this scene, despite much erosion and flood damage.

Shortly after the Williams Cañon hike, Rose goes on a long excursion with Queen Palmer, and in recounting this adventure, gives us a glimpse of the city founder's wife which challenges the common image of her delicate health. Queen Palmer and Rose walk as far up Camp Creek Cañon as possible, now named Queen's Cañon. In an almost childlike way, Rose declares, "Anything more lovely I never saw." The reader feels sure that Rose had just said that about Williams Cañon. With this repetition, one is led to conclude that Rose's appreciation of the landscape is an expression of gratitude toward her hosts. Since Rose and Queen walked in that canyon in 1871, the contemporary reader has been sufficiently desensitized by Grand Canyon-sized vistas and electronic media broadcast of landscapes from around the world that we have become inured to the palpable pleasures of a simple water-cut canyon.

Let's revisit this day 26 November. Rose and Queen "scrambled up, crossing and recrossing the stream every few yards, by fallen timber and boulders under lofty pines and cotton woods." One can't imagine their hiking shoes—Rose never mentions a word about their apparel—but they climb onward:

> The stream has scooped itself out a round path in the red and white streaked rocks, which rise high above the bed of the stream. The basin is about twenty feet across, and fills up the whole cañon. The water falls into it over steps of rock; and above it the cañon winds up into the mountains, no one knows how far, as only a few miles of it have been as yet explored. About two miles up are some beautiful falls, which M. discovered last year: but as the only way across the Punch Bowl was by a single log of pine, very thin and covered with ice, and as I was wet through from wading through the snow, which was quite deep in some places, I did not feel inclined to risk the chance of an icy bath, but determined to see the Falls some

other time, and we turned back to Glen Eyrie for
dinner and dry shoes. (*South by West*, 80)

If Rose was "wet through" then so must have been Queen Palmer—seen here as a rather avid hiker—perhaps only wet shoes are the consequence.

Rose continues her narrative with General Palmer and a surprise visitor. Palmer's vision of Colorado Springs includes creating a college which will engage the minds of students and benefit the city as a whole. "Professor H. of Madison, Wisconsin" is visiting for the purpose of suggesting a site north of town for such a world-class institution. This academic leader is Thomas Nelson Haskell, the founder of Colorado College, whose vision of a home for international education crystallized on that day. Rose explains that Palmer and "Professor H." arrive at the house and they all start out on a hike—another hike that day it seems—"as the sun set and the moon rose, to explore the upper end of Glen Eyrie." It doesn't seem possible or advisable: Two long hikes on steep hills and one after sundown both on a winter day? The reader feels certain that these foothills hikes took place on separate days:

> The moon looked so tempting over the crest of the
> hill that we set off on a track that leads up the high
> ridge dividing Glen Eyrie from the Upper Garden
> [of the Gods]. After we had passed the great Echo
> Rocks, and made them sing two or three songs a
> couple bars behind us, a narrow track led us to the top
> with a scramble; and once there the view was really
> superb. To the right, on the crest of the hill, was a
> group of pines, through which the moon shone so
> brightly, it was like white daylight. Behind us lay the
> Glen, with its strange red rocks, and the hills rising
> up to old Pike all covered with snow; and in front
> of us another deep valley, shut in with another wall
> of rock, widening out into a park above, and below

narrowing into a cañon which apparently had no exit. None of us had ever been there before: but we plunged down the hill through deep snow, with here and there a Spanish bayonet sticking up to prick the unwary, down to the bed of the cañon. It was so narrow that only one person at a time could squeeze along between the rocks; and I began seriously to fear it would soon get too narrow for us to escape, and that we should have to stay there for the rest of our days. Suddenly, however, out of the intense black shade, we came into a streak of brilliant moonlight, which streamed through a cleft in the rocks before us not more than three feet wide; and we saw we were at the gate of the cañon with the outer valley in dazzling light beyond. (*South by West*, 81)

They hike homeward, "wading through the snow and mud up to the stable, where the P.'s are still living, as their house is not finished." The reader feels sure that Rose exaggerates for humorous effect when she says she felt trapped in the cañon; but rather than doubt her accuracy, we should see that her enjoyment of the time, the place, and the company is obvious—and her pleasure at recollecting the scene while writing. The quality that comes through in this passage is the mystical beauty of the evening landscape.

If Rose was indeed an exemplar of the mid-19th-century belief that outdoor exercise is conducive to mental and physical harmony, while also a spiritual practice, she was not acting out a program. Her long walks and high-altitude hikes were her romantic experience of a landscape-in-transition while she, too, was a work in progress. Through these examples of walking on the prairie and in the piñón-covered foothills, she experiences herself beyond her social role as a minister's daughter, though her life was conditioned by the expansive outlook of her father's Broad Church perspective. Moreover, she's experiencing the Pike's Peak region just after it's been compared to the Swiss Alps but before mass tourism advertising. At the same time,

Rose's public writing is a part of that process of defining a region for the purpose of attracting visitors. There is no avoiding the fact—expressed by social historian Haley—that outdoor exercise had become central to the self-image of the rising middle-class. While we can and should take Rose's writing on its surface as the enjoyment she describes, no hiker in the foothills can escape being associated with the broader societal trend of health-resort tourism.

The era for which Haley describes the new holistic understanding of physical health and mental well-being was also the period during which the national political ambitions of middle-class tradesmen were being recognized in Parliament for almost the first time. The Second Reform Act of 1867 extended voting rights for men, while women accordingly expanded their civic role and responsibilities; people were feeling their individuality, and outdoor exercise expressed it. In addition, the development of industry and the resulting profits—and the public debate on how to best manage technological change and fairly distribute those profits—had increased the discretionary income of enough people, including many rising out of the working classes, that they became aware of what they could accomplish. For working people, concepts of leisure time evolved with lighter hours—ten hours work per day instead of twelve or fourteen, plus only a half-day on Saturday. Local rail transport increased the movement of people enabling an afternoon at the new amusement parks and science exhibition halls. Rose Kingsley's life was shaped by these developments.

Churchmen like Charles Kingsley understood that for the well-being of the mind and body, government had to work on sanitation infrastructure, a topic he advocated during his entire career, particularly the role of science in solving disease caused by poor sanitation. In 1848, when Rose was almost four years old, the Public Health Bill passed by Parliament stated that new houses must have proper drainage, and a dependable clear water supply, particularly in the London metropolis. But citizens in general had to keep the pressure on government. In the 1840s, in addition to the Public Health Bill, Parliament passed the Waterworks Clauses Act and the Metropolitan

Sewers Act. The Health of Towns Commission was formed, and in 1847, Viscount Ebrington (after 1859, a near neighbor of Dr. Bell on Hertford Street), addressed the Health of Towns Association with a lecture titled "Unhealthiness of Towns, its Causes and Remedies"—as a survey of internet document archives reveals. Ebrington's son, Dudley Fortesque would become an investor in several Manitou Springs resort hotels. As one can see, the interconnected topics of health, education, medical science, and the increasing consciousness of human potential are a vast area of 19th-century studies.

Charles Kingsley had taken up the cause of sanitation reform because, in Bruce Haley's words, he saw that "the laws of health" were "theologically imperative; that is, to be constitutionally whole was to be, strictly speaking, holy" (Haley, 19). Kingsley was an early reader of the philosopher Thomas Carlyle who popularized the notion that the "body is the temple of the living God" though many accused Kingsley of "glorifying the body" (Haley, 117). When Kingsley was in his sixth year as Rector of Eversley, a cholera epidemic in London threatened the countryside; he acted quickly and preached three sermons on avoiding cholera (Kingsley, Frances, v. 1: 414-5). In 1853 and 1854, cholera again swept through London. Kingsley wrote that sanitation reform was a religious duty. He demonstrated that while outdoor exercise and spirituality were connected, people's lives could not be complete without government restructuring of sewers and streets. Given these conditions, Colorado appeared as a paradise of clean air and water.

If Rose Kingsley's hiking and landscape-seeking adventures are meant to appeal to the rising middle-class, a paradox becomes obvious, namely, that the working-class British who emigrated (and the laboring Americans they associated with) may have believed that the concept of outdoor exercise was an activity for comfortably well-off urbanites. In other words, railway track-layers, stockmen, herders, stable keepers, barrel makers, carpenters, and shopkeepers would have thought that their physical labor was their exercise, with the saloons in Colorado City as a place of masculine leisure. As we recall, Palmer wanted to attract English people of financial means, but the tone of the town was to be maintained by the community at large. Palmer knew that Rose Kingsley's leadership would ameliorate the perceived boundaries between the well-to-do and the laboring population.

As suggested earlier, advertising and promotional material on Colorado appealed to a variety of people across the social, economic, and work-related spectrum. In newly-forming towns like those along the Front Range of Colorado, the social divisions between laborers, tradesmen, and middle class businessmen and their wives and children were not as great as they were in the settled Midwest from which most of Colorado Springs's early residents originated. Anyone settling in Colorado Springs would have expected social interaction. The railway itself physically linked once-remote outposts with the growing town. Individuals arrived who understood that cultural events such as music concerts, popular science pursuits, and reading rooms softened the rough edges of frontier life.

Anyone who participated in the cultural events Rose Kingsley planned witnessed the extraordinary evolution of the town.

Of reading and music—and laughter—in Foote's Hall

In the overall picture of cultural pioneering I'm sketching, Rose's role in creating Colorado Springs's first reading room, a nascent library, and the first natural science club must rank alongside—rather, above—her hiking and walking exploration, since organizing a music concert to benefit the reading room required a proven talent that only Rose possessed. In the new towns of Western America, reading rooms were usually sponsored by literary societies which formed after the pioneer stage of the town, and were a way of "improving" the minds of those living in raw conditions, as scholar Robert Haywood has shown in *Victorian West*, his study of Kansas cattle towns, in which cattle ranching produced wealth that was used in creating class stratification (Haywood, 126-32). In the case of the Springs, which had no 'pioneer' stage because it was a colony, no single profession dominated in which those at the top could determine social life, as in the ranching empires. To use Haywood's phrase, the city beneath Pike's Peak had a "unified personality" based on everyone being there for the same reason (to found the town together), a purpose that Haywood said cattle towns lacked (Haywood, 7). In contrast to the wives of cattlemen, Rose Kingsley had the egalitarian standards of a liberal and inclusive social order. The Fountain Colony management intended that everyone participate in cultural activities, not just those cattle kings with high income, fine clothes, and a grand attitude.

Rose wasn't in Colorado Springs much more than two weeks when she took steps to create the town that would live up to General Palmer's dream. People living anywhere in the region wanted to cultivate their highest potential, and an opportunity had to be given laborers to take a break from road, railway, and building construction. The "we" Rose refers to includes William A. Bell and Maurice:

> As the population is increasing every day, we and some of the colonists have been trying to devise some plan to get up a reading-room, where the young men may spend their evenings, instead of lounging about the town, or going up to drink in the saloons at Colorado City. So we sent out [announcements] to invite the colonists to meet together and discuss the subject this evening. We carried chairs, lamps, and benches over to the railroad office, and had a capital meeting of thirteen. (*South by West*, 72)

While Rose's elbow in the ribs of young men loitering in Colorado City is unmistakable she is also making a statement to her British readership that there is work to be done. Rose knew from Eversley parish that she had to keep her emphasis on community formation (rather than scolding young men) since enrichment had to be made attractive rather than based on denial.

One purpose of the reading room, aside from being a small library, would be to host a natural science club. Rose describes how this plan evolved. In the following passage, "Mr. F," who played a significant role at the meeting, has not been identified, but probably is Mr. Foote, owner of Foote's Hall, the all-occasion, community assembly room which will become the reading room, or Mr. Field, co-owner of Field & Hill's store on Cascade Avenue. "Mr. M. F." was the multi-talented Matt France, a stockman and telegraph operator, and one of three El Paso County Commissioners, as well as one of five Trustees of the Town of Colorado Springs, and later Mayor, and founder of Franceville, a small town east of the Springs. Rose recounts that "Mr.

F. made a good speech" about the necessity of a reading room and gathering place:

> ... and when M. and Mr. M. F. were appointed to frame the constitution and bye-laws, and some one raised the question of what could happen if they did not agree, Mr. F., in the most gallant manner, said of course M. "would do nothing without his sister's advice, so there could be no difficulty," —a sentiment which caused much laughter. $143 were subscribed on the spot, and I had the honour of naming the Society the 'Fountain Society of Natural Science.' (*South by West*, 72).

Later, December 2, Rose recounts that "in the evening we drew up a sketch of the constitution and bye-laws for the 'Fountain Society of Natural Science'" and the membership list was kept in the Fountain Colony Company office. The membership is "increasing every day, as every one [of the new settlers] who comes in is immediately attacked for a subscription, $3 giving a yearly membership, or $20 a life membership" (*South by West*, 85). The natural science society, hosted in the reading room, became a leading amenity of the new town.

Once again, Rose had a model in her father. For Canon Kingsley, when growing up in Devonshire on the edge of the moors, and later in the Fen country, walking and collecting plants was child's play. The young Charles had absorbed nature into his heart and soul as only a child can, without calculation or purpose. Later in life, Canon Kingsley claimed that his botanizing habit as an adult owed much to John Stevens Henslow, the Cambridge University professor who helped transform the science of botany from classifying plants back to its childlike origins: a love of nature for itself. Henslow led students on inspirational botanical field trips around the countryside near Cambridge, and counted among his most devoted students one Charles Darwin (Searby, 210-1).

Still inspired by Henslow years after his own student experience, Charles Kingsley wrote *Glaucus; or, the Wonders of the Shore* in the winter of 1854-5 (four years before the publication of *On the Origin of Species*), when the study of natural science "was an almost unknown quantity in the lives of all classes in England," Rose recalled years later (Kingsley, Rose, *Glaucus*, "Introduction" vii). Scholar Francis O'Gorman found that the botany classes Kingsley conducted for the general public "attracted unprecedented numbers of students." Throughout *Glaucus*, Kingsley presented natural history "as a moral activity which pleasurably reveals engaging fact but also strengthens personal virtue," a very familiar theme in the nineteenth-century. In an 1867 lecture on the topic, Kingsley "emphasize[d] not the élite nature of empirical investigation but its accessibility, insisting that it requires merely the proper application of common sense . . . . natural history both requires and strengthens moral faculties" (O'Gorman, 147-9). One feels sure that Professor Henslow, and after him Kingsley, studied specimen plants in class, and on country walks left the plants alone to grow unplucked for all to enjoy.

Like botanizing, rock collecting combined science with exercise and a simple interest in one's surroundings, which one could call spiritual. In Colorado Springs, Rose stressed the "accessibility" of the natural sciences, and the "naturalness" of being interested; otherwise, hard working carpenters, roadbuilders, cattle and sheep herders and their children would not have gone to a social event which appeared to be for the well-to-do. In *Glaucus*, her father had emphasized the "manliness" of "the pleasurable pursuit of natural history" as though to "preserve its masculine credentials" (O'Gorman, 152), however, the majority of participants were women.

By her own account, Rose didn't have to persuade people to join the Fountain Society of Natural Science: While at a "roadside boarding-house" north of town, run by Lydia Teachout, a refined lady of Massachusetts, one of the women boarders, whose ill husband came out for the "pure mountain air," showed Rose her specimens of "smoky quartz, satin spar, and white chalcedony" which she had found while hiking (*South by West*, 89). Reading Rose's account, one experiences the allure of a rock-hound romance, but as a word of caution, I would advise leaving the rock samples and the plants in place—and not re-move them from their habitat—for the population of El Paso County is now much nearer 400,000 than four-thousand.

Earlier, I had mentioned historian Bruce Haley's description of the mind-body harmony as a model for spiritual health, as a topic that runs through mid-Victorian middle-class perceptions. In draw-ing another association between Rose Kingsley and the leading ideas of the age regarding physical exercise and natural science pursuits, it's important to understand that in addition to healthy conditions, the upwardly-mobile middle-class sought to improve their minds, men as well as women (a point not lost on the cultural pioneers of Dodge City, Kansas, as Robert Haywood shows). In an essay comparing Charles Kingsley with the Americans Ralph Waldo Emerson and William Ellery Channing, scholar Susan L. Roberson points out that in 1826 (when Charles Kingsley was seven years old and his father's rectory was on the edge of the Rockingham Forest), Emerson stated that "self-cultivation and the formation of character" require a "relent-less pursuit of moral perfection" (Roberson, 152). There is much of Emerson and Channing that crossed the Atlantic to England—and back again—for Kingsley and his contemporaries saw self-cultivation and moral conduct in their hiking through the countryside.

Rose Kingsley embraced this notion of personal development throughout her life, although "relentless pursuit" seems a condition which doesn't characterize her. Roberson also states that in the nine-teenth-century people believed that "the individual is responsible for cultivating all areas of life, the intellectual, social, and vocational as well as the spiritual" (Roberson, 152). Social historian Geoffrey Best is even more specific when describing the increasing population of England's big cities. Individuals in the government and society were worried about what masses of industrial workers would do with their new spare hours off from work (after various Acts of Parliament re-duced working time from sixty or seventy hours per week). The upper middle-class concern about respectability generated classroom-style activities such as "catching up on lost schooling, technical instruc-tion, self-improvement in secular as well as religious respects" and, in short, "the merely amusing or relaxing, the utterly uneducational, was deprecated as morally feeble . . ." (Best, 211). The young Colorado Springs needed people like Rose Kingsley to demonstrate how to balance work and quality recreation.

Rose seems never to have been idle. No sooner was the natural science society underway when she recounts that a Pueblo, Colorado, clergyman, "Mr. E." was coming up to conduct the first Episcopal service on Sunday, January 14, 1872. Colorado Springs was hoping to have an Episcopal service once a month until a permanent church building could be constructed. "We are determined to begin with as good a service as possible," Rose observed. "Mr. E.," the Reverend Samuel Edwards of St. Peter's in Pueblo (and, after August 1872 of St. Paul's Episcopal in Golden, Colorado), arrived on the north-bound stagecoach. To Rose's delight, he is an Englishman from Berkshire, specifically, the Thames-side village of Marlow (which Rose spelled with a final 'e'). She tells us that the service is to be held in Foote's Hall, of course, since the church building on East Pike's Peak Avenue would not be finished until July 1874.

The congregation numbered sixty-five that Sunday in January 1872. For musical accompaniment, Queen Palmer brought a harmonium over from the school and played two hymns and canticles. Rose had her "English Prayer-book with our dear Queen's name open before me," and explains humorously to her readers that her "emphatic Amen" at the end of the prayer for President Ulysses S. Grant had been for Victoria and not him. After the service, many of the congregation adjourn to the brand new Colorado Springs Hotel, where all the doors and windows were thrown open, and everyone is "glad to get into the shade" as relief from the strong winter sun (*South by West*, 118). Referring to this same hotel—Colorado Springs's first city-style building—Rose recalled that two weeks earlier, on the opening day, January 1, she "ate with English knives and forks, off English china, a first-rate dinner" (*South by West*, 104).

Knowing that she was the only person to chronicle the first days of Colorado Springs, Rose noted the growth of the town which she witnessed during the four months of her sojourn. The raw village hadn't remained the dozen or so shanties and cabins which she had reported in November. "The town certainly is growing prodigiously," Rose notes. "I find it quite difficult to keep pace with all the new arrivals, or the new buildings which spring up as if by magic." The Colorado Springs Hotel is full of visitors from Denver and the East Coast, and a hotel had been erected in Manitou Springs, referred to as the "Temporary Inn" at the time. The Palmers move into it while their Glen Eyrie house is still under construction, having quitted their previous domicile in rooms above the stables.

With the grand opening of the Colorado Springs Hotel and the Reverend Edwards's sermon at the Foote's Hall church service, excitement about the Pike's Peak region increased. Rose kept the pace going. She and her most devoted townspeople finalize the plans for the concert which will ensure that the reading room serves as the permanent home of the Fountain Society of Natural Science. Rose and Maurice had "enlisted all the musical talent in the neighbourhood to help us" (*South by West*, 119). Rose went out to Manitou to enlist Queen Palmer's aid in the musical event which she, Matt France, and Mr. Foote are organizing. A music concert could not be complete without the talent of Queen Palmer. For the ease of rehearsing with her, Rose stays with the Palmers in the temporary Manitou hotel since it's easier to do so than travel the round trip of eight miles from the Springs and back.

The winter cold of January 1872 seems to have been severe, but Rose writes of the concert preparations, unconsciously revealing herself to be a pioneer like any other:

> On the 24th there was a dense snowy fog, and the thermometer never rose above zero all day, and when we met in the evening at the L.'s [the Liller's] for a practice, it was 19° below. We were nearly frozen. We put the piano close to the stove, and between each verse of the songs which I was accompanying, I had to jump up and put my fingers into the open stove door to thaw them; for they were quite numb from touching the keys.

> My warm room with a hot stove in the F.'s well-plastered house, and two "comforts" (quilted cotton-wool covers) on my bed, was delightful, after the cold struggle home through the snow. (*South by West*, 122)

Rose doesn't recount the evening concert until after its conclusion. The day of the concert the weather warmed a bit. Everyone had practiced their songs on their own musical instruments in groups or individually, and a full rehearsal was held in the afternoon as soon as the southern stagecoach arrived bringing the "bass viol and its owner from fifteen miles down the Fountain," referring to the village of Fountain. The bass player "made a most imposing foundation" to the "valses and écossaises played by the owners of the livery stables on two violins, Mrs. H. [probably Mrs. Holmes] on M's guitar, and Miss B. at the piano" (*South by West*, 123). Though uncertain, "Miss B." could be the daughter of Mr. A. H. Barrett, the first drug store owner and soon to be the first secretary of School District 11, established September 1872. Rose recalls that "the tenor from Colorado City came to tea at the F's" as did Maurice, known of course as "M." By 8:00 p.m., the audience was seated in Foote's Hall.

"Captain de C."—that is Marcellin DeCoursey, Gerald's brother—bent the temperance rules, as was allowed on special occasions, and "brought a jug of egg-nogg under his coat, which was cunningly deposited under the piano, so that as the performers went up to the very shaky platform they could stoop down and refresh themselves unseen." Rose recalled:

> . . . Everything went well. The bass viol, who I found had only tried his instrument a fortnight before, scraped away and tuned his strings, which insisted on getting out of tune every six bars. Our prima donna Mrs. P., and M., got rapturous applause. Mrs. P. sang a scena of Verdi's and two or three popular ballads; and M. began with "The Fox went out on a Moonlight Night," which was so successful that he

had to sing two other songs as encores. We wound up
with the "Men of Harlech;" after which loud cries for
M. began; and he was obliged to sing again. (*South by West*, 123-4)

Folk song collections show that Rose might have substituted the
word "moonlight" for "chilly" or the word "moonlit." Even today, we
can imagine Maurice Kingsley tossing his handsome head, singing
with 'manly' grace, as his father might have described it. Two stanzas
of the song that thrilled the audience of Colorado Springs's first
benefit concert are as follows:

> The fox went out on a moonlight night,
> He prayed to the Moon to give him light,
> For he'd many a mile to go that night
> Before he reached the town-o, town-o, town-o,
> He had many a mile to go that night
> Before he reached the town-o.

> He ran till he came to a great big pen
> Where the ducks and geese were put therein.
> "A couple of you will grease my chin
> Before I leave this town-o, town-o, town-o,
> A couple of you will grease my chin
> Before I leave this town-o."

If Maurice Kingsley was as charming as photos of him indicate,
this concert would not have been forgotten by anyone. Moreover, no
one attended this concert simply to "improve" their minds, for everyone wanted to hear the hypnotic voice of Queen Palmer.

Rose reported that 150 people attended the Foote's Hall concert,
people "of all classes, down to 'bull-whackers' who dropped in after
their day's work with the ox and mule teams." Rose experienced creative fulfillment at organizing the concert and attracting a wide-ranging audience, as well as bringing the evening to a financially success-

ful conclusion. "All went home delighted with their evening," Rose recalls, and that "The result to the reading-room was most satisfactory, as after all expenses were paid we netted $60 (£12 sterling), a creditable amount for a town only five months old" (*South by West*, 123-4). The fact that "all classes" of people attended this concert pleased Rose Kingsley, the Palmers, the Nettletons, and the devoted editor of the *Out West* newspaper, J. Elsom Liller, for it was never their intention to create an event that excluded anyone.

In December 1873, a year and a-half after Rose had returned to England (after the railway adventure in Mexico which concluded her travel account *South by West*), J. E. Liller would wonder what had happened to the grand intentions of the reading room. In the *Gazette* successor to his occasionally-published newssheet *Out West* (the full title of which was *The Colorado Springs Gazette and El Paso County News*), Liller states "There is some talk of establishing a Circulating Library here." He asks the community, "Now, where is our 'Fountain Society of Natural Sciences,' which was set on foot almost with the foundation of the Town, and liberally endowed by the Colony, for the purpose of promoting all kinds of literary and scientific institutions?" We have the books, he claims, and "the want of a Library is being felt," and "can it not bestir itself into new life, and meet this want, as a first step towards fulfilling the objects for which it was put into existence?" (*Gazette*, Dec. 6, 1873, 2).

In other words, Liller was missing the leading light of the town: Rose G. Kingsley.

Top floor observations: "the amusement of seeing all that goes on."

The families and individuals who traveled through or stopped in the Pike's Peak region were of diverse backgrounds from the beginning. Rose recounts the services of "Butler the office-negro" (*South by West*, 58-9), when she is under no compulsion to name anyone, though her use of the image "office-negro" sounds as though for her emancipation had not yet begun. Mr. Butler was not the same person as the Palmer's African-American employee who waited on Rose and Maurice and the Palmers in Glen Eyrie in early November; Rose later gives his name as George (*South by West*, 109). On several occasions, Rose refers to "Leroy" the French cook and gardener who helped Maurice move the Fountain Colony office from the shanty-tent (on Huerfano Street) into the second story of the new Field and Hill's dry goods building, three blocks away on Cascade Avenue (near the new hotel). Rose mentions a "young Dutch master carpenter" (*South by West*, 52, 54, 61), who remains unidentified.

"Mr. von M." is certainly Albert *van* Motz from Amsterdam, a Dutch civil engineer, apparently not connected with Wertheim & Gompertz, perhaps subcontracted by them, living briefly in Manitou Springs. As noted by scholar Augustus Veenendaal, Albert van Motz wrote a book on Colorado, well-known in Dutch, though never translated into English, with the title *Colorado uit een geographisch en huishoudkundig oog punt beschouwed*, roughly meaning "Colorado from a geographical or agrarian and economic point of view," published in 1874 (Veenendaal, 73). The identity of "M. von W." Rose mentions remains unknown but possibly a Dutchman from the Maxwell Land Grant and Railway Company.

Had Rose Kingsley more thoroughly described the individual settlers in the area and the railway or land agents crossing the region, the reader would be happier for the detail, but she has left us with much to investigate. A "German-Russian" engineer arrived in the Springs from Denver sent by the Russian government to learn as much as possible about narrow gauge railways and bridge construction. Rose explains that the Russian engineer knew little English, so that during his visit they conversed in French (*South by West*, 71-2), which Rose had mastered earlier in anticipation of the nursing position in France.

A careful observer in a new-born town, Rose was especially pleased with the new second-story location for the Colony office to which people were drawn from the rail station at the bottom of Pike's Peak Avenue. "The front room is the office, the middle M. and Mr. N. share, and the back one has been allotted to me," Rose recounts happily. "I have a splendid stove in the middle, which keeps me quite warm; and have two windows looking over the town east away to the plains with the white bluffs at Jimmey's Camp showing twenty miles away"; in addition, "From the office windows we look on the whole range, with Pike's Peak as a central point, and have the amusement of seeing all that goes on at the depot and on the line a quarter of a mile below us" (*South by West*, 62). The Field and Hill's store at ground-level was also the new stage coach stop bringing people from the Maxwell headquarters at Cimarrón to connect in the Springs with the Denver-bound train (until the day, soon, when the rails could be completed to Pueblo).

After three months experience responding to inquiries about town lot and small farm purchases, Rose recounts two notable interactions at the end of February 1872 involving new arrivals who go to the Fountain Colony office in the Field and Hill's building to accuse the Colorado Springs Company of misrepresenting the opportunities. In the first of the incidents, Rose is waiting for Maurice to return when a husband and wife with a small baby just off the train take the stairs up to the office. They have come all the way from Southampton, England, in response to the Colony advertisement, and enter the office "utterly disgusted and disheartened, of course, by the place at first sight." Rose's sympathies are with them, however, the new English arrivals had expected a completely built up town, not a place of a few dozen buildings; moreover, they have no clothing or agricultural tools for existing conditions. Maurice lets them stay in the vacant shanty, since he and Rose had finished moving. Rose declares: "But never will I persuade people to emigrate after seeing these and other colonists arrive, utterly unprepared for the sort of life they will have to lead." In other words, many came expecting Colorado Springs to be of the same climate as "a rich bit of Hertfordshire or the Vale of the Thames" (*South by West*, 132-3).

The second incident involves two men from the East Coast. Rose is in the office with "Mr. N."—E. S. Nettleton, of course—when two nursery gardeners from Long Island, New York, come in demanding to see General Palmer "and the people who wrote that circular; because, if we catch them we'll *shoot* them." Edwin Nettleton attempts to "pacify them." "Where are the farming lands?" they demand, and Nettleton points out the second story window toward the creek and the irrigation canal. The two Long Islanders aren't satisfied and stand there fuming when in walks a road building supervisor claiming that he can't find enough men to grade the road on the other side of Monument Creek (which would run along the top of the mesa toward Glen Eyrie). "The usual wages for day-labourers," he states, "$2½ a day." "Thereupon," Rose recounts, "a wonderful calm comes over the irate nurserymen, who consider that a place where you can get 10s. a day for common labour cannot be such a very bad place; and in a week they come in . . . vowing it is the finest country in the world" (*South by West*, 133).

In recounting these two cases of unhappy settlers, Rose Kingsley illustrates the situations new residents might find themselves in, while she demonstrates that the Fountain Colony Company can resolve anyone's dissatisfaction.

Writing home of "... wonderment at this strange country"

Rose Kingsley's sojourn in Colorado Springs was coming to a close only because she had been invited by the Palmers to accompany them on their Mexico railway expedition. By mid-February, 1872, Rose is working at the unfamiliar activity of making cotton dresses, "excessively out of place" in Colorado's cold weather (*South by West*, 126). The plan is for the Palmers and Rose to travel by train with the ever-capable Alexander C. Hunt to San Francisco, then by sea to Manzanillo, then overland toward the Gulf Coast via Zapotlan, Guadalajara, Ocotlan, Piedad, Irapuato, Guanajuato, Celaya, Salamanca, Guachipi, Queretaro, San Juan del Río, Arroyo Zarco, Tula, Mexico City, Puebla, and Orrizaba, and continuing from Vera Cruz to arrive in Cuba for a stopover, then to Florida, and by rail to New York City. Maurice will take a separate route from Colorado Springs (possibly overland) to Mexico City accompanying the railway reconnaissance crew to meet up with the Palmer entourage there.

When the reader searches for an indelible image of Rose Georgina Kingsley which will bring us to the point at which we find her in February 1872, I must consider that I've not mentioned Rose's excursion to land owned by William A. Bell in a place then called Bergen's Park (along modern Highway 67 North) renamed Manitou Park. And I've neglected to tell you of "Miss J.," William Sharpless Jackson's sister from Philadelphia, who stayed two nights with Rose in the shanty, and I haven't recounted the Christmas week that Maurice and Rose spent with friends in Denver, nor of their 4-mile trek which Rose called their "scramble" from Manitou Springs across three ridges and canyons, looking for a short cut to Glen Eyrie. And I haven't described her brother's acquaintance Dr. Henry Gatchell, a practicing physician from Chicago who benefited the new town. And though I've touched on "Professor H. of Madison, Wisconsin," Thomas Nelson Haskell, I have skipped over much of Rose's account of his visit. Overall, I find that the most enduring image of Rose is as a solitary hiker. Our very Victorian lady went hiking, always with sketchbook in hand, and made the simplest sort of line drawings; she should not be called the first sketch artist, however, she led the way for professional artists.

On a chilly February afternoon, while staying in Glen Eyrie with the Palmers, she climbs to the top of a hill to finish coloring the sketch she had made with the Garden of the Gods in the distance, a mile away. She clambers among the red rocks, jumping from ledge to ledge, mentioning only briefly her phenomenal winter climbing abilities. With four weeks to go before the departure to Mexico, Rose had much preparation to do, and yet, she takes time at Glen Eyrie to write a meditative letter home as a way of summarizing her experience thus far. Rose addresses her parents and home audience:

> I fear my admiration and wonderment at this strange country must be growing too wearisome to you. But every day I find some fresh puzzle or curiosity that I have not seen before, and long for you to see it too, and explain it to me. For instance, I found a hill of gypsum, 500 feet high, within a quarter of a mile of this house the other day; and borrowing a pickaxe from one of the workmen, toiled up to the top of it, and spent an hour in clumsily picking out specimens, some white, some satin spar, some a faint pink, of which I have since made you a paper weight. We had no notion that there was any gypsum in the glen

before this week: but it is a land of surprises, and there is always the delightful possibility, if one goes out for a walk, of making some new discovery in geology or botany, or of finding some fresh view or way over the mountains which no one has ever thought of. One of the great charms of a new country is the feeling that one is looking on places which probably have never been seen before . . . So you must have patience with me if I grow prosy over our wonderful mountains and rocks. (*South by West* 128-9)

What comes through on every page is that Rose G. Kingsley was a gracious observer—never a perfect one. While she got around on foot far more than any person since has recorded, hiking could not get you everywhere. Rose loved horseback riding and was very sensitive to the work horses did—as we shall see—in the following adventure.

With Captain Howard Schuyler to Cheyenne Cañon

About two weeks before Rose's departure to Mexico with the Palmers, one of her wishes is at last fulfilled: to ride to Cheyenne Cañon, a rugged foothills area about five miles south of downtown Colorado Springs. Captain Howard Schuyler, the Denver & Río Grande's assistant engineer, had ridden into town to file a report on the construction of the line south to Pueblo and to submit an expense account, and on hearing that Rose would like to see the rock formations where North and South Cheyenne Cañons meet, at the north base of Cheyenne Mountain, he offered to escort her there. Rose's contemplation of the scenery initiates the reputation of the place as a favorite tourist haunt. Because of her father's later reaction to her ride with such an eligible bachelor, additional background on the American civil engineer polishes a facet of Rose's travels in the Pike's Peak region.

As noted earlier, Howard Schuyler was a protégé of Palmer's, who took steps to see that Schuyler would have railway management expertise beyond the apprenticeship he served on the Kansas Pacific, as historian Brayer suggests. In October of 1870, Palmer appointed Captain Schuyler a trustee of the Denver & Río Grande, but Schuyler declined the same day, saying that he would instead "accept an assignment to study European railways," which enabled him to acquire the same experience as Palmer. Though Schuyler had turned down the role of trustee, he was still secretary and treasurer of the D&RG (until William Sharpless Jackson took the position the following year) and also assistant engineer, with Greenwood in his new role as manager of railroad construction, while Mersereau remained as chief engineer (Brayer, v. 2: 25-36). Schuyler was given great responsibilities for someone not yet 26 years old. Palmer could attest to his undeniable energy and skill, though other engineers such as Mersereau and Greenwood were older and were promoted first.

The circumstances in which Howard Schuyler took a leisured afternoon ride with Rose to South Cheyenne Cañon may have been a pause in his supervisory role, the track having been constructed far along toward South Pueblo, since the surveying and grading of the route had commenced almost as soon as the tracks had reached the Springs on October 27, 1871. Piecing together Schuyler's work schedule, it's safe to assume that he was in town at least as often as other surveying engineers, and that he attended the reading-room concert she organized. In short, Schuyler was in the vicinity of Colorado Springs for at least three months—far more often than Rose's one ride with him suggests. Schuyler was born in December of the same year as Rose, 1844, and they were in the same rising professional middle-class, though Schuyler would have attached himself to Colonel and Mrs. Greenwood for social appearances.

On a bright February day, Rose and Howard rode south of town, along the new railway tracks on the east bank of Fountain Creek, then they crossed the creek to a marshy, alkali area, now encompassed by the Fort Carson military reservation, and along South Cheyenne Creek to the pink granite gateway rocks, and the as-yet-unnamed Mt. Cutler, that separate the south and north cañons. Here's how Rose evolves the scene in the company of the assistant engineer:

> *Colorado Springs*, Feb. 21 .... The last few days at Glen Eyrie have been lovely—quite summer weather; and we have been panting for summer garments. After dinner to-day Captain S. and I started for a long ride to Cheyenne Cañon. It is close to Cheyenne Moun-

tain, about six miles from here; and the huge blue cleft in the hills has looked so mysterious and awful that I have always longed to explore it ever since I first came.

We went across the railway track south of the town, inspecting the track layers' work on our way; over the Fountain, through ploughed land, and past alkali springs, up a long flat valley to the mouth of the cañon. We tried to ride up it a little way: but found the horses could not keep their feet, the sides were so steep. So dismounting, we led them back; tied them by the reins to two pine trees; and then walked up along a side-hill on one side of the little stream, pushing our way through bushes and trees, on such a steep slope of pulverized granite that I could not keep my feet without a hand to help me. We scrambled along till we reached a side cañon, and here sat down to rest.

The rocks are magnificent; far finer than any I have seen before—of red granite straight up many hundred feet in smooth rock walls, so worn by water that they look quite polished. Wherever there is a crack, fine pines grow in it, if there is a place for a root.

We sat some while enjoying the grandeur and solitude, the silence broken by the stream below tumbling over the great boulders, and then turned back, as further progress up the valley was impossible without a hatchet to clear a way through the brushwood; to find our horses safe by their respective trees. Then mounting, we turned up to the right over a mesa into a second valley, which would make the most perfect site in the world for a house, with a wall to the west of red and green rocks considerably over 1000 feet in height, crowned with pines, over which circled a huge pair of bar-tailed eagles.

We forded a stream, with a scramble over fallen logs and boulders, which made me respect my horse's power of keeping her feet, and toiled up the great mesa which stretches down from the foothills into the plains. At the top we stopped to breathe the poor horses, who seemed to feel climbing up 1000 feet as much as human beings do, and there we got a fine view. The mountains rose behind us in rugged masses to the very sky. The plains east and south stretched away and away like a purple ocean in the sunset. To the north-east we saw over the Divide, which rises nearly 2000 feet above the plains, to Cedar Point on the Kansas Pacific Railroad, ninety miles off. We kept along the mesa for some two miles, and then up and down rolling hills and valleys of short buffalo grass, full of prairie-dog holes, which made careful riding necessary, till we struck the Fountain again, and got into town just at sunset. (*South by West*, 130-1).

For people familiar with the romantic potential of North and South Cheyenne Cañons, Rose's daring ride of late February 1872 so far from town has genuine appeal. Of course, there were no footpaths in the area, let alone a road, and the existence of the Seven Falls was unknown.

Considering that travel accounts are carefully crafted before publication, Rose may have written Howard out of much of it when preparing her final draft of *South by West* in 1873, knowing that readers would expect a balanced narrative and not too much on any one person. For the success of her book, it was crucial to show as complete a social picture as possible, though having the Palmers, Bell, and her brother feature prominently. It's reasonable to assume that the executive engineers, who put in long days before the track crews arrived, would have enjoyed some leisure at the Foote's Hall reading room, or the Denver & Río Grande office, and the lobby of the Colorado Springs Hotel. Of course, horseback riding with an educated English lady would have been a special occasion for Howard Schuyler who had been in Britain the year before. Whatever the case may be, for fear of cheating her future readers, Rose could not cut the scene to Cheyenne Cañon.

Because evidence shows that Schuyler was career-oriented, it's truly unlikely that Rose "fell in love" with him as scholar Patricia Lorimer Lundberg suggests (Lundberg, 44). Years earlier, Susan Chitty originated the unfortunate phrase that Rose was in love with Schuyler as though 'sexing up' history makes it more entertaining. Robert Bernard Martin, when collecting and editing Charles Kingsley's 1874 letters to his wife from the United States, repeated the gossip in a footnote, stating that Schuyler was a "young man with a romantic past which must have appealed to the ladies" (Martin, *Notes*, 45). Of course, we should allow that Captain Schuyler may have had some affection for Rose Kingsley, but all the suggestions that Howard had a "romantic past" are highly unlikely up against proof that he was thinking of resigning from the Denver & Río Grande to leave for California. In fact, every career move Schuyler made from the D&RG to the North Pacific Coast Rail Road to his work on the Mexico National Railway took him from survey engineer up to Supervisor of Construction, the same title as General Palmer when with the Kansas Pacific.

Even though I find Professor Martin over-indulging in that one instance, his scholarship is otherwise very responsible; he assists us to find information about Howard Schuyler when he refers to a two-volume work written by Howard's uncle, George Washington Schuyler (1810-1888) published in 1885, *Colonial New York: Philip Schuyler and his Family*. Howard's family tree is almost as detailed as Queen Victoria's. He was a descendant of Philip Schuyler II, and was related to the Van Rensselaers, the Ten Broecks, and the Scribners. Howard's parents had moved the family away from New York City to settle in Ithaca, New York. Then, like many younger sons, Howard headed west to seek his fortune in Kansas. In May 1861, at the outset of the Civil War, he joined a regiment—while not yet seventeen years old—to engage in the military service which distinguished so many of his ancestors.

Schuyler was in several battles in Missouri and in Arkansas, and when not yet twenty years old, he "accepted the commission of captain in the 11th United States Colored Troops." Howard's uncle suggests that he got into a fistfight with a white male who had insulted the "colored" soldiers (however, such a noble tale is difficult to verify). Whether Howard resigned because of that or not is unclear, but in any case, the war ended shortly afterwards, and in May of 1865, he mustered out of the service "before he reached a higher grade or the twenty-second year of his age" (Schuyler, v. 2: 383). In addition to Herbert Brayer's account of Schuyler's work in volume 2 of *William Blackmore*, George L. Anderson adds details about the Captain's early Kansas Pacific survey work along the Smoky Hill valley, his role as Resident Engineer during the final stages of the KP extension to Denver, and his presence on the first train to arrive in Colorado Springs, the ceremonial train with Nathan Meeker of the Greeley *Tribune*, Byers of the *Rocky Mountain News*, and William S. Jackson, in addition to Bell and others (Anderson, 18-21, 66-7). An 1872 Asher & Adams map of Colorado railways shows a whistle stop named "Schuyler" on the Kansas Pacific tracks near Sand Creek at the current intersection of Smith Road and Havana Street (northwest of the old Fitzsimmons Army Medical Center).

In April of 1873, with his most important work for the Denver & Río Grande complete, Schuyler said farewell to Palmer in order to accept the coveted position of Chief Engineer on a railway to be constructed from San Francisco northward, the aforementioned North Pacific Coast Rail Road. In late 1873, Rose was finishing the manuscript for *South by West* before sending it to her publisher, W. Isbister & Company, then packing to accompany her father on his American tour, to depart England in January 1874. At about this time, Canon Kingsley perused his daughter's book manuscript, and if he didn't know about her ride with Captain Schuyler before, he did then. Usually, unmarried ladies never spend four minutes alone with an accomplished bachelor, let alone four hours riding in rugged terrain. It's impossible to imagine Canon Kingsley not asking his daughter about the railway engineer. Moreover, Kingsley would have told Frances that Rose wrote of her ride with Schuyler to an isolated canyon, and how the two of them had paused for a while to look at the view. Probably it was the wise Frances, who advised her husband not to censor anything of their daughter's first book.

We know Kingsley's fear of Howard Schuyler lingered because in late May 1874, he writes to Frances from San Francisco, at the time his lecture tour has him scheduled there, while Schuyler is firmly placed in his North Pacific Coast railway office at 319 California Street. Kingsley's tour dates were fixed well in advance (Martin, *Notes*, 7), and newspapers in the Bay Area would have announced his appearance. When Schuyler learned that Rose and her father would be stopping in San Francisco, he telegraphed to their hotel in St. Louis asking them to accept his hospitality. The Canon then wrote to his wife from St. Louis that he and Rose could pick up mail and telegrams at Schuyler's office (Martin, *Notes*, 45). Canon Kingsley recorded his thoughts in this letter to Frances, dated May 31, 1874, from their San Francisco Occidental hotel that he had met Schuyler, though it's uncertain if the railway engineer escorted them to various sights in the area including the redwood forests.

In this previously unknown letter—the one dated May 31—Kingsley changes topics quickly as though telegraphing and blurts out that "Howard Schuyler is going to be *married*—'so that bugbear is gone, thank God!!'" (Martin, *Notes*, 49; Lundberg, 44). In other words, Kingsley had indeed feared losing Rose to an American. No matter how groundless his negative psychological projection, he was relieved that Frances Kemble Brannan of San Francisco would marry Schuyler. It's equally certain Rose did not know about the "bugbear" epithet until after her father's death, when she noticed it among the letters her mother had saved.

Tragically, Howard Schuyler died in December 1883 one week before his 39th birthday. He had become ill with what seems like malaria while working on the Mexico National Railway, and died in Davos, Switzerland, where he had gone to seek a cure (Schuyler, v. 2: 384-5). He left behind his wife and young son and daughter. We don't know Rose's reaction.

Naming a Mountain after Rose Kingsley

By November of 1873, Rose Kingsley had nearly finished the manuscript for *South by West; or, Winter in the Rocky Mountains and Spring in Mexico*. To write the customary—rather, obligatory—chapter in travel accounts, "Colorado—Its Resources and Progress," she used data supplied by Colorado friends as well as Ferdinand V. Hayden and the 1869 U.S. Geological Survey of Colorado. She noted that the population of "the temperance colony town of Colorado Springs" was now "between 2000 and 2500" with 400 to 500 buildings, a considerable increase from her own experience in early 1872. One feels sure that someone in Colorado Springs—probably the newspaper editor-in-chief, J. Elsom Liller—had sent these latest statistics to her, which she assembles in this "Resources" chapter. Being an English lady, she could not help mentioning that "Indeed, the English and Canadian incomers are now making a marked portion of the population" (*South by West*, 148-9; Baker, 190). Rose sent her manuscript to the publisher and began packing for her father's coast-to-coast tour, her second sojourn.

How Rose and the Canon came to be in the Pike's Peak region for six weeks may have been the result of a fortuitous, seemingly minor illness. In California, toward the end of his tour—which I will detail in due course—Kingsley noticed he had a persistent lung pain which may have begun while riding around the Sequoia forests. After concluding his San Francisco engagements, Rose and her father headed eastward and stopped overnight in Denver where his brother, George, happened to be staying. George went around to Charles's hotel, giving him the diagnosis of pleurisy, thus, precipitating Canon Kingsley and Rose's six weeks in the Pike's Peak region that June and July. Rose renewed her acquaintance with many friends, including J. Elsom Liller, whose *Out West* (actually founded and owned by Bell and Palmer) had already transformed into *The Gazette*, a weekly, but was owned and printed by the Out West Printing Company. Edwin S. Nettleton, the town planner, was there to greet Rose. On this second, though brief sojourn, when Liller and Nettleton were in Rose's company, they perceived something truly distinguished about her: She was central to the origin story of Colorado Springs. They strongly desired to honor her, but waited until she and her father departed the Springs in late July.

On July 24, Rose and her father were in New York City preparing to sail the next day aboard the *Adriatic* for the crossing to England and home. Rose could not have known that on that same day Liller printed in the *Gazette* his article stating that a prominent mountain near Pike's Peak, which had never been named, would now bear the lyrical Italian name of Monte Rosa. Writing without naming himself in the article, Liller describes climbing to the summit with George Summers, the new architect for the Colorado Springs Company, and Nettleton, the appreciative Kingsley watcher. Liller's notice reads in part:

> A party, consisting of Mr. E. S. Nettleton, Mr. Geo. Summers, and the editor of the Gazette, set out on Saturday to make the ascent of the sharp-pointed mountain which appears from Colorado Springs to lie to the north-west of Cheyenne Mountain, and which, though not the highest, is the most prominent peak (except Pike's Peak) that is visible from Town.
>
> The object of the ascent was to confer a name upon the mountain, which, though higher and more prominent than either Cameron's Cone or Cheyenne

Mountain, had previously been without designation. The name adopted was Monte Rosa, and was given in pursuance of a choice made by the early colonists in the winter of 1871-2, in honor of Miss Rose G. Kingsley, who was here in the first days of the Town, and who, as our readers are aware, has just returned [to England] from her second visit. (*Gazette*, July 24, 1874, n. pag.)

How Rose Kingsley reacted to the naming of a mountain for her, we do not know; from her natural modesty she may have been puzzled, certainly deeply touched by the effect she'd had on the Americans there. Liller, Nettleton, and Summers were inspired to name the mountain for Rose, their decision having nothing to do with what she might publish about the Springs. The publication of *South by West* in perhaps May or June made timely shipment of copies impossible; Rose did not see her own book until returning to England after the American tour.

Contrary to assumption, Rose never climbed the mountain named for her. If she had, she would have written about it.

The one and only edition of *South by West* is a curious document. The name Rose G. Kingsley does not appear on any of the title pages, only "Edited with a Preface by the Rev. Charles Kingsley, F.L.S., F.G.S. Canon of Westminster." The words "To my Father and Mother" appear on a separate page without Rose's name. In his Preface, Kingsley never names his daughter. Midway through the Preface, he refers to her obliquely: "Much which the authoress may have longed to say, she could not say, for fear of trenching upon private confidences," and at the end, he merely states, "The whole of the physical facts—botanical, zoological, or geological—were observed or collected by the authoress herself" (*South by West*, x). It's as though, Canon Kingsley wrote Rose out of her own book. And Rose was nearly thirty when *South by West* was published.

Literary scholar Patricia Lundberg states that Rose spent so much of her life caring for her mother when not serving as secretary and travel companion for her father that she became a model for the renouncing women of her sister's early novels (Lundberg, 33). However, one suspects that Rose herself never felt like she renounced anything. Lundberg recounts that scholar Margaret Farrand Thorp believed that Rose had been "described as 'Charles Kingsley in petticoats' and her father's constant companion" (Thorp, 106). Another Kingsley scholar, Susan Chitty, found that Rose's "filial adoration was to have unfortunate consequences, for it tended to discourage suitors ..." (Chitty, 255; Lundberg, 48). While Rose's similarities to her father did not necessarily turn away potential suitors, it could be that Charles Kingsley was so over-solicitous for her that no suitable bachelor dare usurp his role.

Certainly, the Canon was possessive of his daughter, as he demonstrated when reacting to Howard Schuyler as a threat. Whether on land or sea, in the letters home during his busy American schedule in 1874, Kingsley's oft-repeated phrase is: "Rose is quite well," "2.PM Rose still quite well," "Rose seems wonderfully well & happy," "Rose is quite well, & the life of everything ..." and after two colds, "Rose is better again" (Martin, *Notes*, 19-49), just before Kingsley's "bugbear" comment regarding Schuyler. And, two weeks later, in Manitou Park at the Bell and Cholmondeley Thornton ranch just the week before they depart for New York, Canon Kingsley is so delighted with his daughter's love of Colorado that he writes to Frances that Rose's "strength & activity & happiness are wonderful" (Martin, *Notes*, 55).

The Canon's frequent remarks on Rose seem irritating but reveal his dependence on her, paradoxical evidence that she was a seasoned traveler and quite independent of him. Important to note, Rose Kingsley's role as her father's amanuensis mirrored similar relationships in that era. Mary Aitken had been secretary to her uncle Thomas Carlyle; American President Andrew Johnson's daughter Martha Johnson Patterson acted as his First Lady, and President James Buchanan's niece, Harriet Lane, was his First Lady. Since childhood, Rose had the self-assurance to put herself at ease in all social situations, a precious commodity for public appearances.

Rose never found the opportunity to return to the United States a third time. Even so, her experience there haunted her for decades. In 1907, when writing *Eversley Gardens and Others*, Rose's mind winged back to July of 1874 when she had seen "intense cerulean blue" Penstemons growing "on the dry plains at the foot of Pike's Peak"— far from the green fields of England (Kingsley, Rose, *Eversley*, 231).

How such a memorable lecture tour unfolded for Rose and her father once again telescopes our view into mid-Victorian transatlantic relations—and is the topic of the next two chapters.

Getting the best of Canon Kingsley for *Out West* 1872

In early 1872, Charles Kingsley's thoughts were full of the mountainous landscape above the infant town of Colorado Springs though he'd never laid eyes on it: His eldest daughter and son were there. Probably as early as March 1870, Canon Kingsley had read something of William A. Bell's *New Tracks in North America* and by February 1871, when the unforgettably dignified Americans General and Mrs. Palmer visited Eversley, the Canon and Mrs. Kingsley had at least glanced over William Blackmore's *Colorado*, and Gilpin's *Notes on Colorado*. They had read much about the United States—or at least the western territories—by March 1872 when they heard from Rose that she and Maurice were taking leave of Colorado for an expedition to Mexico City on railway business.

Characteristically full of his topic of America and Americans—and no longer scornful—Canon Kingsley took up his pen and wrote three articles which he sent to J. Elsom Liller in March 1872 for Liller's *Out West* (after Rose's and Maurice's departure). It's possible that Liller and Kingsley had reached some agreement on the topic of the letters prior to Kingsley having written them, as part of Liller's arrangement with General Palmer to promote the Springs to an English audience (Brayer, v. 2: 150). However, Kingsley never wrote anything to order in his entire career. He composed only through conviction and inspiration. These three articles constitute proof that the Canon had almost completely transformed his views after years of rash opinion, and were written to transcend any utilitarian purpose of promoting Colorado. Moreover, the three compositions served Liller's immediate purpose of keeping the cultural standards of Rose Kingsley on the minds of Coloradans even when she was not physically present.

The three articles Charles Kingsley mailed to J. E. Liller in the Springs take the form of public "letters" which Liller published in three separate issues of *Out West*, with the title, "Letters from the Old Country." Liller promised his readership that "Mr. Kingsley will write upon matters Social, Literary, Scientific, and Political, especially in their *International Aspect*, and we sincerely echo his wish that his valuable letters may increase peace and goodwill between the two great Nations to which they will have special reference" (Matthews, 313). In early studies of Colorado history, these three letters were not unknown but were seldom mentioned, and were most prominently brought to light when reprinted with commentary by Ruth Estelle Matthews of Pueblo, Colorado, in *Stanford Studies in Language and Literature*, published in 1941.

The first Kingsley letter that Matthews reprinted was published in Liller's very first edition of *Out West*, Volume 1, Number 1, which appeared March 23, 1872, just over a week after Rose had left for Mexico with the Palmers. "Letter No. 1" begins with expressions of goodwill that are touching, even if sentimental: "Happy shall I be, if my letters form one more link of cordiality and mutual understanding between two Peoples who are one in race, one in genius, and—as I fully believe—one at heart, and whose differences have been only those which so often arise between a father and a son, when both are full of high spirit and original energy" (Matthews, 314; Baker, 193). It's as though the Canon of Chester had completely forgotten the transatlantic tension stirred over the Civil War. Kingsley gives the context for his goodwill: In 1871, the Prince of Wales had come down with typhoid—from which his father Prince Albert had died   ten years earlier. The entire nation feared the death of Victoria's heir as well. And Kingsley feared losing a friend; he had been the Prince's tutor at Cambridge University.

Kingsley recalls that such a substantial number of Americans expressed deep concern over the Prince's health that "John Bull is looking with cordial respect and affection" on America and that affection "is heightened . . . by the very graceful sympathy which America has shown of late about the illness of the Prince of Wales." As an honorary canon of Chester Cathedral, Kingsley was deeply touched when he, and his entire congregation, witnessed Americans visiting Chester "fervently" saying prayers for the Prince's recovery and that the sight had a "wholesome effect towards drawing the two nations closer together" (Matthews, 315). Kingsley turns toward the notion that the Prince of Wales knew his illness could have been prevented, and that after his full recovery, he might lead a national awareness campaign which would save "two hundred thousand souls perishing needlessly." Kingsley's purpose in this first *Out West* letter was to show how sincere he is that the two nations maintain their common ground. Of course the United Kingdom is a constitutional monarchy and America a republic, but the life of the Prince of Wales could be employed symbolically to "deliver the poor of his realms from dirt, disease, and death" in Kingsley's words (Matthews, 316), expressing the common belief that religious faith and medical science must work together.

Having established his goodwill in Letter No. 1, Kingsley feels it safe to raise the topic of the *Alabama* claims in Letter No. 2, published on April 6, 1872. Kingsley starts out ominously, "I am bound to give you some notion of public feeling in Britain just now, about these 'Alabama' Claims, and the painful mistake which seems to have been made by one or both sides" (Matthews, 316), possibly stating "both sides" to avoid admitting British culpability. By "ill-will between the two Countries," Kingsley means that at the time he was composing this second letter in January 1872, British newspapers were exaggerating the public's anger over the rumor (which they took for truth) that they would have to pay the United States the estimated damages of $110,000,000, as explained earlier in this study. The fact was that no sum could be publicly announced until agreed upon during arbitration. Certain newspapers were playing on British nerves when, in fact, all knew that the purpose of the Geneva arbitration was to have the British and American delegations ascent to the sum that the independent arbiters would decide upon, rather than the Americans demanding *any* amount they could get. Regardless of how the tribunal will turn out, Kingsley establishes the sincerity of his regret that there is any quarrel at all between the two nations.

While Kingsley was writing this second letter to Liller in January 1872, the plan to settle the claims was already publicly known. The American High Commission to Geneva included former Ambassador to Britain Charles Francis Adams as head of the commission with Caleb Cushing and William Evarts as legal advisors; and for the British High Commission, Sir Alexander Cockburn as the leading commissioner with Sir Roundell Palmer as lead attorney. They met in Geneva, Switzerland, for the first time in December 1871 with independent arbiters Count Federico Sclopis de Saleran of Italy, Jakob Stämpfli of Switzerland, and the 2nd Baron d'Itajuba of Brazil (Long, 181).

Despite wide publicity, Kingsley and the general public could not have known certain details. While breaking for the Christmas holiday, Robert C. Schenck of the American delegation (an acquaintance of Governor Gilpin) handed a packet of documents to the London Foreign Office for study, while the Americans and English alike enjoyed the holiday season (Long, 182). Historian Renata Eley Long explains that when the Geneva arbitrators reconvened in January 1872 (during the time Rose Kingsley was still in Colorado), the staff in the London Foreign Office had not yet read those documents in preparation for the renewed meetings. When they got around to doing so, they noticed to their shock that the Americans were asking the British to settle the *Alabama* claims section of the Treaty of Washington not for $110 million—but for $2 *billion*, a jaw-dropping sum, which included the indirect claims, namely, the increased insurance costs on all American vessels as a result of the predatory Confederate ships, compensation for the decrease in American trade which resulted from the depredations, plus the cost to the American taxpayers of tracking down the *Alabama*. The shock to the British was that they were under the impression that according to the Treaty of Washington, the indirect claims were to be excluded (Long, 177-82).

The British delegation felt that such a sum as $2 billion endangered the continuation of the arbitration tribunal and they called for an adjournment, suspecting a "deliberate ploy" on the part of the Americans. Charles Francis Adams was practical and inspired; he consulted his colleagues, and when in agreement, they declared that "on the principles of international law, the indirect claims ought to be excluded from their consideration" (Long, 182-3). It would seem that the American demand was indeed a strategic move; they didn't actually expect to get the $2 billion sum but included it in the State Department papers in order to make a point. The tribunal met again in Geneva and within three months concluded in September 1872, as related, for a paltry $15,500,000 million, or £3.2 million (Long, 185).

We recall that Charles Kingsley had heard only of the rumored sum of $110,000,000 when he wrote his Letter No. 2 for *Out West*; however, he didn't need to know all the details in order to finally understand that the British Foreign Office had been negligent in transatlantic relations during the Civil War. Thankfully, Kingsley summoned his better talents as a mediator to his Colorado audience. He explained his views concisely hoping that his daughter's and son's new friends would understand. And yet, Kingsley's statement that a "painful mistake . . . seems to have been made by one or both sides" is a weak argument intended to have Americans believe that the insults and injury were not all inflicted by the British. How much Charles Kingsley actually knew may be impossible to determine, however, the following details which will complete the narrative of the *Alabama* show that Queen Victoria's subjects behaved very badly.

First of all, the Confederate States did not have a battle-ready navy until English enterprises built ships for them. In late July 1862, Liverpool cotton brokers Fraser, Trenholm & Company financed the building of the Confederate States Ships the *Alabama* and the *Florida* and several others through Confederate States agent James Dunwoody Bulloch. Shipbuilders John Laird & Sons constructed the *Alabama* at the Birkenhead shipyards across the Mersey from

Liverpool, and later expressed pride in helping the South. Originally christened the *Enrica* to conceal the ship's purpose, and also called by the pseudonym "the 290," the *Alabama*, a.k.a. *Enrica*, was launched on May 14, 1862 (Long, 74). Renata Eley Long explains that as soon as the *Enrica* was officially launched, it was guided to another nearby dock where crews began the alterations for a ship of war. Intrepid American Foreign Office employees had been monitoring any construction activity at Birkenhead, and gathered intelligence to alert the American Ambassador Charles Francis Adams that the vessel 290 was nearing completion. While Adams began his urgent efforts to have the *Enrica* seized for violating the Foreign Enlistment Act of 1819, the newly-formed Confederate States Navy and their British supporters began fine-tuning their evasive strategies.

Ambassador Adams sent an official packet of papers to the Foreign Office in London, and just the sight of the package alerted a mole in the department that it might contain the feared legal documents proving that the *Enrica* was in violation of international law. Sensing urgency, the mole aiding the Confederate States—who was a British subject—sent a telegram on Saturday, July 26, from London to the Birkenhead dock that the *Alabama* would not be safe another two days (Long, 98-100). Early in the morning of Monday, July 28, "with no further ominous tidings forthcoming from London, the *Enrica* was brought out of her dock on the tide," and towed to "the river off Seacombe" to await additional preparations for setting out to sea.

On July 29, the *Enrica*—soon to be rechristened the CSS *Alabama*—took a trial cruise on the Mersey, then sailed to the isolated Moelfre Bay off the Isle of Anglsey. Only then, by accident or intention, the Foreign Secretary Lord Russell and Crown law officer Roundell Palmer realized the *Enrica* was intended for war and tried to stop it from sailing—but too late (Long, 104-5).

Once again, the mole in London's foreign office reached the Confederate agent Bulloch communicating that the game might be over after all, however, Bulloch was able to avoid detection and arrest because he had been tipped off that the USS *Tuscarora* was sailing out of Southampton and would attempt to apprehend the *Enrica* if it sailed southwesterly, out of St. George's Channel near Queenstown, Ireland (now called Cobh). Beginning early in the morning of July 31 (1862), Bulloch ordered the *Enrica*'s crew to take a lengthy detour around the northern coast of Ireland. Now unimpeded, the *Enrica* or 290 reached Terceira in the Azores where the fitting out for war was completed, as historian Long explains in detail. On August 24, the *Enrica* was rechristened the CSS *Alabama* and began its two-year career of destruction (Long, 106-7). Though the British public would not have known all these details, as soon as the *Alabama* began to harass and destroy American merchant ships (with or without loss of life is unclear), American newspapers began to print the details.

It was known that the new commander of the ship, Captain Rafael Semmes, who came on board in the Azores, was an American commissioned by Confederate States President Jefferson Davis. While the exact number of British sailors involved remains unknown, many were in Confederate States uniform. In a period of nearly two years, the CSS *Alabama* had destroyed or released on ransom 65 American merchant vessels during raids conducted from New England to the Gulf of Mexico and the South Pacific.

On June 19, 1864, the CSS *Alabama* was sunk by the USS *Kearsarge*, commanded by Captain John A. Winslow, in a duel in international waters outside the harbor of Cherbourg, France. The *Kearsarge* had been well-prepared and overpowered the CSS *Alabama*, but the American victory was only partial; while the *Alabama* was sinking, a private British yacht, the *Deerhound* rescued forty-one of the officers and crew and escaped to England (Long, 133-6). The Confederate men involved and their British abettors lived openly, without consequences.

The career of the *Alabama* was known during the Civil War as was the damage caused by the other ships, namely, the *Florida* and the *Shenandoah*. Nearly ten years later, by early 1872, Charles Kingsley could have finally comprehended the harm caused to international relations through incompetence in the British Foreign Office. In his second letter to the Colorado Springs *Out West*, he would have to demonstrate that he understood what Sumner had publicly called "gross negligence" in April 1869. But, judging from Canon Kingsley's Letter No. 2 to the *Out West*, he could not make himself feel disgusted at his own country's behavior, or maybe he feared British criticism if he admitted too much. More than likely, he was tired of getting into arguments and instead took the easier role of middle-man. Kingsley felt an obligation to tell the Colorado audience that English people were astonished at the rumored damage claims. He states that while Americans have national pride, so do the British. However, in an attempt to soften his statement about English pride, Kingsley states that even if the sum is outrageous, the British people want to do the right thing, and they suspect that their government could have done something to stop the sailing of the *Alabama*.

Kingsley knew that various factors complicated the settlement of the damage claims; there were Americans who wanted to take Vancouver Island from Canada "on account of certain Coal Mines therein." Go ahead and take it, Kingsley states, if such an action will "really and honestly put an end to miserable squabbles between two Nations who ought to be marching shoulder to shoulder in the same path, and whose interests are, and always will be, identical . . ." Kingsley linked Colorado to international economic relations when he stated that ending these disputes was absolutely crucial "for the interest of America, as well as of Britain, that this uncertainty [about international relations] must hinder the free flow of British capital (and our wealth just now is enormous) to the far West, and so check seriously the development of your own Colorado and of the other Territories."

Kingsley concludes by pointing out that "If England has been somewhat of a goose, she is still laying golden eggs: and it will be a bad policy to try to kill her in order to get them all at once" (Matthews, 317). In other words, Britain has lots of money for economic development and the United States needs it. And, the fact is—Kingsley seems to say—that the English are excited about investing in the western states and territories, and, therefore, if money is the concern, surely we can reach an agreement, though there are emotions on both sides. Kingsley ends this *Out West* letter by stating simply that he trusts the statesmen to find a just settlement.

On close perusal, Canon Kingsley's point seems to be that two nations who desire to do business will find a solution, even while the *Alabama* claims are unsettled. Kingsley suggests that because American businessmen themselves what to secure the goodwill of Britain, the American government should let the British invest in western mines and railways. While such a notion seems benevolent— that Britain kindly offers its help to develop American resources— it was not, if we take William Blackmore's subsequent career of land grant exploitation as an example. In other words, British investment wasn't an offer with integrity but more like a sly request that Americans allow themselves to be further exploited (since no nation develops the resources of another without expecting profit to themselves).

Historian Adrian Cook found that American entrepreneurs were convinced that "The real inducement to peace [with England] was that America needed more foreign investment." Cook shows that American businessmen with gold mining interests, like Jay Cooke of the Northern Pacific Railway, were contacting their Congressional representatives and pointing out the loss in sales due to the ongoing *Alabama* controversy (Cook, 241-2). This notion that the seven-year process of the *Alabama* settlement was hindering investment (as Bell claimed in *New Tracks*) was impossible to prove since the vast majority of business transactions went forward as before, that is, based on the previously establish practices of verifying the presence of the stated natural recourses and ensuring that the contracts were defensible, and that trustees fulfilled their oversight role.

In Letter No. 3 for *Out West*, published June 20, 1872, (around the time Rose was back in England after the Mexico railway expedition), Kingsley turned to a much lighter topic, that of American tourists gazing at historic buildings in the city of Chester and "the eager reverence of the Americans for Old England" and for "all antiquity"

(Matthews, 320). Canon Kingsley's conclusion to his third letter in *Out West* rings with his passion:

> We are the same people; we speak the same tongue; our surnames—truest test of race—are the same; and the more we know of each other the more we shall find that our instincts and intellects are the same, that we see with the same eyes, and feel with the same hearts, that the only permanent difference which ought to remain between us is this—that the one nation should be the complement of the other and learn from the other: that as America should learn from us—what the cultivated persons of whom I have been writing have learnt—faith in, and reverence for, the magnificent Future. (Matthews, 320)

Kingsley's words were from the heart. And his final image—"the magnificent Future"—was interpreted as an American future. It would seem in this Letter No. 3 that Kingsley was ensuring—without conscious intention—that less than two years later, in every major city of the East Coast where he spoke, he would be warmly received by every cultural leader in America including William Cullen Bryant, Henry Ward Beecher, John Greenleaf Whittier, Mark Twain, Henry Wadsworth Longfellow, and the philanthropist Francis George Shaw among many others. Amusing to note is that while Kingsley was observing Americans in Chester Cathedral, a youthful Henry James was watching the Canon from the choir loft and produced his essay "Chester," published in *The Nation*, July 4, 1872, later collected in *Transatlantic Sketches*.

With these three *Out West* letters, Canon Charles Kingsley made a conciliatory appeal to the new settlers and businessmen of the American West. But not everyone was convinced. Even though many thought leaders welcomed Kingsley as soon as he arrived in New England, scholar Robert Bernard Martin found that the ever-vigilant journalists of the day were not so kind, that "The newspaper accounts of Kingsley's lectures are frequently condescending, and sometimes forthrightly rude." The New York *Daily Tribune* of February 28, 1874, was the harshest, mentioning Canon Kingsley's mannerisms and nervous ticks, thus personalizing their criticism rather than addressing the ideas he presented. Of course, the passage of time has made the *Daily Tribune* portrait of Rose's father as "a shy gentleman" who "blushes in his arm-chair" a valuable insight into Kingsley, the vulnerable human being (Martin, *Notes*, 9-10).

In the following chapter, I will show that Kingsley's tour of the United States was watched carefully as though it were a royal progress.

Charles Kingsley: ". . . air almost too fine to breathe . . ."

While preparing *The Dust of Combat*, Robert Bernard Martin was sifting through the Kingsley Family Archive and found the Canon's letters home written between speaking engagements, and organized them for his handy volume, *Charles Kingsley's American Notes: Letters from a Lecture Tour, 1874.* Martin found that Kingsley's active commitments were so wide-ranging that many American social, political, and cultural figures who wanted to meet the Canon were familiar with only one area of his work. As an early supporter of the Christian Socialist movement, Kingsley had "tried to combine the ideals of the Church of England and of the labor unions; at the same time he campaigned ardently for sanitary reform and the Sunday opening of museums" in addition to being a lecturer in modern history at Cambridge University and a writer of complex social novels.

Notwithstanding the consternation caused by his bad judgments, the Canon's achievements in essays and novels were occasionally brilliant, though the sentence structure or syntax of his work reads very awkwardly for 21st-century minds. Significantly, Martin notes that at the time Kingsley began his lecture tour, in January 1874, he was "beginning to slow down after a lifetime of hectic activity, his mind and body strained from too much work" (Martin, *Notes*, 3-4). In 1873, as the newly appointed Canon of Westminster Abbey, after Queen Victoria reassigned him from Chester, he gradually let go of "the notoriety which had surrounded his name during the days when he was known as a political and social radical" (Martin, *Notes*, 4). And yet, he hardly seems to have mellowed; before leaving for America, he gave at least twenty-seven sermons at Westminster Abbey which were collected and printed in book form in time for Bostonians to have copies when he arrived there in March 1874.

When Kingsley sailed out of Liverpool with his daughter, England had been riding a nearly forty-five year wave of dramatic change of which the Canon had been a part. The era had been painful for many but scholars specializing in the times called it generally prosperous, characterized by industrial and technological development, advancements in medical science, and hope for financial justice for the laboring classes. In 1831, when a school boy of barely twelve years, Kingsley witnessed part of the riots in Bristol, the violent reaction of working men to the House of Lords' rejection of the first Reform Bill. Fortunately, the bill was passed the following year giving some power to the men who had always been excluded from voting though they were perfectly capable of responsibility. In 1833, slavery was abolished throughout the British colonies, though unevenly enforced. The hours a child should work were limited but not ended. In the 1840s, the men of the Chartist Movement demanded—among the reforms mentioned earlier—that voting by secret ballot should be the standard practice so that a man's vote would not be exposed to his employer's view as was the custom, since retaliation often resulted.

The Irish Famine had been devastating for the nation, and finally led to government reform. Religious controversy was always a feature of public life, however, in 1871, Church of England taxes were abolished in Ireland. For decades government ministers, professors, and many graduates of Oxford and Cambridge universities were calling for stricter attendance standards, new curricula and examinations, though these reforms were not complete until the 1870s. Generally in Britain, there was a feeling that everyone was called forth to create the nation they believed worth living for. While Britain was constantly evolving, perhaps Kingsley had been trying to be as great as his nation and gave his energy to so many areas.

Traveling in the United States should have been a relaxing experience for Kingsley; there were no causes for him to espouse, and all of his public engagements were conveniently fixed in advance by James Redpath, the Scottish-born founder of the Redpath Lyceum Bureau. The lecture tour underway, pleasant visits and spontaneous meetings should have eased Kingsley's mind. At the Massachusetts Press Association in Boston, he and celebrated writer Mark Twain—his opposite in so many ways—were guest speakers. When a reporter for the *Lowell Daily Citizen and News* reviewed the event, he was kinder to Kingsley than the same newspaper had been on June 16, 1863, when calling him a "pampered fawner upon the nobility" (Issue 2185, n. pg.).

The Lowell, Massachusetts, paper printed Kingsley's informal address verbatim, noting the moments of laughter and applause. Kingsley stated, "I can only say very briefly that the courtesy and kindliness and generosity which I have received already in my short sojourn in the United States" he continued, "deserves from me the strongest expressions and the deepest feeling, and that gratitude which has been well described on the other side of the Atlantic as 'the lively sense of favors to come'" (Feb. 18, 1874, issue 5540, n. pag.).

On March 10, 1874, in Washington, D.C., Kingsley was present at an open session of the United States Senate which Charles Sumner was attending against the advice of his doctor. Kingsley found the Senator to be "most cordial, & we had much talk about Gladstone, & the Argylls," public figures who, in addition to Kingsley, had made rash statements during the American Civil War (Martin, *Notes*, 31). Later that very afternoon, the Senator had a heart attack and died the following day; Kingsley noted that the nation mourned. Three years later, Frances Kingsley would recall the importance to her husband of encountering Sumner. Frances states (while quoting Rose's recollections of her father's tour) that in the Senate that day, despite virulent transatlantic disagreements, "the moment the two came face to face all mistrust vanished, as each instinctively recognized the manly honesty of the other, and they had a long and friendly talk" (Kingsley, Frances, v. 2: 426).

Later that week, after a stay in New York, and a brief visit to Hartford, Connecticut, Rose and her father returned to Boston—or, so it seems, based on available documentation of their movements—as the guests of James T. Fields, the editor of the *Atlantic Monthly*, and his astutely observant wife, Annie Adams. Literary scholar Arthur Adrian found Annie Adams Fields's archived diary in which she recorded her impressions of Canon Kingsley, suggesting that though the Canon was well-received everywhere, Kingsley could not quiet the constant working of his mind, even when the Fields created the most sympathetic environment for him.

The Fields had traveled extensively in England, knew the cultural traditions, and already had an "affinity for any Englishman on tour in America" (Adrian, 94). That March 1874, when the Canon and Rose stayed a week—rather than simply a few days—the Fields were delighted. Mrs. Fields immediately befriended Rose, and they toured "hospitals, schools, missions, and came home tired as dogs!" (Adrian, 95). Later, Annie Fields recorded that after dinner Rose Kingsley sang *The Sands of Dee*, her father's own words set to music, with the first line "Mary, go and call the cattle home." Rose also sang Percy Shelley's words set to music, "I Arise from Dreams of Thee." Annie Fields stated plainly that Rose's singing "we thought very beautiful" (Adrian, 96).

But Rose's father was a troublesome matter, as Annie Fields noted. She summarized that Charles Kingsley ". . . is what Wordsworth might have called a marvelous machine," she explained. "A great eater and drinker, [and] the engine being well fed, the best thinker and talker probably on the ground. And so modest and appreciative" (Adrian, 95). But Kingsley was also cautious. Another dinner guest, Oliver Wendell Holmes, raised the topic of boxing, and Kingsley as the Canon of Westminster would not confess to Holmes until they were in private (evidently with Annie Fields listening in) that he was familiar with certain boxers because he'd taken up the sport when an undergraduate at Cambridge University.

Annie Fields was very concise in her summation of the Canon:

> Kingsley is full of hastily made opinion as I suppose
> all strong individuals are, which may frequently be

quite wrong and unjust to his own higher judgment, but to which he clings with a sudden tenacity quite appalling to one who may wish to persuade him to the contrary. But he is a great and good man and to those who understand him well not difficult to get on with. He is his own greatest discomfort, being excessively nervous, ceaselessly in motion, and apt to get into sudden little storms of temper which he appears to work at in a corner by himself, bringing no harm to any one.

He is an overworked man and finds this travelling and lecturing the greatest possible rest. He has no time to write, an endless series of new impressions are continually presented to prevent him from thinking in the old ruts, and tired and sleepless as he often is, he is still rested by change of occupation. (Adrian, 96-7)

For scholar Robert Bernard Martin, Annie Fields was too gracious. Martin emphasizes that Kingsley's native irritability resurfaced in America. Similar to the American travel experience of novelists Charles Dickens and Frances Trollope, Canon Kingsley "began every undertaking in enthusiasm, which slowly degenerated as the novelty wore off" (Martin, *Notes*, 7). In fairness, Martin also shows us a vulnerable Canon of Westminster, one not afraid to remember his undergraduate weaknesses and former desires.

After having met so many wonderful Americans, Rose and her father depart—at first, regretfully—heading westward. Crossing the Mississippi and entering the mysterious prairies, Charles Kingsley wrote to his wife that their daughter was travel-worn from the excitement, but "Rose looks better already, at the mere idea of being in her beloved West" (Martin, 43). In another letter to Frances, written from Omaha, Nebraska, on May 11, as his lecture tour pauses, the Canon reviews exquisitely painful memories of his youthful Cambridge days—as I recounted earlier—from his reading of Washington Irving's *Tour on the Prairies*. The Canon begins "My own beloved":

> We have just got—in this delightful Hotel, your
> whole budget of delightful letters—Oh how dear you
> are for writing so much, both you & Poll [daughter
> Mary St. Leger Kingsley]. . . .
>   And we are at Omaha!!! a city of 20,000, 5
> years old made by the railway—& opposite us is
> *Council Bluffs*!!! 30 years ago the palavering ground
> of trappers & Indians (now all gone)—& to that very
> spot—which I had known of from a boy, & all about
> it, I meant to go—*if I had not met you*—as soon as I
> took my degree, & throw myself into the wild life,
> to sink or swim escaping from a civilization which
> only tempted me, & maddened me with the envy of
> a poor man! Oh how good God has been to me. Oh
> how when I saw those bluffs yesterday morning I
> thanked God for you, & everything, & stared at them
> till I cried—with thankfulness & repentance. (Martin,
> *Notes*, 45-6)

In these private letters to his wife, Canon Kingsley is merely Charles, breathless with gratitude and religious feeling, longing to return to his simple parson's life at Eversley.

When summarizing the letters he'd collected for *Charles Kingsley's American Notes*, Martin claims they reveal to us the "unflattering remarks which his wife thought unsuitable for publication" (Martin, *Notes*, 7), which included Kingsley's disparagement of his daughter's friend, Captain Howard Schuyler. When considering the pace of Canon Kingsley's lecture tour, the Canon seems to have expressed his fear of Schuyler in a moment of haste while worrying about money. Writing from the Occidental Hotel in San Francisco: "Here we are, safe after such adventures & such wonders in the Yo Semite & Big Trees, & found your dear letters waiting for us. Now as for money, I have written today to Duncan & Sherman to send you off £50 *more to the Cheque Bank*, beside the £50 I sent a few days ago . . . These generous people absolutely refuse to let Rose or me pay for a single thing . . ." (Martin, *Notes*, 49). Canon Kingsley runs his phrases and sentences together hastily in an impulsive or telegraphic way: "Rose is better again. She caught a cold in the plains, but it is going—& Howard Schuyler is going to be *married* . . ." etcetera. While Martin's collection of Kingsley's letters sheds light on the Canon's nervous frame of mind, one feels embarrassed for the man who valued high achievement.

Obviously, with Canon Kingsley, insight and blindness run in the same mold. He was in top form at the University of California at Berkeley. Introducing himself, Kingsley remarked pleasantly on the name of the town being the same as the philosopher and churchman Bishop Berkeley who "was one of the noblest, calmest, and kindest of all philosophers" (Kingsley, Frances, v. 2: 440). As Frances Kingsley relates, her husband found a balance between appearing to instruct the university audience while addressing them as fellow world citizens. Kingsley raised the very topic that still concerns us in the 21st-century when students focus exclusively on science and engineering: Young Americans must lead the nation in balancing technological advances with cultivation of the arts and literature. Frances Kingsley quoted from excerpts of the student-written article which appeared in the university newspaper, *The Daily Californian*, founded in 1871.

The student who introduced Kingsley, W. R. Davis, "addressed to the Canon a few remarks appropriate to this rare occasion" and Kingsley responded with "an eloquence and earnestness in his utterances that elevated them to the plane of oratory." The student reporter wrote:

> The man was inspired, and felt every word that he spoke. And he spoke to a purpose. Though the tone of his voice was low, and his manner of delivery slow and quiet, there was a magnetism in his presence that held the attention of his hearers. He desired to speak

for the other cultivated English people present. They saw a new world beyond the new world, containing much that tends to make a world great and good. But behind this fact was one equally potent: the old world was the seat of culture and learning, and to her the young men could look for many useful lessons.... He endorsed the dissemination of technical knowledge, and yet desired that his hearers should strive for a moral as well as intellectual education, and the culture so highly appreciated by the ancient Greeks and Romans and the Japanese of to-day. Such an education would humble them in the present and render them hopeful of the future. And the better would it adapt them to the struggles of life in the world. Out of darkness would come light. (Kingsley, Frances, v. 2: 439)

Though 21st-century readers would need to research Kingsley's 19th-century reference to the Greeks, Romans, and modern Japanese, the student-writer (in his rendering of Kingsley's presentation) seems to be confessing that student attitudes toward learning had been too utilitarian and empirical, lacking sufficient interest in what were then called the 'moral sciences' including Modern History and Classical Literature.

The overall truth should not escape the contemporary interpreter of Kingsley's lecture at Berkeley that in California the Canon of Westminster Abbey felt the rising tide of America, and he wanted to shape its energy. "The University ought to be the glory of California, and the coast, as a common civilizer of the Pacific," the Canon said, as quoted by the student reporter. He assured the students and the faculty gathered that "Culture meant true freedom." Canon Kingsley "exhorted his hearers to cultivate the true, the beautiful, and the good, if they would succeed in life, and thus closed his beautiful address" (Kingsley, Frances, v. 2: 440). The Berkeley students found the Canon to be what they had heard he was like at Cambridge University in the

1860s: not an "intellectual dealing with complicated ideas" but "an exciting *teacher* . . .[who] had more to give to them than an unexciting scholar, however accurate" (Searby, 258).

California touched the complex European mind of Kingsley in many ways. The beautiful redwood trees were majestic, and the rock formations and abundance of geological features unparalleled: ". . . Geologizing in England (except perhaps Wales) is child's play to this" the Canon wrote home (Martin, *Notes*, 48). His irritability may have passed quickly while in northern California, and his missteps were few, but he longed for his Eversley home and the four-square pinnacled tower of St. Mary's church. He could not refrain from expressing homesickness and an occasional complaint. More than likely, Captain Schuyler was not in their company, even at Yosemite, if he sensed he was still an irritant to Rose's father.

In the San Francisco Bay Area—in town if not earlier when in the country—Kingsley caught a cold, and in a day or two had pain breathing. Either because of this increasing illness or that he was exhausted with speaking engagements and longing for home, Kingsley wrote to Frances, from San Francisco, June 9, to tell ". . . all the servants I wish heartily I was through, & safe home; for there is no place like England—& all the superior Americans say so themselves." The speaking engagements concluded successfully, Rose and her father departed from San Francisco, heading eastward, on June 10 (Martin, *Notes*, 50). Two days later, crossing the prairies outside Cheyenne, Wyoming, or strolling the streets of the frontier town, Charles Kingsley quietly celebrated his 55th birthday.

The Canon and Rose arrived in Denver the next day, on Saturday, June 13, and stayed two nights at a modestly-priced hotel, the Grand Central. Coincidentally, the same evening that Rose and her father arrived—the 13th—the 4th Earl of Dunraven and Dr. George Kingsley, M.D., were at the more expensive Charpiot's hotel (*Rocky Mountain News*, June 14, 1874, n. pag.). George had been in Denver several times since 1870 when Dunraven had first heard of Estes Park, and hastened to the Grand Central Hotel—easy enough to do since Denver had few main streets near the railway depot, though the 1874 population had risen considerably from the official 1870 U.S. Census of 5,000. George explained to his brother that he and Dunraven would be heading up to Estes in the next day or two (Martin, *Notes*, 52), about fifty miles north-northwest of Denver. George's delight at seeing Charles quickly changed to concern when he noticed his brother's weak breathing. A brief examination confirmed that Charles's cold had turned to pleurisy, a troubling lung complaint. George recommended immediate rest, preferably away from the mid-summer temperatures of Denver and the heat waves radiating off the dry plains of gramma and wheat grass surrounding the town. As scheduled, George and Dunraven left on June 15 for the mountain village of Estes Park, this time accompanied for a few days by artist Valentine Bromley (*Rocky Mountain News*, June 16, 1874, n. pag.), who would produce illustrations for Dunraven's planned—but unannounced—book on the nation's very first national park, the Yellowstone.

Rose knew just the place for her father to recuperate. William and Cara Bell were at their Briarhurst home in Manitou Springs, and were reachable by telegram; more than likely, they knew of the Canon's lecture tour dates and expected a communication. The Bells felt the call to rescue Canon Kingsley. Rose and her father rested in Denver another day, and arrived at Colorado Springs on June 16, via the now familiar Denver & Río Grande narrow gauge railway. We can safely assume that Bell met the Canon and Rose at the log cabin railway station in his private carriage (rather than send only a servant). For Rose and her father, the drive from the depot, through Colorado City would have been instructive. A secure bridge had been constructed over Monument Creek, connecting downtown Colorado Springs with the westside. The road to Colorado City had been stabilized, with new houses and businesses going up there, too. Rose might have felt some guilty apprehension as the carriage approached the small town she had called a "gambling and drinking den," but the Canon commented on the magnificence of Pike's Peak and looked in wonder on the area in which his eldest daughter and son had a part.

On the carriage ride through Colorado City, the Canon of Westminster might have thought that the two or three saloons were rather quiet—all the men out doing the work of town development—and didn't look at all like the dens of iniquity he'd imagined. Dr. James Garvin had an office on the main street, and Royce's El Paso House hotel looked like a respectable establishment, though one or two hostelries on side roads could be called into question. A glance at Wallihan & Company's *Rocky Mountain Directory* for 1871 suggests that all along the main street on which they passed, there were the signs of a fine community coming into being. The office of the surveyors Albinus Z. Sheldon and Robert Finlay was busy with people looking for town lots. Though Emile Gehrung had closed his dry goods and clothing store, another was opening. Anthony Bott was advertising services as a carpenter and house builder, as was Ike Yoho, Maurice's friend. One Reverend William Howbert had built a church on the next corner up. In fact, there were several churches. The saloons were definitely outnumbered.

Charles Kingsley's mind winged back thirty years to the Eversley of 1844 when he was a new Rector in his first year of marriage and found the village without leadership. He and his beloved Frances had begun their own kind of pioneering, creating "New clubs for the poor, shoe club, coal club, maternal society, a loan fund and lending library." There was no school house in the immediate area of Eversley, and under Charles's guidance "an adult school was held in the rectory three nights a week for all the winter months . . . and weekly cottage lectures were established in all the out-lying districts for the old and feeble." At the beginning of his ministry, "there was not a grown-up man or woman among the laboring class who could read or write. . ." and the Kingsleys took on the responsibility of addressing basic human needs (Kingsley, Frances, v. 1: 122-3). Bringing his thoughts forward to Colorado, Kingsley might have wondered if the magnificent outdoors was a distraction from school work. Rose's experience there in 1871 had proven otherwise. In the summer of 1874, the Canon was conscious of his marvelous daughter's accomplishments in creating a reading room, a natural history society, and a music concert which encouraged the townsfolk to desire more.

Arriving at Bell's Briarhurst home in Manitou Springs, Kingsley

was welcomed with every domestic appointment of an English domicile, as maintained by Bell's wife of two years, Cara Scovell. While
Bell had recently written pamphlets and news articles encouraging
under-employed tradesmen and farmers to emigrate to the Springs
and South Pueblo, he had ample time for his guests that summer, who,
in addition to Canon Kingsley and his daughter, included Dudley
Francis Fortescue, the MP for Andover, Hampshire, and Fortescue's
nephew, Viscount Ebrington, a new student at Trinity College (not
to be confused with Trinity Hall). Also arriving in Manitou Springs
as a summer visitor was the Canon's friend, Henry Cadogan Roth-
ery, a Cambridge man employed by the British Admiralty in solving
maritime cases (Martin, *Notes*, 29, 53-4). And if Cara Bell's memory
is correct of that same year, guests included Cyrus Field and Asa Gray
(Bell, Cara, *Diary*, 16).

In the Springs the next day, Rose Kingsley was welcomed back
by old friends, E. S. Nettleton, Matt and Anne France, Captain and
Mrs. Marcellin DeCoursey, Mr. & Mrs. Gerald DeCoursey and other
officers of the Colorado Springs Company town developers (many
of whose wives' names have not been traced), and especially J. Elsom
and Rachel Liller. Canon Kingsley was greeted by well-wishers who
hoped he would feel fit enough to lecture. Maurice's acquaintance
Dr. Henry T. F. Gatchell, the homeopathic physician, was now the El
Paso County Coroner. Gatchell had fond memories of Maurice, and
graciously mentioned to Kingsley that he had been impressed by his
son's "extraordinary range of general information" (Martin, *Notes*, 52).
Two days later, June 20, the local newspaper noted that Dr. Gatchell had recently held a conference to determine if the death of one
Samuel Carmack by gunshot was murder or the shooter's self-defense
(*Gazette*, June 20, 1874, 2). Whether or not Gatchell told Kingsley
of his work as coroner—and that nearly every type of crime had arrived in the idyllic Pike's Peak region—the Canon was able to divert
his mind from the lecture tour and his illness. For Rose, during her
first afternoon in Colorado Springs, she heard that the indispensable
reading room she'd started in Foote's Hall had been moved to larger
quarters in the new *Out West* newspaper and printing company build-

ing, and in the old reading room Miss Allen had started a "free school" with twenty-five children (*Out West*, Sept. 12, 1872, 4; *Gazette*, Jan. 25, 1873, 2).

From the comfort of Bell's home, Kingsley hastily dashed off a note to Frances, that he was "in perfect peace" after the strenuous lecturing. Bell's house was built "in a lovely glen, with red rocks, running & tinkling burn, whispering cotton wood, & all that is delicious . . . the more so because we get excellent English food—the American is to me more & more disgusting—hear no more the Everlasting yang-twang of the Natives . . . ." (Martin, *Notes*, 51). Of course, in his intense longing for Eversley, Kingsley was tired of Americans—as Americans are often tired of English people when abroad. Writing quickly, in the same letter, dated June 18, Kingsley writes nothing of his illness but focuses on having met George. Charles writes be sure to tell Mary Bailey Kingsley's servant at the home in Highgate that "we saw George for one night at Denver, looking stronger & better than I ever saw him in my life. They were going on next day to Asty's [Estes] Park, behind Long's peak, for *bear*. It was very pleasant to see him again." The Canon continues, "The New York men say he is the most agreeable Englishman they have had there for years" (Martin, *Notes*, 52).

One gets the impression that the Canon never completely rested—if he ever knew how. On June 29 he writes to Frances that Maurice sent a telegram to Colorado Springs saying that he had arrived safely in New York, with newlywed wife Marie Yorke (often referred to as Mary), whom he'd met in Mexico City where her elder brother, Edward, was employed in railway engineering. Then ten days later, the Canon writes home that he just wired Maurice a remittance of £250 to cover his marriage expenses, the journey from Mexico City, including his mother-in-law's expenses, plus Maurice's travel to Chattanooga, Tennessee, to follow up a lead on engineering work.

Kingsley needed rest from worrying about his eldest son, and Bell offered a brief solution—not for Maurice, but for rest. Bell suggested to Canon Kingsley, and to his other British guests that they see his two-story log cabin hotel in "Burgun's Park" eighteen miles further up

Ute Pass, and another seven miles north. The excursion up the Fountain Canyon (usually called Ute Pass) also showcased the recreation potential of the road that miners used to the Cripple Creek gold mines. The narrow dirt road (now Highway 24) led up past the future resort villages of Cascade, Chipita Park, Green Mountain Falls, and Crystola. Back in early January of 1872, when Rose first visited the area and was en route to Bell's mountain home, she had stopped at "a new wooden shanty near the mill" established by "Dr. D." a Yorkshireman, near present-day Green Mountain Falls, about midway to Bell's hotel. The uphill route from Manitou Springs is quite strenuous in winter, and Rose had been easily persuaded to stop for the night at the shanty or log cabin near a sawmill (a photograph of which has been carefully preserved by the Colorado College). Despite the ramshackle exterior appearance, the long cabin had "a nice large sitting-room, with open hearth and roaring pitch-pine fire, where the ladies of the family made us welcome" (*South by West*, 111-2). It might not be possible to know if the Yorkshire family was still at the Glenwood Mills two years later in July of 1874, but in summer weather the uphill trek would have been pleasant.

Rose and her father stay at the Bell's second home for about a week. Canon Kingsley writes "Burgun's Park" on his letterhead for July 2, with two 'u' letters. This Bergen's Park where Bell situated his hotel is along Trout Creek, just north of present-day Woodland Park, and would be renamed Manitou Park the following year, 1875, to distinguish it from the "Bergen Park" west of Denver. The confusion scholars have between the Bergen or Burgun Park along Trout Creek (in the South Platte watershed) and the Bergen Park to the west of Denver is understandable without the aid of U.S. Geographical Survey maps. Robert Bernard Martin was himself confused between the two Bergen Parks, but greatly aided the scholar when he quoted Rose that she and her father stayed at "Mr. Cholmondeley Thornton's Ranch" for a week (Kingsley, Frances, v. 2: 441; Martin, *Notes*, 55). At the time of Rose's first visit in early 1872, Francis Cholmondeley Thornton—often referred to as F. C. Thornton—had not reached Colorado. Born in 1850, nine years younger than Bell, Thornton graduated from Trinity College

Cambridge in 1873, his B.A. degree topic not given in Venn's *Alumni Cantabrigiensis*. Thornton would have heard of Colorado through the informal Cambridge University network and was attracted by the connection with Bell.

Manitou Park (the Bergen's Park of 1874) was certainly on the Colorado tourism route. Nearly a year earlier, in September 1873, Isabella Bird had taken a side trip from Estes Park to Colorado Springs on Rose Kingsley's recommendation, and on the way there Bird found that "Bergens Park has been bought by Dr. Bell, of London, but its present occupant is Mr. Thornton, an English gentleman, who has a worthy married Englishman as his manager" (Bird, 186); though the manager remains unidentified, he might have been a Thornton cousin (not Thornton's brother). Bird also notes that "Mr. Thornton is building a good house" and will "build other cabins, with the intention of making the Park a resort for strangers" (Bird, 187). This was the hotel at which Rose and her father stayed—which exists only in a haunting photograph taken at twilight with Pike's Peak in the background.

The reporter for the *Colorado Springs Gazette and El Paso County News*, under Liller's management, was more concerned with the wheat and oat crops in Bergen's (Manitou) Park and didn't mention Cholmondeley Thornton at all when announcing that the Bells and Canon Kingsley and daughter would be spending a week there. However, the news article states that "A large building has been put up, with spacious Dining Room and a number of sleeping rooms, and, in close proximity, three tasteful Log Cottages have been erected for the use of families desiring to make lengthy visits" (*Gazette*, June 27, 1874, 3).

While at the Bell and Thornton hotel, Kingsley has a nervous relapse. He is not quite happy in Manitou Park, and writes of it, mentioning a forest fire raging (in the era before fire suppression). Though expressing irritation, Kingsley is delighted by botanizing:

> This place is like an ugly Highland Strath, bordered with pine woods. Air almost too fine to breathe (7200 ft high) Pike's Peak 7000 ft more at one end. . . & alas! a great forest fire burning for 3 days between

us & it—& at the other [northern] end wonderful
ragged peaks 10-20 miles off. Flowers most lovely
& wonderful—Plenty of the dear common Hare-
bell—& several Scotch & English plants, mixed with
the strangest forms. We are (or rather Rose is) making a splendid collection. She & the local botanist
got more than 50 new sorts one morning—Sir C.B.
[Charles Bunbury] will be delighted, I hope. Her
strength & activity & happiness are wonderful. . . .
(Martin, *Notes*, 55)

Three days later, he writes to Frances, again from Bell's Bergen's
(Manitou) Park home, conveying another optimistic projection about
Maurice's unsettled life. The Canon tells Frances that Maurice's Chat-
tanooga railway job with General Wilder ought to be "the turning
point of his life" based upon "the serious tone of his letters" (Martin,
Notes, 54). In his concern for his eldest son, one hears in Kingsley's
voice the sad refrain of so many fathers; less than ten years later the
British General William Feilding (yes, spelled "ei") would write two
essays for a leading magazine, the *Nineteenth Century*, published in
April and July of 1883, titled "What Shall I do with My Son?" and
"Whither Shall I Send My Son?" In each of these two essays, Feilding
writes of the concerns of middle-class parents whose sons with high
aspirations cannot find career-track employment in Britain. Feilding's
answer to the nagging questions was that the youth of Britain should
get appropriate training and emigrate to Australia, New Zealand, or
Canada (not naming the United States). However, for many—like
Maurice Kingsley—emigration was not the solution.

During the Canon's American tour, his son, Maurice, was of
constant concern. One feels apprehension for the relationship between
father and son when reading how Canon Kingsley wrote to Sir Charles
Bunbury, March 15, 1870—four years earlier—that Maurice had just
come back from Argentina's Río de la Plata or Entré Ríos province
(in fact, quite a vast area) and was "so delighted with the life that his
only wish is to return [to the occupation]; though not, probably, to the

same place." Kingsley boasted to Bunbury that "My boy would make an admirable explorer, and, it may be, win himself a name." A month later, the Canon wrote to geologist friend William Pengelly, dated April 15, that Maurice was "just going off to try his own manhood in Colorado . . ." The Canon had been musing on the unpredictability of life, how it "looks often uncertain and utterly lawless." He stated, "You will understand, therefore, that it is somewhat important to me just now, whether the world be ruled by a just and wise God, or by $(\chi + \eta + \zeta) = 0$. It is also an important question to me with regard to my own boy's future, whether what is said to have happened to-morrow (Good Friday) be true or false." However, Kingsley adds, ". . . I am old-fashioned and superstitious, and unworthy of the year 1870." And a few days later, he wrote to Bristol-born philanthropist Susanna Winkworth that Maurice "has started three days since full of heart and hope, for the Rocky Mountains" (Kingsley, Frances, v. 2: 316-9). In these three letters, the Canon had written with hope that Maurice would settle down in Colorado. And, four years later from his lecture tour in 1874, he's written in the same vein, hoping that Maurice would fix on the reputable Chattanooga railway. Perhaps the father's choice of words for these letters indicates that, unwittingly, he habitually irritated his elder son and would also trouble Maurice's eleven years younger brother, Grenville Arthur, born in 1858.

On Sunday, July 5, the Canon gives a service in the large dining room of the Bergen's (Manitou) Park hotel, and the next day he and Rose return to Colorado Springs to spend several days with General and Mrs. Palmer at Glen Eyrie, where the Canon continues to recover. A week later at the Palmer's home, Kingsley is more eloquent in letters to Frances: "This is a wonderful spot," Kingsley marvels, "Such crags, pillars, caves—red & grey—a perfect thing in a stage-scene—& the Flora such a jumble—Cactus, Yucca, poison-sumach, & lovely strange flowers, mixed with Douglas & Menzies pine & *eatable* Pi-ñon—& those again with *our own* harebells, & roses, & all sorts of English flowers"—seemingly impossible in Colorado's arid climate (Martin, *Notes*, 56). This descriptive passage is one of the few in which the Canon is his old self, experiencing the joy of describing nature.

Feeling well, Kingsley fulfilled a request to speak on July 12 at the newly-completed Episcopal church in Colorado Springs's growing downtown, on East Pike's Peak Avenue, which had its inauguration the week before. The topic of Kingsley's presentation was the much-anticipated lecture on American's admiration of old buildings, "Westminster Abbey." Of that July 12 event, Rose wrote that "The church was crowded, many men, young Englishmen chiefly, having ridden in twenty miles and more from distant Ranches to hear my father preach" (Kingsley, Frances, v. 2: 441-2). Documentation is unclear if the weekly *Gazette* reported on Kingsley's Episcopal Church presentation of July 12, or if the report was of another Kingsley appearance. The weekly *Gazette* reporter does not state the location: "It would be useless for us to attempt to give any résumé of the Lecture," the reporter wrote quite innocently, "for it not only sketched, with masterly power, the chief features of Westminster Abbey, . . . but touched upon an almost innumerable number of suggested subjects" (*Gazette*, July 18, 1874, p. 2).

During his tour, in addition to presentations like the one Kingsley specifically tailored for the University of California students, he carried with him the drafts of five lectures of the travelogue variety that were enormously popular with audiences which included his best, "Westminster Abbey," also a lecture on the Athenian theater titled "The Stage as It was Once," in addition to "The First Discovery of America," "The Servant of the Lord," and "Ancient Civilisation" (Martin, *Notes*, 4-5). These five lectures were collected by Frances as *Lectures Delivered in America* and published shortly after her husband's death.

Canon Kingsley's time in Colorado drew to a close. He felt reconstituted, and shortly after July 14, the date of his last letter home, father and daughter depart for Denver, and on to New York, to sail for home on July 25, while, as we recall, Edwin S. Nettleton, J. Elsom Liller, and George Summers christen the third highest peak in Rose Georgina Kingsley's honor. "It was sultry August weather when he returned to Eversley from America," Frances writes, ". . . and he was out among his people twice and three times a day in the burning sun and dry easterly wind . . . his great joy at being with his poor people again made him plunge too eagerly and suddenly into work, . . . before he had regained his strength after his illness in Colorado." Charles Kingsley went to Westminster Abbey in September to fulfill his duties as an honorary Canon, however, "a severe attack of congestion from the liver came on, which alarmed his friends, and prevented his preaching in the Abbey on the first Sunday of his residence" (Kingsley, Frances, v. 2: 449). He seemed to recover, and then in October his beloved Frances was suddenly ill, and his own illness returned. His anxiety for her was overwhelming, and Kingsley may have had another characteristic nervous attack of prolonged fatigue. After another supposed recovery, and to unwind before his November work at the Abbey, the Canon was able to visit a friend in Bedfordshire and another in Essex. Kingsley returned from Essex refreshed, but he became ill again, this time with no will to recover, according to Frances. Kingsley coughed and his lungs hemorrhaged, probably from bronchitis and recurrent pleuro-pneumonia. Kingsley took to bed, never to rise again. Rose and her sister Mary attended his bedside (Lundberg, 52). The Canon thought his wife would die before him. Frances was unwell and unable to be at his side when he passed away, January 23, 1875. She recovered her health to live another sixteen years.

Decades later, Rose focused on her father's strong points. As a child in his company, she absorbed nature so completely that her 1908 introduction to a reprint of her father's 1855 *Glaucus; or, the Wonders of the Shore* stands as her tribute to him. Rose would recall her father's role as a popularizer of nature studies: "To foster this delight in the wonders of nature and encourage sound scientific research, was one of my father's ceaseless aims," she stated (Kingsley, Rose, *Glaucus*, viii). "Many a grown man recalls the days when, as a small school-boy, his first interest in natural science was awakened in walks over the Hampshire moors catching butterflies with my father, or in long spring afternoons carrying his basket for him." Rose continues, "And townspeople of Reading or Winchester still say that their own delight in the study of natural history dates from hearing some of his lectures forty or fifty years ago, which revealed a new life to them" (Kingsley, Rose, *Glaucus*, ix).

Other scholars and writers remembered the importance of nature to Charles Kingsley. In an evaluation of his career, man of letters Leslie Stephen, President of the Alpine Club at the time, wrote that Kingsley was a half-hearted novelist, but "his appreciation of nature remained true and healthy to the end" (Stephen, 439). Stephen was "half tempted to wish that Kingsley could have put aside his preachings, social, theological, and philosophical, and have been content with a function for which he was so admirably adapted" (Stephen, 441). In his review, Stephen quotes at length Kingsley's descriptions of the Devonshire coast; his evaluation suggests how easy it was for the next generation of readers to set aside Kingsley's novels and keep his natural history work: "The men who can feel and make others feel the charms of beautiful scenery and stimulate the love for natural history do us a service which, if not the highest, is perhaps the most unalloyed by any mixture of evil" (Stephen, 441). Stephen's praise of Kingsley made the natural sciences lyrical.

New readers could not resist Charles Kingsley's recommendation that natural science be studied "on grounds which may be to you new and unexpected—on social, I had almost said on political grounds." Elspeth Huxley quotes the Canon from his "Town Geology" of 1873 that if we love "the names of Liberty, Equality, and Brotherhood . . ." and want those qualities to "come true for the whole world, by practicing them ourselves, when and where we can . . ." then "in becoming scientific men, in studying science and acquiring the scientific habit of mind, you will find yourselves enjoying a freedom, an equality, a brotherhood, such as you will not find elsewhere . . ." (Huxley, 155-6). In short, long forest walks create community and nation.

If a love of nature and a scientific mind made Charles Kingsley a popularizer of the natural sciences, his brother George was an example of the scientific mind turning his gaze onto lands far from London. On the June evening in Denver in 1874 when George hastened to his brother's hotel to find him ill, and in a familiar attitude of homesickness, their situations were quite different. At 48, George was still in top form and had a reputation as a cosmopolite and world traveler. While his brother and niece, Rose, were spending one more day in their hotel before departing for the Springs, George and his employer, the 4th Earl of Dunraven, got an early start and were approaching the mountain village of Estes Park where they intended to relax before departing for a hunting expedition and a tour of the Yellowstone country.

Only one of the actors in the Estes Park drama, George, saw the approaching conflict with Jim Nugent—and he was powerless to stop it.

Dr. George Henry Kingsley, M.D.: "The papers tell such lies about us"

The lives of the clergyman Charles Kingsley and his medical doctor brother, George, were so different that after they had gone their separate ways as young adults, they never could have planned to meet at any point on the earth. Their encounter in Denver was a serendipitous event with a deeper story going back to their childhood years in the lovely villages where their father, Charles Kingsley, senior, held curacies and rectorships, every one of which—from Barnack to Clovelly and Chelsea—enriched the children's experience of the natural world. Charles, junior, as we recall, was born in 1819, in Holne, Devonshire, but Herbert, born in 1820, died from an illness at 14, and very little is known of him. Gerald, the third child, died at sea in 1844 at the age of 23 onboard a ship of which he was a junior officer, so far away on the other side of the world that none of the Kingsleys knew of his death until the early months of 1845. Louisa, born in 1823, died the following year. George came into the world in 1826—some archived records claim 1827 or 1825—born in the Rectory of Barnack, as was Charlotte in 1828 and the youngest, Henry, in 1830 (Lundberg, 466). Each of the three surviving sons of Charles, senior, and Mary Lucas—Charles, George, and Henry—had in common their love of rendering life into writing. Henry, the novelist brother, sought a novel-writing sanctuary and lived periodically with George and his family, though Henry often lived with his brother Charles as well. As the years went by, Charles and Frances tired of seeing Henry and his wife, Sarah; that left George as the brother that Canon Kingsley liked to hear from.

The contrasts between Charles and George were many. George never wrote novels, never advocated social causes, never made public speeches or held a teaching position, did not share Charles's religious views, and rarely had strong opinions—except those I will show in due course. During the summer of 1848, while George was in the midst of the Paris revolution and leading a semi-Bohemian life, Charles had been Rector of Eversley for four years, had two small children, was deeply involved in social reform, and was a contributor to the penny periodical, *Politics for the People*, edited by F. D. Maurice and John M. F. Ludlow, a publication meant to bridge the gap between the clergy and the common laborer (Pope-Hennessy, 75, 77-9, 82). And, unlike Charles, George did not marry until into his thirties when he wed a woman also in her thirties, Mary Bailey—his housekeeper. Her father was an innkeeper, thus making the Baileys socially unacceptable from a class, occupation, and economic position. Moreover, she and George married less than a week before she gave birth to their first child, Mary Henrietta.

While men of all classes admired George's cultural knowledge, he could not present his wife socially—an embarrassment for her—but doing so was not a requirement of his aristocratic employers. Writer and scholar Lila Marz Harper suggests that because of this "socially unequal marriage" George "stayed abroad as much as possible" (Harper, 187), though the fact is that George traveled because he was employed to do so. These contrasts between Charles and George kept each brother interested in—or at least intensely curious about—the other. Specifically, what held them together was their undeniable bond of childhood experiences of nature and love of literary and historical legend.

During the Reverend Kingsley senior's time in Barnack, 1824 to 1830, the village was in wild country at the eastern edge of the Rockingham Forest and the western edge of the Bedford Level near the road from Peterborough to Stamford, along which Barnack was situated mid-way. In addition to the nearness of untamed nature, the regional capital of Peterborough was rich with ancient stories of Hereward the Wake, which captivated Charles, junior. Even though George was barely four years old when, in 1830, his father left Barnack to take the Rectorship at Clovelly (before transferring to Chelsea in 1836), he stored away childhood memories of Peterborough Cathedral, the burial site of Queen Catherine of Aragon, and the first burial site of Mary, Queen of Scots. Later, as a literary antiquarian, George returned to his fascination with the Tudor and Elizabethan eras.

The key element in Charles's and George's mutual esteem was the desire of each to have as much knowledge as possible and to act on it. George's daughter Mary Henrietta recalled after his death that her father combined literature and medical science because of his "many-mindedness" and a "kindly desire to do good" (Kingsley, Mary H., 16). As we've seen, Charles Kingsley knew that a healthy congregation was a form of social justice; and yet, freedom from fear of disease required the specialized knowledge that only the medical profession could provide. Charles was in awe of his brother's medical achievements. In contrast, George was more objective about his medical skill; he was an intellectual, pursuing medical knowledge as a way of knowing humanity.

And yet, George's romance with nature and the intrigue of medical science cannot alone explain his path in life. It would be paradoxical but not unusual to say that George found a model of stability and structure in the published documents of the Established Church, the Articles of Faith, which he first experienced in his father's strict Anglican household. The family's move to the Chelsea Rectory on the edge of the London metropolis was good for George's future. From 1834 to 1839, he attended the Western Grammar School in nearby Brompton, then for two years the King's College School to 1841 (Williams, A., e-mail to author). It was probably when twelve years old at the school in Brompton that George turned to science, for by May of 1843, at 17, he was a student at St. George's Hospital Medical School, now called St. George's University of London (Manson, e-mail to author). Then, for three challenging and fruitful years, George attended the University of Edinburgh Medical School, which, according to historian Peter Searby, offered "advanced scientific instruction with clinical experience in local hospitals" (Searby, 423) such that later in the 1850s Edinburgh would provide a model to the Graham Commission (and to Prince Albert and Lord John Russell) for how Cambridge University should be reformed.

In contrast to Oxford and Cambridge, the Scottish universities offered "intellectual adventurousness" since the wide range of topics of study fostered a Renaissance "generalist tradition"; moreover, Edinburgh did not impose religious tests on new students, and the modest expense encouraged tradesmen's sons to attend (Searby, 423-6). George Kingsley's cosmopolitan world view grew from this progressive atmosphere which included young men coming from Ireland and Scotland, and English men residing outside the British Isles—individuals whose social, economic, and political status made them much more different from one another than British and Irish men today.

George graduated M.D. in 1847, at the age of 21, with a specialization thesis "On Dropsy." Known today as edema, dropsy or hydropsis is characterized by inflammation due to water retention beneath the skin and in body cavities, a common complaint of urban dwellers in the 19th-century. At Edinburgh, George Kingsley was not alone in his study of dropsy, and fellow students graduating M.D. in 1847 included specialists in pleurisy, pericarditis, dyspepsia, necrosis, kidney disease, and gunshot wounds (Anderson, e-mail to author). Given George's university exposure to other students' areas of study, some knowledge of gunshot wounds helped Kingsley in the summer of 1874 when in Estes Park, Colorado, he was the first on the scene to help Jim Nugent, "Rocky Mountain Jim," a complex scenario which I will address shortly.

Since George Kingsley never kept a journal and he seldom took notes, what we know of him is largely due to Mary Henrietta's "Memoir"—the first 208 pages of *Notes on Sport and Travel* (1900)—in which she quotes generous excerpts from his private letters home, while she recreates the context in which he wrote them. From Edinburgh, George did not settle down into a medical practice; he went to Paris to "carry on his beloved study of anatomy . . ." and, as Mary Henrietta explains, "Paris, in those days being considered the best place for this, owing to the greater supply of bodies to be had there." "During the following spring" of his graduation, 1848, her father found himself "in the midst of the turbulence and disorder which drove Louis Philippe from the throne of France." Young Dr. Kingsley was "deeply imbued with the liberal sentiments which were then rousing the enthusiasm of half the young men of Europe" and could not be "a quiet spectator of the fierce conflict round him . . ." He took a musket ball in his left arm while attending to the wounded among the men who were manning the barricades (Kingsley, Mary H., 17-8).

In 1849, at barely twenty-three years old, Dr. Kingsley was in Flintshire, Wales, to minister to the ill during a cholera epidemic for which there was no known cure except urban infrastructure reform. Then from 1850 to 1852, the doctor was traveling in the Alps and Eastern Europe. He produced an article for *Fraser's* Magazine, "Chamois-Hunting" in the Tyrol, published in August 1851, and in September 1853 another of his sociological travel essays appeared, "A German First of September." By the time George was twenty-seven, there was sufficient evidence that he had no interest in a medical practice either in a hospital or an office in London, but as a traveler offering his skill freely.

Mary Henrietta explains that had Dr. Kingsley "established himself in a London practice," he would have risen to the top of his profession because he possessed "many of the qualities which go to the making of a great physician . . ."; however, "he also possessed many other qualities which rendered it impossible for him ever to become one, or, indeed, ever seriously to attempt to become one." For example, he loved too much the "roar of a salmon river and the music of the brae the sweetest of all sounds; a man whose soul loved to dwell in the magnificent dreams of the old dramatists, and to sail, with the old voyagers, past sandy bays and verdant islands over 'the sunlit sea,'" for, if Dr. Kingsley had a practice in London, he "could hardly have looked forward with complacency to the prospect of days spent in prescribing for the diseases of a multitude of patients in a consulting room in

Harley Street, driving in a brougham from one house of sickness to another through the din and turmoil of the vast city, and passing from one bed of suffering to another, with a group of medical students following behind him, . . ." (Kingsley, Mary H., 27). In this way, the daughter explains that her father could not settle down into a medical office with the intention of becoming a teacher of medical students, a clinician, nor a writer of scientific treatises. Perhaps George felt that he could do little to benefit humanity at large, and that British clinical physicians like Parkinson, Addison, Hodgkin, and Bright had already done so much to identify certain characteristic symptoms that these diseases were named for them.

In 1852, following his Alpine adventures, Dr. Kingsley was back in England, and came to the attention of Charles Brudenell-Bruce, the 1st Marquess of Ailesbury, who employed him as a private physician. Born in 1773, the Marquess was fifty-three years older than George and died in January 1856. With high recommendations as a gentleman physician, George came to the attention of other clients. The 1st Earl Ellesmere, Francis Egerton, was born in 1800 and was already a seasoned traveler when he hired George to accompany him to Scotland and Ireland.

With ample leisure time, George maintained numerous interests while serving Ellesmere. For example, he wrote letters to *The Field* Magazine regarding his observations of nature and wildlife, and on December 16, 1856, he was elected a Fellow of the Linnean Society (Charwat, e-mail to author). It was just like George Henry Kingsley to downplay his own achievements; he might have recalled with amusement how he earned attention from the Linnean Society by classifying fish while actually fishing, that is, noticing new taxonomies of the fish he caught in various parts of the world, thus combining pleasure and research while researching what was pleasurable.

One might wonder how Mary Henrietta knew so much about her father. When quite young, she began to take over her father's library when he was gone, delving into Captain Cook's and Hakluyt's travels. Though George's lengthy absences from home seem negligent, such expeditions were not unusual; and, he did not leave his wife and children in financial trouble or without resources. Mary Henrietta's "Memoir" of her father often seems her attempt to explain him to herself. She assures the reader that even while in Edinburgh, before graduation, as soon as her father had a break from medical studies, he was "off for a long ramble in Germany or Switzerland or Austria, through the Rhineland or through the Thüringen Wald" or "the Swiss or the Tyrolean Alps, and once through Bohemia and Moravia, and far away into the Carpathian mountains" (Kingsley, Mary H., 13).

Traveling alone in this way, pilgrim-like, George learned to speak and write fluent German, enough to translate Paul von Heyse's *Four Phases of Love* into English, published by Routledge in 1857. Since Heyse was honored with the Nobel Prize for Literature in 1910, one can see that George Kingsley brought Heyse to the attention of the English reading world. Around the time he translated Heyse from the German, George was a librarian in residence at the Earl of Ellesmere's Bridgewater House, Cleveland Square West. While at the Bridgewater, George wrote an article on Christopher Marlowe, and edited Francis Thynne's book on Chaucer, for the Early English Text Society, which they published later, in 1865. Eventually, the Ellesmeres gave up the entire Bridgewater Library to the Huntington Library in California.

All the while George pursued scholarly interests, he was observant of medical advancements and practice. To comply with the 1858 Medical Act, and to maintain his aristocratic connections, he passed the exam to become a Member of the Royal College of Physicians in 1859. George's name appears in the RCP Medical Directory at least until 1871. The autumn of 1862 found Dr. Kingsley unwinding in the Mediterranean after the death of his patron the 2nd Earl Ellesmere, who had passed away at only 39 years old, less than five years after his father, the 1st Earl. The exact dates are unavailable, but sometime afterwards, George was employed by the Duke of Sutherland to accompany him on what must have been a brief sailing expedition to Egypt and the coast of Syria, since George was back at home in Islington to marry Mary Bailey on October 9, 1862. Mary Henrietta was born a few days later on the 13th. One imagines that Dr. and Mrs. Kingsley agreed to tell Mary Henrietta that they had married in 1860.

Mary Henrietta is unclear as to whether or not her father traveled anywhere other than Scotland with the 2nd Duke of Sutherland, who died in 1861, or the 3rd, who was Kingsley's contemporary and died in 1892. In 1864, George Kingsley moved his family to Highgate, London. Mary Bailey Kingsley gave birth to a son there in May 1866, Charles George, called "Charlie." The year 1866 also found the doctor with the Duke of Rutland in Egypt, and then in Spain with the Lady Herbert of Lea and her eldest son, George Herbert, then age seventeen who became the 13th Earl of Pembroke. Within a year, Dr. Kingsley bade farewell to his family in their beloved Highgate home for a three-year voyage to the South Sea Islands with the youthful Pembroke, which resulted in the Earl's book, *South-Sea Bubbles*. By 1870, Dr. Kingsley was well-known in the aristocratic travel network and was hired as an expedition physician and erudite companion by the Ireland-born 4th Earl Dunraven, Windham Thomas Wyndham-Quin, to accompany him on the first of what would be at least four hunting and travel adventures in Canada and the United States.

If we summarize the life and career of Dr. George Kingsley including his travels with Dunraven, we can't do better than return to Washington Irving's book of 1834, *A Tour on the Prairies*, in which one can find Irving's portrait of the George Henry Kingsley type:

> Another of my fellow travelers was Mr. L——, an Englishman by birth, but descended from a foreign stock; and who had all the buoyancy and accommodating spirit of a native of the Continent. Having rambled over many countries he had become, to a certain degree, a citizen of the world, easily adapting himself to any change. He was a man of a thousand occupations; a botanist, a geologist, a hunter of beetles and butterflies, a musical amateur, a sketcher of no mean pretensions, in short a complete virtuoso; added to which he was a very indefatigable, if not always a very successful sportsman. Never had a man more irons

in the fire, and, consequently, never was a man more busy or more cheerful. (Irving, 14-5)

Truly, George became this person—buoyant and adaptable—and more willing, perhaps, even than Irving's Mr. L. to research any scientific or literary study that appealed to him. It would be worth following up if George Henry Kingsley shared these qualities with Charles Joseph Latrobe, the model for "Mr. L."

The day came when George willingly forsook the high seas for the High Plains. Traveling in the American West would certainly have been easier than, say, the South Seas, but then the western territories could throw in some twists. The unexpected meeting with his brother at the Grand Central Hotel in Denver was delightful, but after Dunraven and Dr. Kingsley proceeded on to Estes Park, the fateful encounter between Jim Nugent and the Earl's employee, Griffith Evans, tested George's medical knowledge—and his *sangfroid*.

George Kingsley took letter writing seriously as a literary form, and put a kind of *bonhomie*, a light-hearted fun into every line. Writing to his wife, Mary Bailey, from Estes Park, dated 13 July 1874, Dr. Kingsley gently raises the topic that Dunraven's employee, Griff Evans, has taken a few shots at Jim Nugent, the now famous "Rocky Mountain Jim," the same man Isabella Bird had befriended the year before, in the autumn of 1873. In writing home, George attempted to lighten the tension with exaggeration—not a good idea. The context is that he's responding to his wife's letter which "reached me in the heart of the Rocky Mountains":

> We have been hunting and fishing, but have not done much, only killed three mountain sheep and an infinity of trout. We had a little difficulty the other day: one of our friends had a row with a wild man of the woods and shot him with buckshot, actually knocking out some of his brains. They sent up the mountain for me, and when I saw the man I thought that, of course, he must die. Not a bit of it, he got round so far

that I have been able to send him to Denver Hospital, with a possibility of recovery, though I assure you that there was at least a teaspoonful of brain oozing out of the wound. It is the most wonderful climate in the world for wounds; there was no suppuration whatever. I have ridden down to the confines of civilization to-day to write you this hasty note, as there is a man going to Denver. A mountain lion comes by our shanty every night; we could have shot him once, but thought, in the darkness, that it was Plunk, our sheep dog; it was a pity as we may never have such a chance again.

We talk of going round to Fort Steele [Wyoming], thence to the Ute Indian Reservation, and then round here again, which will be a hard but very pleasant trip. The weather is awfully hot, 90° in the shade, and both Dunraven and I are burnt to cinders. (Kingsley, Mary H., 171-2)

Retellings and distortions of the episodes of the mountain lion stalking the tent and Dr. Kingsley being first on the scene after Nugent was shot were magnified out of proportion by newspapermen who considered them good for sales. Mary Henrietta explains that "A certain enterprising Western journalist hearing of this incident elaborated it into a story of the most thrilling character" which had reached her mother's ears and worsened her nervous disposition. In Mary Henrietta's attempt to disentangle truth from fabrication, she quotes her father's letter verbatim. In a separate letter, Dr. Kingsley re-emphasizes his concerns, repeating some of what he'd written earlier:

What is this legend you have got hold of about a blood and thunder battle with a bear? It was not a bear we were after, it was a mountain lion, and there was neither blood, thunder, nor battle. It was a great pity that I didn't shoot, I thought it Griff's big dog

Plunk; but Dunraven had neither knife nor rifle, and it might have turned out nasty for him. I suppose that this business is the origin of the wonderful story in the papers. Our lion is the puma (*Felis unicolor*). There are plenty of them, but they are seldom seen, as they prey at night. The papers tell such lies about us. They are very facetious on the subject of Jim and I, "a bold Western mountain man not going to die at the bidding of a British physician, however famous, etc." (Kingsley, Mary H., 172)

The *Rocky Mountain News* was often a gossipy daily in that era, in contrast to its later deservedly high reputation, but there was a reason that anything to do with the Earl of Dunraven was exaggerated. A number of Denverites with their eyes on the real estate market were irritated that Dr. Kingsley's employer was buying up enough of Estes Park to create what they thought a princely private domain, but eventually a cattle ranch and a hotel open to the public. Of course, that's what American men in Denver wanted to do themselves, but they accused Dunraven of practicing landlordism, and Dr. Kingsley was considered a fair target for verbal attacks.

Writing in 1899, Mary Henrietta felt compelled to explain more about her father's experience of Jim Nugent. With the same carefree, tongue-in-cheek humor in which her father wrote about himself, she continues her narrative in her chapter "Hunting in the United States," in the "Memoir" section of *Notes on Sport and Travel*:

The Doctor had two patients, at least, while he was staying in Colorado in 1874. One of them was his brother Charles, whom he found, to his great surprise, in an hotel in Denver, suffering from a severe attack of pleurisy, the other was the wild man of the woods mentioned . . . whose real name was Nugent, but who was popularly known as 'Rocky Mountain Jim,' one of the notorious and the most picturesque of all the Western desperadoes, truly a man as wild and as strange and as full of contradictions as the most Bourbon-inspired novelist ever dreamt of! An extremely interesting account of him is given by Miss Isabella Bird in her charming book, *A Lady's Life in the Rocky Mountains.* He was a Canadian—a man of considerable natural ability who had received a good education, but for some reason he found it expedient to leave his native land and to go to the Western States . . . (Kingsley, Mary H., 173)

Mary Henrietta never visited Colorado to experience the Estes Park setting, hence her admission that she got the essence of the Jim Nugent story from Bird's narrative and her father's letters. With her blend of humor and objectivity, Mary Henrietta records that Nugent had "sixteen golden curls, eighteen inches long, hanging over his shoulders" and, in imagery that imitates that of other western characters, she states, "At a later period of his life he joined a gang of border ruffians in Kansas"; however, "when Miss Bird and George Kingsley made his acquaintance he was a trapper living in a hut—'it looked like the den of a wild beast'—at the only entrance to Estes Park" (Kingsley, Mary H., 173-4).

Despite the overdrawn illustration of Nugent, one finds that the Earl of Dunraven and Dr. Kingsley knew him well beginning with their first sojourn in Estes Park in 1872, while Isabella Bird met Nugent only on her one visit there from September through November of 1873. In that autumn of 1873, Dunraven and Kingsley were on a hunting expedition in Nebraska, and, as a result, missed Bird by only a few weeks, just the time she needed to form her own opinion and construct her rendition of Rocky Mountain Jim and his context. After Bird had left the area, the *Rocky Mountain News* noted on November 20, 1873, that Dunraven was expected to arrive at Charpiot's Hotel on his way to Estes Park with an additional guest, Viscount Parker. The hunting season had extended into November, just long enough for Bird to leave the Estes Park area before Dunraven and Kingsley arrived.

Dr. Kingsley had written home from Fort McPherson, Nebraska, the letter date unclear—"November 15, 187 ?"—but of course 1873. The hunting trip letter is rather standard, almost like another tour on the prairies. Dunraven and Kingsley were guided by Buffalo Bill Cody before his celebrity days with the Wild West show. "We have been hunting for nearly a month . . ." George continues:

> . . . and have had some wonderful sport. Our first hunt lasted for fifteen days, out by the wildest part of the Platte River, north of the Station. We killed elk, white-tail and black-tail deer, antelope, swans, immense geese, ducks, and small game without count. This elk running is perfectly magnificent. We ride among the wild sand hills till we find a herd, and then gallop after them like maniacs, cutting them off, till we get in the midst of them, when we shoot all that we can. Our chief hunter is a very famous man out West, one Buffalo Bill. To see his face flush, and his eyes 'shoot out courage'—as his friend and admirer Texas Jack says—is a sight to see, and he cheers us on till he makes us as mad as himself. (Kingsley, Mary H., 124-5)

So the letter goes, like a tale of men in paradise shooting at anything that moves. But the letter is much longer, with Dr. Kingsley's passages of landscape description as well as notes on the manners of the American men of the military escort that accompanied the Dunraven party from Fort McPherson, plus detailed portraits of both Bill Cody and Texas Jack. Regarding this hunting expedition of late 1873, Mary Henrietta stresses the contrast in age between the energetic Dunraven and her father, who, by many standards, should have retired.

Just a year earlier, 1872, around the time when Maurice and Rose were still in Colorado Springs, the Earl of Dunraven had stopped in the Chicago headquarters of General Phil Sheridan to discuss the Irish Earl's western travel plans when he, Dunraven, "happened to see the head of a magnificent Wapiti stag, which had been sent as a present to General Sheridan from the officer in command of some western frontier post." On the sight of the antlers, Dunraven said to Dr. Kingsley that " . . . nothing would satisfy me but I must be off at once to the fort,'" Mary Henrietta recounts, "whereby it fell out that George Kingsley, at the age of forty-six, found himself clad in fringed buckskins, 'riding like a maniac among the wild sand hills after thundering herds of the American elk'" (Kingsley, Mary H., 124). And Dunraven was only thirty-one.

One can't help being thankful that Isabella Bird visited Estes Park in relative solitude—without Dunraven and Kingsley—for she might not have written her narrative letters home if she had been in Estes at the same time as the trouble-attracting Earl. Fatefully, Bird was the first to put Nugent into a broader story: To narrativize him was to humanize him. However, Bird's account of Jim did not reach the world until her letters were serialized in the *Leisure Hour* in 1878, and a year later collected in the first book edition of *A Lady's Life*. In Letter VIII, Bird includes a footnote thanking Dunraven and Kingsley for their article in *The Field* magazine which revealed the location of Estes Park (Bird, 121), an article I haven't as yet located.

Even before Isabella Bird had met Rocky Mountain Jim, someone must have interviewed him and spoken to others about his background, thus giving Bird some idea of Jim Nugent's picturesque or picaresque reputation. His fate in Estes was all the more startling since he had some college education, was perhaps the "defrocked Canadian priest" and "schoolmaster" who had, in 1871 or 1872, given Dr. Kingsley some "verses of his own composition" (Kingsley, Mary H., 179). In other words, storytelling had already begun to whirl around Nugent before Bird appeared on the scene.

The *Rocky Mountain News* reporters were always on the lookout for items with western flavor, so to speak, and on March 12, 1874, they reported in their "City and Vicinity" column that "Rocky Mountain Jim, the mountaineer and bear fighter, is at Gus. Potter's restaurant," and he "has fully recovered from his last fight with that big 'bar'" (*RMN*, March 12, 1874, n. pag.). On one of the earliest Kingsley-

Dunraven sojourns in Estes Park, Dr. Kingsley had persuaded Jim Nugent to let him examine the eye which the bear had injured. The bear in question had "scratched across" Jim's eye "causing an adhesion between the lid and the eye itself" without injuring the right eye, but causing the lid to hang down like a "permanent curtain" obstructing Jim's vision and thus making it difficult for him to take aim (Kingsley, Mary H., 177-8). Of course, Dr. Kingsley is relating his notation of Nugent's eye injury in a letter home in July 1874 *after* Nugent fired at Griffith Evans, suggesting that Nugent's poor vision was a factor in the shooting incident.

Writing home to Highgate, George—that is, not in his Dr. Kingsley persona—fully explains Evans's shooting of Jim Nugent, in an intricate tale the detail of which serves to build up authenticity. George tells how he was hiking and hunting in a side-canyon near the Estes Park village while Dunraven was elsewhere, and "believing that I was about to kill 'all alone by myself,' as the children say, a reasonably-sized bear" when he heard several local men, "three of the 'hardest cases' in the Park," yelling for him. Dr. Kingsley descended the hill, very angry at the screams from "Bedlam," to hear that Griff Evans had shot Jim, who was lying nearby at the edge of an aspen grove where he had been carried (Kingsley, Mary H., 175). Partly recounting events from what the three "hardest cases" had told him at the scene, Dr. Kingsley writes that Nugent had allegedly advanced slowly along the road toward Griffith Evans's cabin, and either walking and leading his horse—or walking his horse while astride is unclear—paused behind a "timber machine" and took aim at the unsuspecting man sitting on Evans's porch. The "unarmed Englishman" on Evans's porch, William Haigh, was reputed to be a wanderer "dawdling about in those parts under the pretence of hunting," and who happened to pause to sit on the porch of Evans's log cabin while Evans was inside. The seated Englishman, Haigh, called out "Jim's on the shoot!" Evans comes out of the cabin armed, and shoots at Nugent, missing him at first but hitting him with the next round (Kingsley, Mary H., 177-8). Dr. Kingsley explains that Nugent's eye injury in the bear fight meant he could "only shoot from his left shoulder" or "to poke and twist about for a moment or two in order to cross the sights" on his target. A jury convened in Denver might get the picture that Nugent could not aim carefully enough to hurt anyone, though intending to do so.

Since Griff Evans, a Welshman, was Dunraven's resident land manager, he had long known Jim Nugent. Many area residents said the two had a personal feud. In any case, the exact date that Evans shot Nugent seems unknown. Scholar and writer James H. Pickering estimates the date as June 29 (1874) based on the memories of eyewitness William Brown as told to Abner Sprague, but not written down until years later (Pickering, 70; 259 n. 47). The *Rocky Mountain News*, which had shadowed Dunraven everywhere, did not follow him into Estes Park where the population was so sparse as to make waiting for a story unprofitable. And, apparently, Dunraven and Kingsley did not record the date of the shooting either; however, we can estimate that Evans and Nugent shot at each other probably about two weeks after the Dunraven party's arrival in Estes, considering that Dunraven's and Kingsley's departure from Denver to Estes on June 15 was reported in the "Personal Paragraphs" column in the *RMN* of June 16.

One can be thankful that Mary Henrietta Kingsley felt compelled to say something more about her father's knowledge of Jim Nugent. She quotes "the closing scenes" of Jim's life from her father's letter home which she "found among the Doctor's miscellaneous papers." Dr. Kingsley writes:

> . . . Now, though I by no means loved the Mountainous One (as we sometimes playfully called him on account of the extraordinary altitude of his lies), considering him a humbug and a scoundrel, my medical instinct told me, of course, to go and do the best that I could for him. I found the poor wretch stretched out under a clump of silver-stemmed, quivering-leaved aspens, whither he had been carried, with five small bullet-wounds about the head and face, and one of the bullets had most certainly penetrated the cerebellum. He was prostrate, of course, but I must say as

calm and as plucky as any man I ever saw in trouble.
We took him into the neighbouring log-hut, where I
did all that it was possible to do for him, though that
was not much. All the bullets . . . had 'gone through,'
except one which was embedded in the bony process
under the left ear, and the one which had passed into
the brain. One of them had gone right through the
bones of the nose, splintering them at its entrance
and its exit. What a horrible case this would have
been in a polluted war hospital! But up here, eight
thousand feet above the level of the sea, not a single
wound suppurated, and all healed as healthily as the
cut finger of a healthy schoolboy would have done. . . .
some little time afterwards, when I was overhauling
him in the hospital at Denver, I saw to my astonish-
ment that one bullet, the unaccounted for sixth, had
passed right through the biceps of his left arm, and
that the wound had healed without his knowing anything about it. (Kingsley, Mary H., 174-6)

Why the *Rocky Mountain News* didn't publish similar details is
unclear though the reporting staff did have other stories to follow that
week: Vice President Schuyler Colfax was visiting Denver, and there
was silver and gold mining news to report, as well as locusts plaguing
the Front Range of the Rockies near Colorado Springs, and the gathering in Cheyenne, Wyoming, of General Custer and his contingent
of miners preparing to seek gold in the Black Hills of South Dakota
(in violation of the second Fort Laramie treaty).

The Earl of Dunraven and George were anticipating leaving for
the Yellowstone Country by mid-August. Neither ever said that the
Nugent shooting threatened their Yellowstone expedition. In their
code of conduct, for either to have implied that Mr. Nugent was a
problem would have been despicable, and insensitive to the overall
situation of an American citizen being shot by Evans, a British visitor.
As events played out, Nugent was out of the hospital in early August

(about six weeks after the shooting) and was back in Estes Park by about August 7, while—as it happened—the Dunraven party still had three days to go before leaving for Denver and the train to Cheyenne, Wyoming Territory. It was a potentially disastrous three days. Mary Henrietta recounts in her "Memoir" a little-known incident from her father's papers which adds to the controversy over Jim Nugent's behavior, an episode which took place during those three days after Nugent's return to Estes, approximately August 7 or 8, before the Dunraven party departed on August 10. Dr. Kingsley and Griff Evans had to drive a wagon past Nugent's shanty from time to time—perhaps because there was no other road—and on one occasion the doctor feared that Nugent was "drawing a bead on Griff and including me in the shot." It seems unlikely that Dr. Kingsley would invent this.

By mid-August, the *Rocky Mountain News* reported that Dr. Kingsley and Dunraven were in Denver, to meet up with hunting companion Texas Jack on their way to Wyoming (*RMN*, August 11, 1874, n. pag.), with Dunraven's African-American camp cook, Maxwell, and the Earl's Scottish hunting gillie, Campbell, while illustrator Valentine Bromley probably returned to Denver, not intending to experience the rigors of wilderness travel. One wonders how Dunraven knew that he and Dr. Kingsley were clear to leave Estes for the Yellowstone National Park. Of course, if the courts needed only Griff Evans and William Haigh, then the Earl's Denver-resident land agent, Theodore Whyte, could keep an eye on the court proceedings.

After the Dunraven party left Estes, Nugent went to Fort Collins to await the beginning of his court case charging Griffith Evans with assault and William Haigh as accessory. James Pickering presents extensive research on Estes Park and the shooting and eventual death of Jim Nugent in his book *This Blue Hollow* (1999). Pickering found that much of the account was reported in less well-known newspapers, the *Fort Collins Standard*, the *Colorado Sun* of Greeley, and the *Denver Tribune*. The *Rocky Mountain News* seems to have completely forgotten about Nugent until their brief announcement on September 15 that Nugent had died on September 7: "... inasmuch as he had rallied from the effects of the wound, and had been going about the country, his death was mainly due to bad whisky and too much of it" (*RMN*, September 15, 1874, n. pag.). Such a sarcastic comment shows that Dr. George Kingsley and Isabella Bird took Jim Nugent seriously.

The *Denver Daily Times* reported in early September—if mere days before Nugent's September 7 death is unclear—that William Haigh was "fully released from all legal responsibility" while Griff Evans was held under bond to await the outcome of "the wounded man's injuries" (Pickering, 75). Nugent may have gone into a coma a few days before his death. A postmortem examination was ordered, and the autopsy found that a bullet had indeed lodged in Nugent's skull, but the charges against Griff Evans were "discharged on the grounds of justifiable homicide" (*Fort Collins Standard*, Sept. 16, 1874; Pickering, 75). Nugent's threatening actions over the previous few years had contributed to his ruffian reputation, which, in effect, excused all of his adversaries. If writer Pickering's research suggests that there are conflicting accounts of the events of the day Jim Nugent was shot, it's not surprising, though there was no conscious intention of covering up or confusing who did what and when.

Nearly fifty years later, when writing his autobiography, *Past Times and Pastimes*, the Earl of Dunraven stated that he was inside Evans's cabin when William Haigh was on the porch as Nugent approached, and that he remained in the house when Haigh called out that Nugent was on the shoot, the call which prompted Evans to grab his shot gun and go outside (Pickering, 260 n. 59; Dunraven, v. 1: 140-1). However, it's unlikely that Dunraven, if he were inside the house would remain there and do nothing. One questions the accuracy of memories related five decades later, especially when Dunraven writes as though he didn't know Griff Evans personally. Dr. Kingsley does not name the men who called out for him to come to minister to the wounded Nugent, and one can't imagine Dunraven shouting in the way George describes. However, in the same papers in which Mary Henrietta found her father's account that Nugent may have been aiming at himself and Griff (about August 8), she found other papers suggesting that her father at times wrote in haste, and could also be sarcastic. Dr. Kingsley recalls that after Jim's death in Fort

Collins, Jim "left me his rifle and his last pony, but as he had stolen the one and borrowed the other I made but little out of the legacy" (Kingsley, Mary H., 178-9). The tone here is the sort of droll humor that makes such a statement seem a fabrication; it's unclear how the doctor would have known of Nugent's death in September or of his dying wish to leave him anything since by late August the Dunraven party was in the Yellowstone wilderness, and did not return to Denver until November.

Several years later, Griff Evans was still in Estes Park in the employ of the 4th Earl Dunraven. George never forgave Evans for not acting as a gentleman should, and wrote disparagingly of the Welshman. In his more exacting Dr. Kingsley persona, George felt that since Evans was in the shoot-out—though not necessarily the first to shoot—he should have stayed on the scene and not ridden like mad to the village of Burlington, near Longmont, to hire a lawyer to file charges against Nugent for assault (Pickering, 72; Kingsley, George H., 457).

Following Nugent's death, there were repercussions to Dunraven from time to time. About two years before Evans and Nugent fired shots at each other, the Earl had formed the Estes Park Company, and through agent Theodore Whyte was buying land, which Evans and Whyte would manage while Dunraven was on hunting tours or in the Yellowstone country and during the time he was writing *The Great Divide*, at his home Adare Manor south of Limerick. Writer James Pickering noted that Colorado newsmongers were already fond of pointing out their views of "English snobs and aristocrats" and exaggerating wealthy men's plans to "take over" Estes Park, and that the shooting of Jim Nugent was done by "a creature of the Earl of Dunraven" for the purpose of "getting him out of the way" (Pickering, 71). It's possible that Nugent believed the number of foreigners constituted an invasion.

Alas, Dunraven could not avoid publicity; gossip about his land acquisition found its way into the Denver papers and helped fuel the 1880's anti-alien land laws which I've mentioned earlier in the context of Bell and Blackmore. To clarify which documents I'm referring to, the chart titled "Number of acres of land purchased by foreigners in the United States within a recent period" which lists about thirty-five syndicates, corporations, and British individuals and their acres owned, is in the Nimmo Report or *Report in Regard to the Range and Ranch Cattle Business of the United States* of May 16, 1885 (Nimmo, 45), and is the more detailed chart on which the information published in the U. S. *House Report* No. 3455 of July 31, 1886, is based (which I introduced in regard to William A. Bell's partnership with Palmer). How the names and acreages were gathered is uncertain but they were used in speeches by Representative Nutting from New York, and Representative Lore of Delaware (and the lists each congressman gives in his report are similar). Scholars like Douglas Nelson found that the 60,000 acres that the Nimmo Report claims Dunraven owned by 1884 were an exaggeration—someone having added an additional zero, as Pickering shows (Pickering, 33–51). But supposing the 60,000 acres were accurate, it's still paltry compared to the numbers which upset so many American owners of 160 acre homesteads across the Midwest. These estates included "English syndicate No. 1 in Texas" which owned 4,500,000 acres, and the Marquis of Tweeddale, and the "C.R. and Land Company of London" which owned 1,750,000 acres; William Whalley, M.P. for Peterborough, 310,000 acres; and Robert Tennent, of London, 230,000 (Nimmo, 45).

Representative Payson from the Committee on Public Lands (quoted by scholars Clements and Nelson) wrote that "In the hands of many of these foreign owners and holders these lands are made subject to a system of landlordism and conditions totally un-American, and kindred to that existing in the Old World, systems and conditions that have spread ruin and misery wherever they have existed in Europe" (U. S. *House, Report* No. 3455). As noted, the alien land law movement was meant to reserve prime agricultural land for American settlers, and legislation would not have been applied to mountainous areas like Estes Park. More than likely, many Anglo-Americans who complained the loudest wanted to be landlords themselves.

Important to note, Dunraven was not yet making any money from the Estes Park Company; he was putting money *into* it. Only research in Wales and in the Limerick, Ireland, archives would show if

Dunraven was funding his travels and Colorado land purchases with money from his coal mines and real estate in Glamorgan, Wales (not his tenants near Adare). For Denverites who wished to attract foreign investment, to harangue Dunraven over the shooting of Nugent was counterproductive, if not simply unwarranted.

If George had thoughts about his employer's plans for the blue hollow of the Estes valley, he did not record them, but more than likely believed that whatever ranch or hotel establishment Dunraven brought into being would be as right as possible—and even have room for a few odd characters. One can't help wondering, if, one afternoon in that summer of 1874, Dr. Kingsley realized that for Jim Nugent, Estes Park was all he had and all he would ever have. The doctor had traveled extensively and wasn't possessive about any of the places he loved: the Mediterranean, the islands of the South Pacific, the mountains and plains of Canada, the Tyrolean Alps. He had cultivated a way of being-in-the-world which Jim Nugent could not.

Two years later, in 1876, the Earl of Dunraven's insightful tale was published, *The Great Divide: Travels in the Upper Yellowstone in the Summer of 1874*, when George was fifty years old. If he read Dunraven's account of their expedition, he may have felt honored to be a "character" in it, and to have acquitted himself honorably—but that, as they say, is another story.

Dr. Kingsley—and others—"under the thrall of the Erdgeist"

Scholars have given so little attention to George that an injustice has been done him by Mary Henrietta Kingsley's able biographer, Katherine Frank. While Frank finds ample evidence that George had "a passion for scholarship" which was nurtured in his own father's Chelsea Rectory library, Frank sums up George's travels in a rather casual way, simply as a "need to lead a wandering life." Frank also dismisses his earliest travels through Germany, Switzerland, and Austria as simply for "an exhilarating sense of liberation" after medical school (Frank, 14-5). Frank's hasty explanations for George Kingsley's travels are a disservice to readers who find in his life the only consistent intellectual the family ever produced, other than Mary Henrietta. Of course, in a book on George's daughter, the reader should not expect a nuanced study of the father; however, interested readers have been dependent on Mary Henrietta's personal and narrowly focused assessment of her father's viewpoint of the American West.

Noticing her father's multi-faceted interests, Mary Henrietta felt a necessity to explain two related things about him, one which I've detailed as his sense of confinement or limitation had he pursued a profession in a private office or hospital, and the other is why, unlike his contemporary, traveler Richard Francis Burton (1821-1890), her father had not produced a book-length "monument of learning in literature" similar to Burton's *First Footsteps in East Africa* (1856). In her attempt to elucidate her parent, Mary Henrietta found the Teutonic image of Tannhäuser readily available, since she and her father were both fluent in the German language and sensibility. Unfortunately, Mary Henrietta's motif of Tannhäuser calls up notions of ideological and physical irresponsibility as the cause of Dr. Kingsley's wasted talents, an image that doesn't actually reflect what she presents of him.

Perhaps Mary Henrietta meant to put more emphasis on her translation of *Erdgeist* as an Earth worship that had gripped her father's intellect. She explains that "The spirit that held his mind in thrall was no one goddess of no one mountain, but the *Erdgeist* Goethe knew of—that *Erdgeist* who has countless thousands of faery palaces in this world . . ." (Kingsley, Mary H., 193). In other words, from his boyhood wanderings in Devonshire, the idea gripped him that he had to see the variety of the world, all its people, land forms, and seacoasts. In his imagination at first, he would launch himself outward from the beauty of the Devon coast, then contrast it with the urban wilds of Chelsea and Brompton; what connected everything was the great dome of sky and the overarching divinity of Earth.

While George acquired German early, and got to know Europe, he pursued the details of medical science as a pathway to observing and knowing humanity wherever he might travel. Everything George witnessed through the limits of medical knowledge, between the cholera epidemic in Wales and the adventure in the Alps, he began seeking globally. He was attached to the effects that every nation had on him, and wherever George went—to Continental Europe, to the South Seas, the West Indies, Tahiti, Singapore, and the Falkland Islands, Egypt, or the Rocky Mountain Front Range of Colorado— he allowed the place to inhabit him.

Within a few years, George knew that he had a love of nature for itself—and didn't want to analyze it too much—and with his cosmopolitanism, and practical medical knowledge, proved to have the qualities that titled aristocrats desired in a gentleman physician and travel companion: a philosophical awareness of the ambiguities of life, a literary and scientific approach to knowing the flora and fauna of the nations through which they traveled, and a practical man in ministering to the accidents and illnesses occasioned by travel.

Even as such an objective traveler, George Kingsley proved to be an urbanized social being who loved a good library and good conversation; his heart was in Highgate, London. He missed it for years after moving to Bexley Heath, south-east of London, for his wife's health, but then enjoyed living in Cambridge the last eight years of his life from the autumn of 1884 when his son Charlie began at Christ's College. When Dr. Kingsley died instantly from a heart attack on February 5, 1892, he was just a week short of his sixty-sixth birthday. One can see that the death of his wife, Mary Bailey, two months later, freed their daughter for her own travels to Africa. After Mary Henrietta produced a book which satisfied her, *Travels in West Africa* (1897), and made numerous public presentations of her work, she was still intellectually curious about her father's trajectory, enough to take a break from her own travels to write the "Memoir" and collect his essays for *Notes on Sport and Travel*. The location of her father's original letters and manuscripts is unknown.

Mary Henrietta's notion that her father was too enthralled with seeking an experience of *Erdgeist* to write publishable travel accounts can never be a completely satisfying explanation for 21st-century readers. Based on the travel essays she includes in *Notes*, she must have known her father was a proto-typical analyst of the cultural predicament, the kind of reader who would a hundred years later be the ideal audience for Edward W. Saïd's book *Orientalism*. As George traveled with aristocratic patrons, he began witnessing the effects of colonization and empire, but also the slow, unconscious expansion of English influence. He knew he was a sophisticated Englishman from a technologically developed nation, observing—regretfully—the slow but irrevocable changes in individuals and their cultures, peoples who were never uncivilized or primitive to begin with. This experienced observer is the George H. Kingsley who will appear in the American West.

One might still wonder how the Dr. Kingsley in, say, New Zealand, is connected to the Kingsley in Estes Park and the prairies of western Nebraska. First of all, as suggested earlier, Mary Henrietta had to become knowledgeable about her father's reading and travel interests and to think like him. In his personal library, she discovered an 1863 first edition of Frederick Edward Maning's *Old New Zealand: Being Incidents of Native Customs and Character in the Old Times*. From this book, she may have been introduced to her first impression of ideas on empire and colonization, which were reflected in her father's essay "Musings on Manning's 'Old New Zealand'" (in which he spelled Maning with two 'n' letters). First published in *Temple Bar*, December 1877, Mary Henrietta Kingsley reprinted this New Zealand essay with her "Memoir."

In his essay on Maning, George reveals his way of seeing and sheds light on his experience of Colorado. George was not afraid to tackle a complex topic such as the effects of the colonizer on the colonized, and also of how native people perceived English men. However, to the contemporary reader trained on postcolonial studies, and used to the direct statements of Claude Lévi-Strauss or Edward Saïd, it's difficult to decide if the purpose of George's word choice is to soften his insights on colonization for the *Temple Bar*'s upper-class readership, or if he retained some feelings of British superiority.

More than likely, George chose his tone of voice in order to point out the insidious tendency of certain British individuals to dominate other cultures. For George, Frederick Edward Maning was "a gentleman of, I believe, good north-Irish blood," he wrote, who lived with the Maori for a number of years, long enough to develop a rare ability, the "power of putting part of your mind *en rapport* with the mind you wish to study—'sympathy' is a good old word . . ." (Kingsley, George H., 334). George trusts Maning's viewpoint, partly because Kingsley believed he himself could not ever be in New Zealand long enough to develop the quality of rapport which Maning achieved. George's tone may be too casual or light-hearted for 21st-century readers, but he's asking his 1870s English readers to investigate their own level of consciousness when interacting with the people whom their consumer habits affect.

In a significant anecdote, George contrasts British interaction in New Zealand with his experience in the American West. He recalls with disgust the corrupt practices of white traders licensed by the United States Department of War to interact with Native Americans at or near western forts, trading posts, and reservations (before the Bureau of Indian Affairs was created in the Department of the Interior). Actually, by the time George wrote his essay on New Zealand, he'd had the experience of many expeditions to Nebraska, Wyoming, and Colorado; in that light, his interpretation of New Zealand is conditioned by his American West experience. In New Zealand, Maning had been a "Pakeha Maori," that is a "white Maori," or, rather a kind of "Maori's white-man" who was "the property of the Maori chief who patronised him, and permitted him to trade with his tribe, and who was, moreover, a species of consul, or communicating agent with the outside world." Using his ornate adjectives, George Kingsley analyzes the U.S. government trader in comparison to the "Maori's white-man," following on from the phrase an ". . . agent with the outside world":

> [The Pakeha Maori is] A very different sort of person from our friend the beachcomber, a runagate rogue without property, position, or influence; but one more in the position of the Indian post-trader of the Far West, a man who had to combine mercantile pursuits with wise policies, and delicate handlings of many questions, foreign and domestic. Not that the Pakeha Maori ever had any taint of the unutterable rascaldom of that scoundrelly representative of that most scoundrelly 'Indian Ring' which Americans so tamely permit to disgrace their country. He [the Pakeha Maori] was 'backed' by no one, and had never to cheat in order to bribe his Government; and, in fact, had he attempted to treat his clients as the [American] traders treat theirs, the sharp-witted and swift-handed Maories would have made but short work of him. (Kingsley, George H., 334-5)

In effect, George admires the way the native New Zealanders have control over the business conduct of the white trader in comparison to the American Indians who are at the mercy of the United States government-appointed traders who cheat both Native nations and the U.S. government (whose conduct George would have witnessed when he and Dunraven were stopping at military encampments). It's difficult to imagine George remaining silent about the injustices, especially when he knew others were observing the same corruption.

George Kingsley offers an insight into how European consumerism infects individuals during the most subtle individual interactions. George stated that he felt reluctant "to part with" certain Maori individuals, who, he suspected were actually glad to see him go. "I think him most curious and worth studying from every side," George wrote, while "he, I am afraid, has got the idea into his head that there is nothing very remarkable about me, but that I am a very commonplace individual" whose only advantage over the Maori may be "having better tools," that is, some sort of technological superiority. George remains vague on this point and recommends we read "Manning's translation of Heki's War" (Kingsley, George H., 351). Regarding George's light tone of voice, when rendering the cultural predicament into print, he has to maintain connection with his audience while showing that he believes he's also a carrier of the virus of British influence. His jovial tone fulfills this purpose of putting himself *en rapport* with his upper-class male reader who is also aware of the paradox.

Mary Henrietta found that her father was not enthralled by any one landscape, and that he visited so many places on the globe that he simply loved the place he was in. For certain vistas, certain exhilaration, there was nothing like the Alps or a South Sea's island, or Mount Etna. Writing home from an island in the Mediterranean, he meditated, "Could I but have an island of my very own, I would have a bit of Sicily, but not too big a bit, cut out, and set in the bright blue sea all by itself." In letters home, his musings on landscape suggest that he did not need the sublimity of the Yellowstone country, as Dunraven did; the merely picturesque would do, which George admits is sentimental. Regarding his imaginary island paradise, George states ". . . there should sweep the splendour of the sunlit sea, flecked with a bright sail or two, gliding by as if storms were unknown. Yes! this *is* sentimental. But you should never turn a sentiment away from your door. Take them all in,—good, bad, and indifferent,—and make the best of them, for, maybe, if you slam the door in the face of one she'll never come again." Mary Henrietta explains "That was written in the Balearics . . . a note, apparently, for the book which was to have been, yet never was,—long before he had seen the Island of Pines and 'the Island of Beautiful People,'" as Pedro Fernandes de Queirós called Tahiti (Kingsley, Mary H., 61-2).

In contrast, there is nothing sentimental about a hunting adventure in Nebraska. Writing in that same November of 1873 (the winter before the Estes Park debacle and the Yellowstone adventure), it's impossible to figure out if George knows he's describing the violence of the colonization of the American West or if he's part of the problem himself, however, someone has to be a witness to the paradox of Dunraven's hunting expedition. "The gale has blown itself out and the day is lovely," George writes, "though intensely cold, but with plenty of blankets we shall do very well, though soldiers' tents are hardly the sort of thing for this climate." The officer in charge of the western military department, General Sheridan, has required that the Earl of Dunraven have a military escort through the High Plains:

> I suppose that people would be considered mad at home were they to leave their houses in the coldest mid-winter and betake themselves to tents for a fortnight together; but here, where every man is a soldier or a hunter, no one thinks anything about it. . . . One comfort is, that this cold will keep the Indians quiet, but next spring they expect a big war, particularly about the North Pacific Railroad, which runs right through their hunting grounds. After all, one cannot be surprised at the poor wretches fighting; they depend wholly on the buffalo for food, and the railway and its consequent settlers will soon drive them away for ever. (Kingsley, Mary H., 127)

George Kingsley's letters seem not to be addressed to family, but are carefully crafted essays for a wider audience. It may be that George preferred islands in one letter, but writing from near Fort McPherson, Nebraska, in November 1873, he demonstrates that his description of the travel setting could be his proven strength:

> Our first hunting ground was not real prairie, rolling away to the horizon, [but] a mass of wild, sandy hills, with patches of rank grass on them here and there, and having, as often as not, abrupt little cliffs some fifteen or twenty feet high on one side of them, which made it mighty pleasant riding. To the south the land was better and firmer, sparsely timbered with gray-barked, gnarled elms and cotton-trees, and cut by shallow valleys containing sluggish, green, alkaline streams fringed with thickets of red willow and large sun-flowers, now dead and dry. A snow bird or two, an occasional flight of handsome, long-tailed magpies, and a few wary willow grouse stretching out their necks . . . ready at the slightest alarm to fly clucking away to the wild prairie . . . (Kingsley, Mary H., 128)

George completes the prairie scene in this letter home with "an infinite variety of moles, gophers, and ground squirrels . . ." With this evidence that her father could have written well, Mary Henrietta repeats the refrain that he had intended to write a book about the High Plains of Nebraska, but "this scheme went the way that so many of the best laid schemes . . . go, and we have only a set of disconnected sketches" (129).

Perhaps it's best that George confined his experiences to the audience of his wife and children. On returning home, he could have perused his own letters and realized that he could not revise them into a tale that would suit the expectations of magazine editors with set notions of Buffalo Bill Cody. George wrote what he saw in the moment—more like a journalist—and none of the 'characters' like Cody or Texas Jack Omohondro come out looking good, but rather more paradoxical than the magazines wanted. George gives us the complete context for his experience of Cody who appears alongside the military escort which includes Irish and German immigrant men (who probably could not find employment other than that which would harass indigenous people). The "only men who can cope with" the "nimble, quick-witted Indian" are "men like our friends Buffalo Bill and Texas Jack" who are "two perfect specimens of the western professional hunter" not of James Fenimore Cooper's "leather-stocking type" (Kingsley, Mary H., 133).

George describes the appearance and actions of the two men as earning their dime novel heroism, which Mary Henrietta quotes from his letters home. "Buffalo Bill . . . is a noble Vandyke stepped from its frame. . . . Half hidden by their long black fringes, his large, lustrous eyes so full of slumbering fire, . . ." George doesn't need the "pen of a lady-novelist" to describe Cody—George already has that ability: "I have never met with a thorough gentleman, quiet, calm, and self-possessed, full of memories of strange adventures, yet never thrusting them too prominently forward, but telling them with a far greater reality than any highly-wrought description could possibly give" (134-5). Having advised the reader, George breaks with the traditional view of Buffalo Bill when revealing that Cody will occasionally wear a "civilian and civilized garb . . . which makes him look like the aforesaid Vandyke nobleman trying to disguise himself as a steamboat steward" and with a sombrero tied down under his chin with a handkerchief "assumes a prudish and poke-bonnet-like appearance which entirely unprepares you for the noble face and flashing eyes . . ." (Kingsley, Mary H., 136).

But if Bill Cody "belongs to the school of Charles I., pale, large eyed, and dreamy, Jack, all life, and blood, and fire, blazing with suppressed poetry, is Elizabethan to the back bone! He too is an eminently handsome man, and the sight of him in his fringed hunting buckskins, short hunting shirt decorated with patches of red and blue stained leather . . . would play the very mischief with many an eastern girl's heart" (137-8). Be that as it may, Omohundro would establish a home in Leadville, Colorado, with his wife, Giuseppina Morlacchi, an actor with Jack in *Scouts of the Prairie*. In the light of Jack's career, it would seem that the military escorted hunting expedition for which Cody and Texas Jack were hired was also a performance for entertainment, but George Kingsley hones in on a sharper portrait. "Jack, being a southern man, thinks it necessary to suppose that he has Indian blood in his veins, a very popular idea in those parts":

> If he has, he is rather rough on his relatives, for he is deadly on Indians. Indian hunting is, in fact, the real profession of both Jack and Bill [Cody], they being retained as trackers, aye, and as fighters, too, in the case of horses being run from the neighborhood of the Fort; though, from time to time, they are put in charge of a band to see that it does not exceed the limits of its Reservation . . . They have the strangest feelings about Indians, these two. Though, when on the war path, they would no more hesitate to shoot down an Indian off his Reservation, than they would hesitate to throw a stone at a felonious chipmunk, they have a sympathy and tenderness towards them infinitely greater than you will find among the greedy, pushing settlers, who regard them as mere vermin who must be destroyed . . . (Kingsley, Mary H., 138-9)

In summary, it's unclear what to make of George H. Kingsley except if one sees him as a journalist or writer of critical feature essays. Like the traveling British writers before him who observed genocide, Dr. Kingsley knows he's on the side of the doomed indigenous people. While Cody and Texas Jack are nearly always 'on stage,' their darker side is similar to that of the in-migrating settlers he describes, especially the "Indian agents" appointed by the U.S. government whom he finds are "extremely evil" (139). Within a few years, readers would see a different Texas Jack Omohundro, not the one in Dr. Kingsley's letters. In the planning stages for the Yellowstone expedition, Dunraven contacted Texas Jack in Leadville requesting his services leading the hunt, memorialized in *The Great Divide* (1876). I must say in passing that Dunraven's account of the Yellowstone is a spiritual search for a sublime connection with landscape, not an account of carnage in the high country.

Even by the winter of 1873, Dr. Kingsley would have noticed that the tourist-hunter's lifestyle was coming to an end. In November 1867, the Union Pacific rails had been completed to Cheyenne, Wyoming, from Omaha, Nebraska, along the Platte River (when the Northern Pacific railway was in its infancy), and as is familiar, the Kansas Pacific Railway linked St. Louis, Missouri, with Denver in August 1870. Another challenge to cross-country hunting parties were the massive cattle ranches, but even long cattle-drives would lose a sense of the picturesque (for the magazine reader) when they ended at railway stockyards. As the herds of buffalo diminished to the point of becoming objects of pity, men like Buffalo Bill would turn to the entertainment business which commodified the vanished West. American types similar to Texas Jack, such as Ike Yoho, would become accustomed to new occupations, for Yoho, guiding the rich English financier William Henry Blackmore around Colorado and New Mexico.

Drawing this chapter to a close, George H. Kingsley's essays were more focused than his letters home, as, for example, "Chamois-Hunting" from *Fraser's Magazine* of August 1851, in which he demonstrates his powers of reflection on self and society. After he bags his chamois, he pauses: "Now I believe, in all propriety, we ought to have been melancholy, and moralized over the slain." He continues, "That rich, soft, black eye filming over with the frosty breath of death, and that last convulsive kick of the hind-legs ought perhaps to have made us feel that we had done rather a brutal and selfish thing; but they did not." Whatever the case may be, after some "rejoicing" at their killing, the chamois hunters sit around the camp and gaze at the dead chamois for quite some time, with only the sound of a nearby waterfall. Dr. Kingsley is sure that the ghost of this lovely animal will haunt him (Kingsley, George H., 528).

Perhaps, the haunted feeling was a sudden realization of his own mortality, a foreboding he would hide for decades in the tone of amused detachment which characterized his published essays as well as his letters home from Nebraska and Colorado. The following year, in the summer of 1874, the shots fired between Jim Nugent and Griff Evans would seem to have shot the nonsense out of Dr. Kingsley. Though he returned with Dunraven to the Yellowstone country in 1879 (unless this date is his daughter's typographical error)—proven by a single letter home from Rawlings, Wyoming—he never wrote of it or of any of his subsequent voyages.

Thankfully, Mary Henrietta Kingsley took the time to curate her father's letters and essays before she, too, was propelled outward bound again. She probably never saw the completed volume of *Notes on Sport and Travel* with her "Memoir"; it was published sometime in 1900. Tragically, Mary Henrietta died of enteric fever in South Africa, June 2, 1900—a wasteful end which all of scientific London mourned. She was buried at sea off Simon's Town, Cape Colony, South Africa.

Maurice Kingsley: "I have done with making fortunes in this country"

For Rose Kingsley, the year 1910 began well. Her book *In the Rhône Country* was published by George Allen & Sons of London. Unfortunately, travel writing didn't generate enough income to live on, nor did any of her other books, if Rose wished to remain in her own house in the village of her birth, Eversley (Lundberg, 337). Thirty-five years had elapsed since her father's death in early 1875, after which she and her mother left the rectory, and Hampshire, and soon settled in a spacious home called The Grove in Tachbrook Mallory, Warwickshire, near Leamington Spa. Friends might have felt that Rose had done little while caring for her elderly mother other than co-founding the Leamington High School for Girls and acting as Provisional Secretary until a full-time specialist was hired. However, she cultivated varieties of roses while at The Grove and published two volumes on the topic. After her mother passed away in 1891, Rose returned to Eversley and a new house called The Keys, the construction of which had in large part been paid for by her novelist sister, Mary St. Leger Kingsley (Lundberg, 194). The French government awarded Rose the title of *Officier de l'Instruction Publique*, for her popular English-language work on French art and culture, *A History of French Art, 1100-1899* published in 1899. Never a novelist, Rose was not a productive magazine writer either, and after her sister's novel-writing income declined, Rose depended on money inherited from her mother and royalties from her father's work.

Rose Kingsley had reached sixty-six years old experiencing rheumatism and liver complaints, but was otherwise fit when the news came in late November 1910 from New Rochelle, New York: Maurice Kingsley was dead from cancer at age 63. Catherine Oothout, a dedicated American friend of her novelist sister, Mary, had mailed copies of the obituary from the *New York Times* and the *Evening Post* (Lundberg, 331). In the *Times* article, "Death of Maurice Kingsley" was in all capital letters, then "Eldest Son of the Late Canon Kingsley Dead at New Rochelle." With such a prominent headline, you'd think that Maurice was well known, but the obituary was composed of a number of fabrications. Most noticeable is that Maurice was not a graduate of Cambridge University; he had stayed for only a year. And there was no mention of his attendance at the Royal Agricultural College in Cirencester. Rose would recall with some embarrassment for Maurice that though he took examinations in his first year at Cirencester in Inorganic Chemistry, Agriculture, Surveying, and Drawing, he left for Argentina without a diploma (Williams, K., e-mail to author).

And while it's true that Maurice had been elected a Fellow of the Royal Geographical Society in 1873, if he didn't have the money to pay the annual dues, his membership would have been dropped by the R.G.S. It's unknown why the obituary writer mentioned Maurice's connection with Colonel McFarland of the United States Engineering Corps when McFarland had died in 1888, twenty-two years earlier. Again, it's unclear what employment Maurice finally settled into except that by 1910, his New Rochelle, New York, address seems to have been of long standing. Evidence suggests that Maurice did accomplish something as a civil engineer of harbor works. He had written several pamphlets regarding the upgrading of harbors, collected in 1898 as a booklet, *The Defence of Our Great Cities*. Noticing "our" in the title suggests that Maurice did indeed become an American citizen.

Relaxed in her own home in Eversley, Rose might have wondered where Maurice's life had gone wrong. She would have looked back on their fulfilling days in Colorado and wondered if there were signs then that he would not be able to find success or satisfaction. Their father naming Maurice after his early mentor in Broad Church social activism and relations with the poor, John F. D. Maurice, may have been an unfortunate start, suggesting an ideal that the younger Maurice could never live up to. On reflection, Rose would not have denied that their father, with his own nervous disposition, demonstrated to his sons how to over-react to perceived challenges and pressures—traits described by Una Pope-Hennessy and validated by Patricia Lundberg's research in the Kingsley Family Archives. Lundberg records that the Kingsley men were prone to be overwhelmed for a period of time, a condition mid-Victorians called "shattered nerves" (Lundberg, 39) which might today be described as chronic fatigue or adrenal stress. And for an intelligent man like Maurice, the irritating periods of inactivity to heal the fatigue—perhaps a few hours or a day or two—could have been compounded by his over-analyzing the situation, which Canon Kingsley called his own "over mentation" or over-thinking.

Perhaps Rose hoped that Maurice would outgrow the anxiety attacks which he seems to have learned from their father, whose nervous responses definitely affected the youngest child, the son whose name, Grenville, reflected his mother's Grenfell heritage. As a sign of a sad story to come, Grenville Arthur Kingsley was removed by his parents from the Harrow school for nervous exhaustion (Lundberg, 50). Canon Kingsley's letters home from the 1874 American tour suggest that he infantilized Grenville to such an extent that, in retrospect, Grenville may have faced obstacles when transitioning into adult autonomy, and certainly was unprepared to navigate his way through human relations in Queensland, Australia. Like his uncle Henry before him, Grenville fled England for Australia with some hope, but died there in 1898 at the age of 40, a suicide, leaving his sisters to pay the massive debts for the land he had purchased in a place called "The Hollow" or York's Hollow (Lundberg, 33-4; 194). Grenville's fate weighed heavily on Rose, Maurice, and Mary.

When reflecting on Maurice's relationship with their father, Rose might have concluded that Maurice was on tenterhooks his entire life, that is, in a state of agitated suspense, the son's nerves rattled when his father overstepped in conversation or in print. In contrast,

Edmund William Gosse, only two years younger than Maurice, established a secure sense of self from which he launched his conscious inquiry into his relationship with his father, and produced an intimate memoir, *Father and Son*, published in 1907. Edmund's father, Philip Henry Gosse, was a zoologist and fundamentalist Christian whom Charles Kingsley had befriended many years earlier based on their scientific interests. Rose recalled that when the Kingsleys visited Torquay, Devon, on a brief holiday in the mid-1850s, Maurice, just a boy, had hunted beach specimens requested by Philip Gosse (Martin, *Dust*, 170-1). But unlike the younger Gosse, Maurice could not have written a sustained exploration of his relationship with his own father if he did not first know himself.

Given that Maurice felt insecure, neither emigration nor life in England would have completely satisfied him. He could have cultivated numerous high-placed connections such as the 8th Duke of Argyll with whom the Kingsleys went fishing at Inverary, Scotland, when Maurice was about fifteen (Pope-Hennessy, 208), around the time Maurice showed lackluster aptitude at Wellington College. When Maurice dropped out of Trinity Hall, Cambridge, his father had to adjust his expectations of his eldest son (Thorp, 105-6). As the years went by, Maurice may have become extremely self-conscious about his Kingsley name and overreacted to criticism from employers, and as a result could not think his way out of difficulties. Rose recalled her brother's reappearance in Eversley in March 1870, after Argentina, during which he asked for £2,000 of his mother's estate, and was refused by Frances's trustees (Lundberg, 43), around the time Maurice did not immediately take up Bell's suggestion of going to Colorado. Surely, this demand for such a huge sum of money foretold of her brother's future employment complications.

Rose would have remembered how resourceful Maurice had been in the foundation of Colorado Springs, but the exact reason he left the employ of Palmer and Bell may be lost to posterity. His restlessness in the Fountain Colony and Colorado Springs Company employment could not have been that they weren't paying enough—on the contrary. The Denver & Río Grande Railway retained experienced employees right through the period when they could have failed due to economic crisis, defaults, and competing railways during the years 1873 to 1878 (Brayer, v. 2: 163-216). After a few years of steady employment in the Colorado Springs Company, Maurice could have come away with at least a few letters of reference from Palmer and Bell and E. S. Nettleton as well as their associates such as William E. Pabor.

After Maurice Kingsley met up with the Palmers and his sister in Mexico City in mid-1872, he may have considered staying on and working for the Mexico National Railway (after Rose returned to New York City with the Palmers and then to England on her own), especially after he met Marie Yorke there, living with her mother, Sarah Hanna Yorke, and brother, Edward Yorke III, a railway surveyor, the "Mr. Y." in *South by West* (not Edward Yorke, Jr., their father, who had died in Vermont in 1868). When Maurice married Marie to everyone's delight, on April 1, 1874, in Mexico City, Rose assumed that her brother's habits would become settled.

There are many suppositions for Maurice's continuing lack of steady employment after marriage, and one is that Maurice might have become irritating to potential employers, though many Englishmen had found a way to become American citizens without sacrificing their values and standards. For example, Bell's associate, Francis Cholmondeley Thornton, introduced earlier, a Cambridge graduate, became well-known in the Pike's Peak region and purchased his own ranch near the village of Wigwam, along the D&RG line about midway between the town of Fountain and the city of Pueblo. More than likely, Maurice developed the habit of general dissatisfaction. Remaining in Mexico City for survey engineering work did not appeal to him, even though his wife's brother, Edward, was there, supposedly offering family support. The fact that Canon Kingsley had to wire £250 to his son for his marriage and travel expenses could have been another warning, but it made sense at the time to help Maurice.

After getting Marie's mother settled in New York City, Maurice and Marie went to Chattanooga to follow up on employment there. This assignment in Chattanooga, which the Canon referred to in the

July 1874 letter from Colorado to Eversley, was the railway work with General Wilder which Canon Kingsley stated would be "the turning point" of his son's life based upon "the serious tone" of Maurice's letters. The Canon had met General John Thomas Wilder—a near contemporary of Palmer—on board *The Oceanic* crossing to the United States in January at the beginning of his lecture tour, when Wilder was on his return trip to Chattanooga where he owned a rail mill he'd founded in 1870, and had served as both mayor and postmaster (Martin, *Notes*, 22, n. 18). The ten-day Atlantic crossing had enabled Kingsley to converse with Wilder on Maurice's qualifications, and Wilder offered exactly the sort of engineering work the son could do, but the brevity of Maurice's employment with Wilder puzzled his Eversley family. Seven months after Canon Kingsley's death that January 1875, Rose recalled how Maurice admitted that he'd lost the job in Chattanooga because he'd had a falling out with General Wilder (Lundberg, 53-4).

In a letter dated, July 14, 1874, Maurice wrote to William A. Bell from the Chattanooga office of "Major T. J. Carlyle," a letter which Bell received while Rose and Canon Kingsley were packing to leave Manitou Springs for the return to England. Maurice begins "I believe I never write to you but to ask a favor & the one being this time—is there any work to be had in Colorado." Maurice continues, "This affair that daddy has been humbugged into thinking so good is 'bogus' utterly—This great Wilder is a land speculator who has done very well in the business for himself but not very well for his principals" (Scamehorn, 7). Maurice isn't more specific on these accusations which are probably unfounded. Bell saved this letter as he did all business correspondence, and his heirs bequeathed many boxes of similar papers to the History Colorado library in Denver; Lee Scamehorn and his staff catalogued the correspondence and business documents in a finding aid titled, *A Calendar of the Papers of William Abraham Bell*.

In this same letter, after Maurice expresses regret that he could not meet Rose and their father in Manitou Springs, he writes, "Will you ask Palmer if he has got anything—you may assure yourselves [and] him that I have changed a little for the better since being spliced &

can be reckoned on a little better than before." Maurice uses the term "spliced" for getting married, which suggests the intimacy of being interwoven but also seems sarcastic, while confessing that he has not been reliable but promises to be so. He complains about Chattanooga, "The iron trade is on its last legs here and the coal trade is purely local ..." statements which may be true, and yet, "The country seems cursed by sloth & ignorance & I had not a notion things were as they are." If Bell responded, Maurice did not preserve the letter.

Maurice stays on in the Chattanooga area employed by Major Walter McFarland (the Colonel mentioned in the obituary) as Assistant Engineer on a project evaluating the Little Tennessee River to its source near the Chilhowee Mountains, a report which he completes and files February 22, 1875. A paragraph of uncertain date in the *Gazette*, though probably early 1875, written in J. Elsom Liller's style, suggests that Maurice returned to Colorado Springs for a brief uninvited visit to "shake hands" with Liller, perhaps on a round trip from Chattanooga. In January 1876, Maurice writes to Bell again from Chattanooga, evidently still with McFarland, but complaining about "economic conditions" in Tennessee, and asking about work at the "furnaces at Grape Creek" near Cañon City, Colorado (Scamehorn, 14).

A few weeks later, Maurice writes again from Chattanooga, addressing Bell as "My dear old chap" a familiar tone which they have apparently agreed upon. The letter dated February 12, covers a number of topics. He thanks Bell for giving him a "thorough insight into Colorado affairs" while announcing the birth of a boy "weighing 10 1/2 lbs & is in every way a stunner!" attesting to the son's good health. He asks Bell to be the infant's godfather, and yet, he states that "I am in such a general state of idiocy that I am incapable of writing any sense" perhaps due to the child's birth, but "with deeper regrets than you can imagine, I must refuse Colorado." In other words, Bell *did* offer Maurice employment. "The wife was wild over it and so should I have been if I had been able to make the move—but I am compromised absolutely to go with the [unclear] engineer here, (who has been a great friend of mine) to Oswego on the Lakes, & I don't feel like breaking it." Here, the word "friend" probably refers to McFarland. Maurice resumes the topic of Bell being godfather to his son, and that he and Marie have not decided on a name (Scamehorn, 16).

A month later, Rose receives a letter from Maurice, dated March 12, one of emotional collapse—and he is not yet thirty years old. Maurice recounted that "with the baby" he and Marie were "roughing it sadly" and that "I have done with making fortunes in this country [with its] fearful state of corruption . . . . This year has nearly killed me with anxiety—& I can[']t go through anymore.'" Maurice was not more specific (Lundberg, 56). Judging by a letter of May 5 to Bell when it was obvious the newborn baby was ill, Maurice advised Bell against the journey to Chattanooga. He explains to Bell that he should not come to Chattanooga "for the children's sake"—clearly plural (Scamehorn, 16, 21), indicating that the baby now ill was the second son, whose name Marie and Maurice were still debating (Frank having been born in early 1875). In that May 5 letter, Maurice states he will not go to Oswego as planned until the end of May. Tragedy was to follow anxiety on 28 May 1876 with the death of baby Charles Yorke Kingsley, who succumbed in Chattanooga at only four months old, as confirmed by David Dobson in *Scots in the American West* (Dobson, 76).

After the infant son's death, Maurice and Marie stay on in the area to recover before moving to Buffalo, New York, then Oswego for civil engineering work with McFarland. When Maurice wrote to Eversley from Oswego announcing that a son would be christened with traditional Kingsley family names, Ranulph Charles, the year was 1877 not 1876, since the birth and death of baby Charles Yorke Kingsley was not known by previous writers attempting to trace Maurice's movements. In September of 1878, Maurice wrote to England from the U.S. Engineer's Office at Oswego, still employed there but looking for another position (Lundberg, 56, 74), which is unfortunate since Maurice had written to William A. Bell in February 1876 that he was going to Oswego as a confidential clerk for "a friend," Major McFarland, a licensed civil engineer.

Maurice's inability to settle down has interested other scholars.

Margaret Farrand Thorp found an 1878 letter from Frances Kingsley to a friend, in Gabriel Vallings's letter collection (now the Kingsley Family Archive), in which Frances states that her eldest son "Being a strong conservative, . . . the institutions of America social and political are naturally repugnant to him though he has made many friends there" (Thorp, 106; Lundberg, 73-5). While honoring Frances Kingsley's note on her son, one gets the impression that in the disagreement with General Wilder in Chattanooga, Maurice was at his breaking point, and could not be patient while coping with baby Frank and the death of infant Charles. Then, in early 1878, the arrival of Ranulph (also called Ralph), put pressure on Maurice while he was working with McFarland in Oswego.

By December (evidently 1878) Maurice and Marie with two sons—Frank, nearly four years old, and Ranulph, just under one—set sail from the East Coast for England, permanently Maurice hoped, obviously no longer working with Major McFarland. Evidence suggests that Marie and sons sailed to England first and Maurice soon joined them (Lundberg, 74-5). But Maurice couldn't settle on work in England either, and was still looking in 1879. Maurice, with Marie and sons, returned to New York and fixed on New Rochelle, where he found seacoast engineering to be more to his liking than railways and riverways. Overall, while Maurice was understandably unable to follow in his father's career, he put himself under too much pressure to succeed in an honorable profession.

The Kingsley Family Archive revealed to scholar Lundberg that Marie Kingsley wrote a troubling letter, dated August 31, 1890, to her mother-in-law, Frances, to the effect that Maurice had run away from home with another woman (somewhat incredibly to Europe). The letter Marie wrote to Mrs. Kingsley shows that Marie had taken her two sons to Paris, France, evidently to look for Maurice there, and would arrive in London shortly—with or without Maurice is unclear (Lundberg, 134). In 1891, Frances Kingsley knew she was dying, and removed Maurice as co-executor of her will, leaving Rose as sole executor, motivated now because of what appeared to be Maurice's habitual instability. Though Frances Eliza Kingsley was often unwell with a heart condition and lacked the stamina to travel, she has been present in this study of the Kingsleys in Colorado as the home anchor for Rose and the chronicler of her husband's life. Mrs. Kingsley died peacefully at The Grove, December 11, 1891; Rose was present.

As the days of 1910 elapsed, Rose meditated on the news of her brother's death and recalled her mother's suspicions of the path he'd taken. Rose would also have been thinking that Maurice had not followed through on his considerable writing talent because of his insecurities about having his stories rejected—so different from the persistent Henry James, whose sister, Alice, Rose had visited in Leamington Spa.

In *South by West*, Rose had included a long section written by Maurice about his adventure crossing the Ratón Pass, south of Trinidad, Colorado, into New Mexico Territory and meeting rugged frontier types along the way. The tale shows that Maurice understood narrative arc; he wrote scenes with concision, turning each scene into the next with smooth narrative flow. He made good use of the Ratón setting, and he created lively realistic dialogue which moved the plot forward. In a short story, "Tio Juan," anthologized by William Dean Howells in *Under the Sunset*, Maurice introduced now familiar Spanish terms such as *brujo* for warlock; and though the story climaxes at the expense of the Apache people, it's clear Maurice could build tension and keep the reader interested, while creating a setting with sociological details such as shepherding and the life of new western towns. This anthology was reprinted five times between 1893 and 1906. Also in 1893, *Harper's New Monthly Magazine* published Maurice's story, "Gabriel, and the Lost Millions of Perote," another work showing his mastery of the short story form. That year, Maurice would have been only 46 years old, but he seems not to have pursued further fiction writing.

In 1895, Maurice took advantage of the controversy over his uncle's career, and wrote perhaps unwisely about him in an essay, entitled, "Personal Traits of Henry Kingsley," which was to accompany a scholarly article on Henry's novels by Laurence Hutton for the *Book Buyer*, January 1895 (Lundberg, 170-1). Henry had died from throat cancer at 46 in 1876, the year after Charles, and had attracted attention nearly all his life, although there is no firm evidence of excessive drinking or gay sexuality. Patricia Lundberg's research shows that Henry's contemporaries felt he lived irresponsibly, but he was also misunderstood and unappreciated. Henry left his wife, Sarah Hazelwood, penniless and with debts during an era when governments did not provide social services or safety nets for widows. The Kingsley sisters were against Maurice participating in the project about Uncle Henry, and would not have wanted his life exposed to further criticism simply because Maurice had a chance to make a little money.

In 1898, Maurice took some income away from his sisters by writing introductions for edited versions of their father's work, such as *The Novels, Poems, and Memories of Charles Kingsley* (1898), which his sisters most certainly would not have agreed to. In Maurice's favor, it must be said that he did not look for this writing assignment himself but was approached by the J. F. Taylor publishing house of New York City; however, Maurice was aware that his work on this edition of his father's life and letters (compiled by Taylor) would conflict with clauses in his mother's will, and with his father's publisher, Macmillan, which allocated Charles Kingsley's royalties to Rose and Mary (Lundberg, 194-5, 199-200). That same year, 1898, saw Maurice try his hand at what we would call a kind of advocacy writing, which I've touched on briefly, the full title of which is *The Defence of our Great Cities: What the government has done and is now doing to protect them.* In this set of collected essays on harbor defenses, Maurice addressed fears that during the Spanish-American War the East Coast might be attacked, possibly including New Rochelle.

By the autumn of 1900, his son Ranulph was about twenty-three years old, and found the money to visit England, perhaps no longer a student at Yale. To Rose and her sister, it seemed that he might become the family literary executor, especially of his adoring aunt, Mary, the novelist Lucas Malet, but "it was not to be" said Mary St. Leger Kingsley (Lundberg, 75). Further disappointments followed. The Kingsley Family Archives in the possession of Charlotte Kingsley Chanter's descendents, the Covey-Crump family, show that in 1904,

Maurice wrote to Rose from 541 W. 124th, New Rochelle, that his "failed writing"—meaning his fiction—had so "'disheartened'" him that he had not attempted writing "for ten years" (Lundberg, 274). In 1905, Maurice felt sure that his novelist sister was affluent, and he may have tried to persuade her to "adopt" his sons Frank and Ranulph, both now in their thirties, whose talents and aptitudes, Maurice concluded, were wasted in the United States. "I much wish the boys' future lay in England—Ralph is lost here, but would rise in England—Frank would get along anywhere a machine is used—he is a born mechanic" (Lundberg, 291-2).

Frank Kingsley visited England briefly in 1906, about the time that Rose got word that Ralph had moved to Cincinnati, Ohio. From this time on, correspondence dropped off, and Maurice never contacted Rose to say he was ill. After Maurice's death, Rose didn't hear at all from his widow, Marie, nor from her nephews. It's difficult to believe that Marie Kingsley is lost to the historical record. Her younger sister, Sara, had been in Mexico City with the Yorkes in 1867 when the people of Mexico freed themselves from the French, but by Maurice's arrival in 1872, Sara was settled in Philadelphia where she had married Cornelius Stevenson and had become a leading intellectual in anthropology and archaeology. In 1899, Sara published her Mexico experience, *Maximilian in Mexico*: *A Woman's Reminiscences of the French Intervention 1862-1867*. It's unknown if Maurice or Marie ever thought of visiting Philadelphia. Other Kingsley connections are difficult to trace. Rose Kingsley had heard about a William Kingsley who died tragically from a train accident in Shelby, Iowa, in May 1906, but he was not related to them at all, and not related to another William Kingsley, a professor at Yale College her father had visited in New Haven, Connecticut, in March of 1874.

Thinking of Maurice, Rose might have paused and wondered if she, too, had done all she could. Through her father she had met almost every church dignitary from Cambridge University, men of science and literature, and in America had met Mark Twain, John Greenleaf Whittier, James and Annie Fields, and possibly Ferdinand V. Hayden. Charles Kingsley had noticed Rose's success in America and had frequently written home that "R. is very well and is the best of secretaries." Even Matthew Arnold, the poet and education reformer, had written to Rose after her father's death, not to her mother; "I fear your mother is in no state to read letters: you must let me write one line to you" (Kingsley, Frances, 2: 426, 471).

Life had brought great treasures to Rose Kingsley.

The last days: ". . . a woman of an entirely different stamp."

On a summer day August 17, 1925, Rose Georgina Kingsley, 80, lay dying in her room at the Hotel Sanclu in the seaside town of Ramsgate, Kent. As she felt her life slipping away, Rose might have thought of the good years at her very own home in memory-filled Eversley. During the Great War, the cost of living had skyrocketed, property values plummeted, and her home had slipped out of her hands; Rose sold "The Keys" by May of 1918. On her financial assistance application to the Royal Literary Fund, Rose explained that for fifteen years The Keys had sheltered her until she was "obliged to sell my cottage at Eversley at a complete loss." The RLF was a subscription society based in London "for writers in need of monetary assistance" and to which other writers contributed when able (Lundberg, 44-5). On her only known application, she listed only a few of her numerous publications, and received £250 several months before her death. A private evaluation of her application by one G. P. Gooch reported that in February 1925, Rose was "currently living in two rooms [in the hotel], that her expenses clearly exceeded her income," that "she was overdrawn £70," and that her writing had always been "scholarly and knowledgeable about art and her writing up to RLF standards of literary excellence." After leaving her home in Eversley, for a time she had lived at the Hotel Imperial at 122 Queen's Gate, London, then left there to live nearby at the Grandby Court Hotel,

88 Queen's Gate (Lundberg, 369, 420-1). Then early in 1925, Rose left the Grandby for the Sanclu in Ramsgate where she knew she would soon pass to the next world, probably from breast cancer.

In Ramsgate, Rose would have remembered the many hours of companionship with her sister, the times that she, Rose, offered her sister solace during her unfortunate marriage to the Reverend Harrison. Both sisters might have concentrated on better days and other scenes. Rose recalled her fear of firearms long ago in Colorado (*South by West*, 85), and how in Mexico with General and Mrs. Palmer, she overcame that fear, first with learning how to use a Smith & Wesson and then a Derringer pistol (*South by West*, 207, 314). So much had Rose gotten over her apprehensions that in England she had formed a women's rifle team which competed against men's teams in a genteel fashion (Lundberg, 33).

Knowing that she was fading quickly, certain scenes in the Pike's Peak region may have resurfaced in Rose Kingsley's consciousness. At one point, in mid-December 1871, she tested her limits. She records that she's riding further east from the Springs than she has yet been. She's a bit mysterious on this scene in *South by West*; she doesn't say who is riding with her, only "we"; it could have been Captain Schuyler, possibly E. S. Nettleton or another of Palmer's associates, or only her brother, "M." So far east of town, without the conventional social tether, and no sure rescue in case of accident, the adrenaline hypnosis of adventure took over. As the first white woman to discover the Coral Bluffs area, she writes:

> We had a glorious ride last week over the plains, in search of antelope, to the bluffs about five miles from town; and riding up between two bluffs found ourselves in a valley full of monuments, like those in Monument Park. It was quite a discovery, as no one had heard of their existence before. If there is any water there it will be a charming site for a house some day, as the glade is much prettier than Monument Park itself; and the views between the

bluffs, of mountain and plain, are magnificent.

Whenever I get out on the plains and look south-ward to those endless mountain-ranges which stretch away into New Mexico till they are hidden by the roundness of the earth, I am seized with a longing to go south and see them. But the stage-journey is enough to deter any one from going who is not abso-lutely forced to go. (*South by West*, 92-3)

From this vantage point—more like ten miles east of Colorado Springs than five—Rose could see the Greenhorn Mountains to the southwest, and beyond them, the lofty twin summits of the Span-ish Peaks near Ratón Pass, the gateway to the Cimarrón country. In successive tones of blue, the mountains are illuminated far and away. Rose's desire to see them was "cured" when Maurice described his own journey on the Southern Overland Mail in December of 1870. Rose recalled Maurice's tale of the hardships he experienced, though for him it was a "gorgeous wild scene" and a meeting with western character Dick Wootten (*South by West*, 93-4). Today, a paved inter-state highway over the Ratón Pass smoothes one's way, and Wootten and his toll road are the stuff of legends, but the point at which Rose Kingsley pauses to look far and away at the distant peaks is the point at which we see her experience reflected in us. She wondered what life was like beyond the next range of mountains—but does not have to go there. She is satisfied.

Little could Rose have known that a man, a friend, with knowl-edge and experience had been watching her protectively and study-ing what she studied; evidence strongly suggests it was the Colo-rado Springs city engineer, Edwin S. Nettleton. He kept his thoughts to himself, for no known journal exists in which he recorded such memories. In January of 1887, a long article on Rose and Maurice appeared in the Springs *Gazette*, a feature quite startling in its inti-mate impressions of sister and brother. The newspaper archive cites H. S. Rogers as the author, the City Editor in the 1880s, but had the Rogers family been in Colorado City or the Springs at all in 1871 or

'72, H. S. Rogers would have been just a boy, and the census lists no Rogers family. H. S. Rogers reveals no source to his article, but that was the custom for protecting informants in that era. To write as Rogers did, he had to have interviewed someone who knew Maurice and Rose very well in the winter of 1871. The only person who could have known such details about Rose and her brother would have been Edwin S. Nettleton, the man who shared the Fountain Colony Company office with Maurice when Rose moved into the nearby spare room after vacating the shanty-tent (*South by West*, 62).

At four years older than General Palmer, Nettleton would have been fifty-five in 1887. He was beginning to slow down with minor chest pains, but had remained in Colorado, a state he had helped create by being the lead engineer for Greeley, Colorado Springs, and South Pueblo, before working for the Colorado State engineering office. In reflecting on the recent past when talking to Rogers, Nettleton focused on his impressions of Rose, in contrast to her brother. Rogers dared not name Nettleton since the images of Maurice take a negative turn. Recall that Maurice had arrived in the region in October 1870 to manage the Monument Farms, while Nettleton was in Greeley finalizing the town planning; then, when Palmer hired him and Cameron to plat Colorado Springs, Nettleton would have come down to the Pike's Peak region and met Maurice Kingsley in the summer of 1871. Nettleton was also in Denver on October 31, 1871—as described at the beginning of this study—to meet Maurice and his sister the morning after she arrived on the Kansas Pacific.

The article which Rogers produced from the interview with Nettleton is a revelation. Rogers begins, "The sun was setting on the evening of June 28, 1871," suggesting that the key personnel had arrived to complete initial surveying before the first stake for the town was driven in July. Rogers commences with a portrait of Maurice in romantic tones:

> . . . a heavy wagon drawn by four long eared mules,
> rattled down the last little hill and came to a stop

by a solitary log cabin on the banks of the Monument [Creek]. From it alighted the first officers of this colony, General Cameron, Wm. E. Pabor, E. S. Nettleton, John Potter and lastly a tall, graceful young fellow with Spanish eyes and hair and an easy, half-indolent, half alert way of moving, suggestive of a southern race and a life of excitement and adventure. Thus was the first starting of this colony, and the young man was Maurice, son of Canon Kingsley, and its assistant treasurer.

Travel below the tropics and among the pampas of South America had darkened his swarthy complexion to a warm olive. His figure, though slight, was well knit and sinewy; his whole appearance as he stood in the light of the setting sun more that of a Spanish cavalier than an English gentleman. Here, one would instinctively think, is a man for an emergency, for danger, a man for romance rather than for the dull routine of daily life. And yet there was none of the uncouthness of a frontiersman about him. His ease, his grace, his repose, was not that of a picket of civilization but of a man of the world. His English birth, his training, his travels on the continent all had lent their influence in the shaping of his character and the moulding of his manners. He looked like a man with a history, and he had one.

He came here through the friendship which existed between his father and Dr. Bell. He only stayed a year and then went to Mexico in a party whose adventures, as told by his sister Rose, read like a romance of an age long past.

He does not seem to have taken a prominent part in the affairs of the colony. He was lacking in ambition—or seriousness. He preferred a comfortable fire and a couple of boon companions to labor. He was inclined to the sunny side of life and the enjoyment of the moment. He was loath to undertake anything, yet when he had once made up his mind he was most conscientious in the fulfillment of his pledges. He was a clever, almost a brilliant man. In all outdoor sports he had great faculty, and had inherited from his father his literary taste, of which, unlike his sister Rose, he was too unambitious to make much use.

She was woman of an entirely different stamp. Tall, well made and graceful, her manner was full of dignity and repose. She might almost have been called masculine, were it not for a certain sweetness and womanliness which one instinctively felt when they approached her. . . .

Like her brother she delighted in exercise, especially in walking, and was constantly tramping over the plains in search of rare herbs and flowers, of which she was passionately fond. A charming sight it must have been on a sunny morning to come across this solitary English woman as she strode over the dull sage with only her hound and a revolver for company, bold, defiant, careless of where she went or whom she met—for cowardice was not one of the Kingsley failings. (Rogers, *Gazette*, January 30, 1887, p. 1)

H. S. Rogers gives one further observation of Rose Kingsley that only Edwin S. Nettleton could have known: "She enjoyed the frontier life and fell into the ways and customs of the people with most un-English facility." The personal reminiscences end there, and then Rogers adds a long quotation from *South by West* in which Rose recalls the beginnings of the town, the "streets and blocks are only marked out by a furrow turned with a plough and indicated faintly by a wooden house, finished or in process of building, . . . About twelve houses and shanties are inhabited, most of them being unfurnished or run-up for temporary occupation . . . " In this way, quoting a few paragraphs from Rose's book *South by West*, the *Gazette* editor, Rogers, shows how the Kingsleys' friends (like Nettleton) valued Rose's words for the history they related that was disappearing under new layers of population growth and city development.

By 1925, Rose was accustomed to her own approaching demise, and her thoughts would have been for the people she had gotten to know under challenging circumstances. In mid-July 1875, only six months after the death of her father, the esteemed Gerald DeCoursey, one of the early secretaries of the Colorado Springs Company (and a cherished friend of Helen Hunt) passed away suddenly at home from a "hemorrhage of the throat." He had died only three months after the equally sudden death of J. Elsom Liller, everyone's favorite English person, the revered creator of the *Out West* newspaper, who may have been taken away by an accidental laudanum overdose. Colonel William Greenwood, the railway construction supervisor, was murdered by gunshot on August 29, 1880, near Toluca, while working on the Mexico National Railway, having briefly advanced too far from his workmen. Rose might have shuddered recalling that it was also near Toluca that Palmer, Alexander C. Hunt, and Maurice fought off attackers in 1872 on their railway reconnaissance while she and Queen were resting comfortably elsewhere.

Howard Schuyler, as we recall, had attempted to carry on Greenwood's work near Mexico City but became ill and died in Switzerland in December 1883 while seeking a cure. And in England, in the village of Frant, near Tunbridge Wells, the lovely Queen Palmer died in December 1894, at the age of 44, from a congenital heart problem, triggered by pneumonia. The ever-resourceful Alexander Cameron Hunt, whose major work was to ensure that the land purchased for the railway and townsites was legal and successfully filed in Denver, died peacefully in 1894 at nearly seventy years of age. Fate overtook E. S. Nettleton in April 1901 when he overstrained his heart while running to catch a train in La Junta, Colorado; he died a week later in a Denver hospital. General William J. Palmer whose leadership, railway knowledge, and connections, had made the railway-to-town ventures happen, died in 1909.

Rose Georgina Kingsley's desire for adventure and community in Colorado was the last to be extinguished by death. Bell had died peacefully at his home, Pendell Court, in Bletchingly, Surrey, in 1921. Bell's wife Cara lived on into the 1930s, but she had separated from Colorado nearly thirty years earlier, and was involved in the role of grandmother of the children of her daughter and the 8th Earl Glasgow, of the Pearce's children, of the Montagu-Pollocks and her son Archie's children—her life warmly domestic compared to the social pioneering of the Kingsleys. When Rose passed away, her sister, Mary, was present at her bedside (Lundberg, 426). The news of Rose Kingsley's death in August 1925 didn't reach Colorado Springs for several months. The *Gazette* headline for December 26 reads "Miss Kingsley Dies at Her London Home." The newspaper didn't so much cover up the truth as they just didn't know.

If this detailed study on Rose Kingsley and her brother Maurice, and their father the Reverend Charles, and his brother George has had a purpose, it's to show how unique their role in Colorado was from all other British travelers. While scholars have documented how British diplomats and aristocrats, sociologists and novelists, political and military figures came to the American West with the intention of returning home to write about it, thousands of working class men and women came with the intention of staying. The Kingsleys' purpose in coming to Colorado took form because General and Mrs. Palmer were guests of Canon and Mrs. Kingsley at Eversley Rectory in February 1871. Whatever the Kingsleys thought or felt about General Palmer and his English business partner, William A. Bell, their ideas were conditioned by previously existing influences such as Charles Kingsley's knowledge of the natural sciences, his promotion of science, and his recognition—though at times grudging—that the United States was reborn into a tremendous future.

In the post-Civil War era of the foundation of quick-growth towns, the Kingsleys gave shape to the future of Colorado Springs, while perhaps only Maurice Kingsley was sensitive to the fate of dispossessed peoples. William Blackmore and William Abraham Bell followed their desires in different ways but for motivations which seem obvious today, that of making money in an unpredictable business atmosphere; however, they, too, have stories. Though Rose Georgina Kingsley would not have come to the Pike's Peak region without her brother's presence in the Fountain Colony office, her community organization abilities are the achievement most unalloyed with regret.

Whether walking east of town through the breeze-brushed wild grass, or on an uphill hike through piñon and juniper, or preparing for a music concert, Rose Kingsley was there for us—a woman for the moment and the future.

WORKS CITED

Adrian, Arthur A. "Charles Kingsley Visits Boston." *Huntington Library Quarterly*. Vol. 20: 1 (November 1956), 94-97.

Altick, Richard. *Victorian People and Ideas: a Companion for the Modern Reader of Victorian Literature*. New York: Norton, 1973.

Anderson, Denise. Curatorial Assistant. Edinburgh University. Message to author. "George H. Kingsley, M.D." E-mail, March 21, 2017.

Anderson, George L. *General William J. Palmer: A Decade of Colorado Railroad Building, 1870-1880*. Colorado Springs: Colorado College Publication, 1936.

Baker, William J. "Charles Kingsley in Little London." *The Colorado Magazine*. Vol. XLV: 3 (1968), 187-203.

Bell, Cara Georgina Whitmore Scovell. *Diary*. Colorado Springs, Colorado College Special Collections. Typescript.

Bell, William A.[braham]. *The Colonies of Colorado in their Relations to English Enterprise and Settlement*. "The Tenant Farmer and Tradesman's Opportunity." London: *Labour News* Office, 1874. The Newberry Library: The Graff Collection.
- - - . *New Tracks in North America: A Journal of Travel and Adventure whilst Engaged in the Survey for a Southern Railroad to the Pacific Ocean During 1867-8*. London: Chapman and Hall, 1869. 2 vols. New York: Scribner, Welford & Co., 1870. 1 vol. HathiTrust.org.

Bell, William A.[braham], Editor. *The Latest News From Colorado*. London: Witherby & Co., 1871. Colorado Springs: Colorado College Special Collections.

Best, Geoffrey. *Mid-Victorian Britain 1851-1875*. New York: Schocken Books, 1971.

Bird, Isabella L. *A Lady's Life in the Rocky Mountains*. New York: Putnam's Sons, 1879. Serialized in *Leisure Hour*, 1878.

Blackmore, William, ed. *Colorado: Its Resources, Parks, and Prospects as a New Field for Emigration with an Account of the Trenchara* [sic] *and Costilla Estates in the San Luis Park*. London: Sampson Low, Son, and Marston, 1869. HathiTrust.org.

Brayer, Herbert O. *William Blackmore: The Spanish-Mexican Land Grants of New Mexico and Colorado, 1863-1878. A Case Study in the Economic Development of the West*. Vol. I. Denver: Bradford Robinson, 1949. HathiTrust.org.

- - - . *William Blackmore: Early Financing of the Denver & Rio Grande Railway and Ancillary Land Companies, 1871-1878. A Case Study in the Economic Development of the West*. Vol. II. Denver: Bradford Robinson, 1949. HathiTrust.org.

Brown, John Crosby. *A Hundred Years of Merchant Banking*. New York: Privately Printed, 1909.

Charwat, Elaine, Deputy Librarian. Linnean Society of London. Message to author. "George Kingsley elected a Fellow of the Linnean Society." E-mail, May 18, 2012.

Chitty, Lady Susan. *The Beast and the Monk: A Life of Charles Kingsley*. New York: Mason/Charter Publishers, 1975.

Clements, Roger V. "British Investment and American Legislative Restrictions in the Trans-Mississippi West, 1880-1900." *Mississippi Valley Historical Review* 42 (September 1955), 207-228.

Cook, Adrian. *The Alabama Claims: American Politics and Anglo-American Relations, 1865-1872*. Ithaca, New York: Cornell University Press, 1975.

Covey-Crump, Peter. Curator, Kingsley Family Archive, Cheltenham, England. "Maurice Kingsley." E-mail, 22 May 2017.

Dobson, David. *Scots in the American West*. Baltimore, Maryland: Clearfield Company Inc., 2003.

Dunraven, 4th Earl, Windham Thomas Wyndham-Quinn. *Past Times and Pastimes*. Vol. 1. London: Hodder & Stoughton, Ltd., 1922.

Farrell, Ned. *Colorado, The Rocky Mountain Gem, as it is in 1868*. Chicago: Western News Company, 1868.

Fisher, John S. *A Builder of the West: The Life of William Jackson Palmer*. Caldwell, Idaho: The Caxton Printers, Ltd., 1939.

Frank, Katherine. *A Voyager Out: The Life of Mary Kingsley*. New York: Bloomsbury USA, 2005. [1986]

Gerlach, Murney. *British Liberalism and the United States: Political and Social Thought in the Late Victorian Age*. Basingstoke, England, and New York: Palgrave, 2001.

Gilpin, William. *Notes on Colorado and its Inscription in the Physical Geography of the North American Continent*. London: Witherby & Company, 1870. "Spoken at the 'British Association of Science,'" "Liverpool, Septr. 26th, 1870."

Haley, Bruce. *The Healthy Body and Victorian Culture*. Cambridge, Massachusetts: Harvard University Press, 1978.

Hamber, Anthony. *Collecting the American West: The Rise and Fall of William Blackmore*. Salisbury, England: The Hobnob Press, 2010.

Harper, Lila Marz. *Solitary Travelers: Nineteenth-century Women's Travel Narratives and the Scientific Vocation*. Madison & Cranbury, New Jersey; London: Fairleigh Dickinson University Press, 2001.

Haywood, C. Robert. *Victorian West: Class and Culture in Kansas Cattle Towns*. Lawrence, Kansas, University Press of Kansas, 1991.

Hill, Nathaniel P. "Nathaniel P. Hill Inspects Colorado: Letters Written in 1864." *The Colorado Magazine* XXXIII: No. 4 (October 1956), 241-276 (Part 1).

Huxley, Elspeth. *The Kingsleys: A Biographical Anthology*. London: George Allen & Unwin, 1973.

Irving, Washington. *Three Western Narratives: A Tour on the Prairies; Astoria; The Adventures of Captain Bonneville*. New York: Library of America, 2004.

Jenkins, Brian. *Fenians and Anglo-American Relations during Reconstruction*. Ithaca, New York: Cornell University Press, 1969.

Karnes, Thomas L. *William Gilpin: Western Nationalist*. Austin, Texas, and London: University of Texas Press, 1970.

Kingsley, Frances E., ed. *Charles Kingsley: His Letters and Memories of His Life*. 2 volumes. London: Henry S. King & Company, 1878. HathiTrust.org.

Kingsley, George H. *Notes on Sport and Travel*. London: Macmillan and Co.; New York: The Macmillan Company, 1900. HathiTrust.org.

Kingsley, Mary H. "Memoir." *Notes on Sport and Travel*. London: Macmillan and Co.; New York: The Macmillan Company, 1900. 1-208. HathiTrust. org.

Kingsley, Rose G. *Eversley Gardens and Others*. London: George Allen, and New York: Macmillan Co., 1907. HathiTrust.org.
- - - . Introduction. *Glaucus; or, The Wonders of the Shore*. By Charles Kingsley. London: J. M. Dent & Sons Ltd. New York: E. P. Dutton & Co. 1908. [1854-5.]
- - - . *South by West; or, Winter in the Rocky Mountains and Spring in Mexico*. London: W. Isbister & Co., 1874. HathiTrust.org.

Linehan, Thomas. *British Fascism 1918–39: Parties, Ideology and Culture*. Manchester and New York: Manchester University Press, 2000.

Lohse, Joyce B. "Young Palmer Travels Abroad." *Legends, Labors & Loves: William J. Palmer, 1836-1909*. Tim Blevins, et al, editors. Colorado Springs: Pike's Peak Library District, 2009, 12-25.

Long, Renata Eley. *In the Shadow of the Alabama: The British Foreign Office and the American Civil War*. Annapolis, Maryland: Naval Institute Press, 2015.

302

Ludlow, Fitz Hugh. *The Heart of the Continent: A Record of Travel across the Plains and in Oregon, with an Examination of the Mormon Principle.* New York: Hurd and Houghton, 1870. Cambridge: The Riverside Press, 1870.

Lundberg, Patricia Lorimer. *'An Inward Necessity': The Writer's Life of Lucas Malet.* New York: Peter Lang Publishing Inc., 2003.

Manson, Carly, archivist. St. George's, University of London. Message to author. "George H. Kingsley student records." E-mail, April 11, 2017.

Martin, Robert Bernard, ed. *Charles Kingsley's American Notes: Letters from a Lecture Tour, 1874.* Princeton, N.J.: Princeton University Press, 1958.
- - - . *The Dust of Combat: A Life of Charles Kingsley.* New York: W. W. Norton & Company, Inc., 1960.

Matthews, Ruth Estelle. "Three Articles from the Pen of Charles Kingsley." *Stanford Studies in Language and Literature* (1941), 312-320.

Morin, Karen M. "British Women Travellers and Constructions of Racial Difference across the nineteenth-century American West." *Transactions.* Institute of British Geographers. Vol. 23 (1998), 311-330.

Neidhardt, W. S. *Fenianism in North America.* University Park, Pennsylvania, and London, England: The Pennsylvania State University Press, 1975.

Nelson, Douglas W. "The Alien Land Law Movement of the Late Nineteenth Century." *Journal of the West.* 9 (January 1970), 46-59.

Nimmo, Joseph, Jr. Bureau of Statistics, Treasury Department. *Report in Regard to the Range and Ranch Cattle Business of the United States.* Washington, D.C.: Government Printing Office, May 16, 1885.

Noel, Thomas J., and Paul F. Mahoney, and Richard E. Stevens. *Historical Atlas of Colorado.* Norman: University of Oklahoma Press, 1993.

O'Gorman, Francis. " 'More interesting than all the books, save one': Charles Kingsley's Construction of Natural History." *Rethinking Victorian Culture.* New York: St. Martin's Press, 2000.

Old, R.[obert] O.[rchard] *Colorado, United States, America: Its History, Geography and Mining: including a comprehensive catalogue of nearly six hundred samples or ores.* London: The British and Colorado Mining Bureau, 1869.

Ormes, Manly Dayton and Eleanor Reddle Ormes. *The Book of Colorado Springs.* Colorado Springs: Dentan Print Co., 1933.

Palmer, William J. General. *Report of Surveys Across the Continent in 1867-'68, on the thirty-fifth and thirty-second parallels, for a Route Extending the Kansas Pacific Railway to the Pacific Ocean.* Philadelphia: W. B. Selheimer, 1869.
- - - . *Letters.* Colorado Springs: Colorado College. Letter from Charles Kingsley, May 24, 1870.
- - - , and Queen Palmer. *Honeymoon Journal.* Starsmore Center for Local History. November 1870 to February 1871. Colorado Springs Pioneers Museum. Manuscript, n. pag.

Pickering, James H. *This Blue Hollow: Estes Park, the Early Years, 1859-1915.* Niwot, Colo.: University Press of Colorado, 1999.

Pope-Hennessy, Una. *Canon Charles Kingsley: a Biography.* London: Chatto & Windus, 1948.

Roberson, Susan L. "Degenerate Effeminacy' and the Making of a Masculine Spirituality in the Sermons of Ralph Waldo Emerson." *Muscular Christianity: Embodying the Victorian Age.* Cambridge & New York: Cambridge University Press, 1994.

Rogers, H. S. "The Early Days: Personal Reminiscences of Miss Rose Kingsley who visited her brother Maurice in 1871." *Colorado Springs Gazette.* January 30, 1887. p. 1.

Ruxton, George Frederick. *Ruxton of the Rockies.* American Exploration and Travel Series. LeRoy Hafen, Clyde Porter, and Mae Reed Porter, editors. Norman: University of Oklahoma Press, 1979.

Sage, Rufus B. *Scenes in the Rocky Mountains, and in Oregon, California, New Mexico, Texas, and the Grand Prairies; or, Notes by the Way, During an Excursion of Three Years.* 2nd Edition. Philadelphia: Henry Carey Baird, 1854. HathiTrust.org.

Scamehorn, Lee, and R. Pritchard, A. Mercherle, and G. Fowler, compilers. *A Calendar of the Papers of William Abraham Bell, 1841-1921.* Denver, Colorado: Hart Research Center at History Colorado, 1970.

Schulze, Suzanne, editor, compiler. *A Century of the Colorado Census.* Greeley: University of Northern Colorado, 1976 [1977].

Schuyler, George Washington. *Colonial New York: Philip Schuyler and his Family.* 2 vols. New York: Privately Printed, 1885.

Searby, Peter. *A History of the University of Cambridge.* Vol. 3, 1750-1870. Cambridge, England: Cambridge University Press, 1997.

Semmel, Bernard. *The Governor Eyre Controversy.* London: MacGibbon & Kee, 1962.

Sprague, Marshall. *Newport in the Rockies: the Life and Good Times of Colorado Springs.* Athens, Ohio: Sage/Swallow Press, the Ohio University Press, 1980 [1961].

Stephen, Leslie. "Hours in a Library: No. XV. Charles Kingsley." *Cornhill Magazine,* 1877, 424-442.

Sumner, Charles. "Claims on England—Individual and National." "Speech on the Johnson-Clarendon Treaty, in Executive Session of the Senate, April 13, 1869." *The Works of Charles Sumner.* Vol. 13. Boston: Lee and Shepard, 1880, 53-93. HathiTrust.org.

Thompson, F. M. L. *English Landed Society in the Nineteenth Century.* London: Routledge & Kegan Paul; Toronto: University of Toronto Press, 1963.

Thorp, Margaret Farrand. *Charles Kingsley 1819-1875.* Princeton: Princeton University Press; London: Humphrey Milford; Oxford: Oxford University Press, 1937.

Turner, Jan C. Deputy Librarian. Royal Geographical Society. Message to author. "Maurice Kingsley elected a Fellow of the R.G.S." E-mail, May 2, 2017.

United States. *House of Representatives. Ex. Doc.* No. 25, 40th Congress, 3d

Session. "Letter from the Secretary of the Interior." (The Warren and Blickensderfer report.) Washington, D.C.; Union Pacific Railroad, E. D., January 6, 1869.

- - - . *1870 Census of the United States: El Paso County, Colorado Territory.* Colorado Springs, Colorado: Pike's Peak Library District. Microfilm.

- - - . *House of Representatives. Report* No. 3455, 49th Congress, 1st Session. "Ownership of Real Estate in the Territories." Washington, D.C.: Committee on Public Lands, July 31, 1886.

Veenendaal, Jr., Augustus J. *Slow Train to Paradise: How Dutch Investment Helped Build American Railroads.* Stanford, California: Stanford University Press, 1996.

Venn, John, and John Archibald Venn, compliers. *Alumni Cantabrigienses: a Biographical List of all Known Students, Graduates and Holders of Office at the University of Cambridge, from the Earliest Times to 1900.* 10 volumes. Cambridge: The University Press, 1922-1954. Web: *A Cambridge Alumni Database.* www.venn.lib.cam.ac.uk.

Weatherall, Mark. *Gentlemen, Scientists, and Doctors: Medicine at Cambridge 1800-1940.* Cambridge: The Boydell Press, 2000.

Wilkins, Mira. *The History of Foreign Investment in the United States to 1914.* Cambridge, Massachusetts, and London, England: Harvard University Press, 1989.

Willard, James F., and Colin B. Goodykoontz. *Experiments in Colorado Colonization, 1869-1872.* Boulder: University of Colorado, 1926.

Williams, Adriana. Deputy Development Director. King's College School. "George H. Kingsley." Message to author. E-mail, April 28, 2017.

Williams, Ka-Yin, and Laura Butler. Library Services Advisors. Royal Agricultural University. "Maurice Kingsley." Message to author. E-mail, April 19, 2017.

INDEX

A

Costilla Estate (U.S. Freehold Land & Emigration Company) 90, 94, 95, 102-104, 107, 110-112, 117, 120-123, 125, 126

Cushing, Caleb (American international legal advisor) 210

D

D&RG (Denver & Rio Grande Railway Company) 1, 2, 5, 17, 20, 32, 33, 93, 94, 115, 117, 119, 120, 121, 123-126, 130, 143, 148, 194, 197, 279

Dilke, Charles Wentworth (British travel writer and M.P.) 108

Dunraven, 4th Earl (Windham Thomas Wyndham-Quin) xv, xvi, 19, 227, 228, 239, 248-262, 268, 269, 273, 274

E

Edwards, Reverend Samuel (St. Paul's, Pueblo) 180, 181

El Paso, Texas 26

Estes Park, Colorado Territory x, xv, xvi, xvii, 19, 45, 227, 228, 233, 239, 244, 249, 251, 252, 254-258, 260-262, 265, 269

Eyre, Edward John (Governor of Jamaica) 43, 48, 305

F

Farrell, Ned 109

Fenian Raids (Fenian Brotherhood) xvii, 74, 79-82.

Fisher, Morton Coates (Governor Gilpin associate) 99, 101, 102, 103, 109, 112, 113, 115, 121

Fort Craig, New Mexico Territory 26, 68

Fort Lancaster, Colorado Territory 27, 28

Fort Wallace, Kansas 66, 68, 140, 141

Fortesque, Dudley Francis (English investor Manitou Springs) 173

France, Matt (Mayor of Colorado Springs) 20, 176, 181

G

Garden of the Gods (Colorado Springs) xi, 27, *161*, 190

Gatchell, Dr. Henry T. F. (El Paso County Coroner) 21, 190, 230

Gilpin, William (1st Governor Colorado Territory) 9, 29, 30, 31, 32, 99, 102, 104, 105, 107, 108, 109, 112, 113, 114, 115, 121, 122, 207, 210

Gladstone, William Ewart (Prime Minister) 40, 42, 221

Greenwood, Colonel William H. (D&RG Construction Manager) 15, 20, 25, 86, 121, 123, 124, 125, 143, 194, 295

H

Haskell, Thomas Nelson (Founder Colorado College) 170, 190

Hayden, Ferdinand V. (United States geologist) 91, 100, 101, 102, 103, 108, 111, 129, 130, 201, 286

R

Ratón Mountains, New Mexico Territory 26, 62, 66, 100, 115
Ratón Pass 2, 19, 130, 284, 291
Ruxton, George Frederick Augustus (English traveler and writer) 28, 29, 304

S

Sage, Rufus (early travel writer) 27, 28, 32
San Luís de la Culebra, Colorado Territory 104, 107
Sangre de Cristo Land Grant xvii, 16, 90, 99, 101, 103, 109
Santa Fe, New Mexico Territory 13, 26, 28, 31-33, 67, 68, 94, 103, 115, 121, 153
Schenck, General Robert C. (Trustee Costilla Estate) 112, 210
Schuyler, Captain Howard (D&RG assistant construction manager) viii, 15, 20, 25, 86, 124, 193, 194, 196, 197, 198, 199, 204, 224, 225, 227, 257, 290, 295
Shelden, Albinus Z. (El Paso County land surveyor) 108, 109
St. Louis, Missouri (Headquarters Kansas Pacific Railway) 13, 23, 29, 66, 67, 77, 101, 137, 199, 273
Sumner, Charles (United States Senator) 25, 71, 72, 73, 75, 76, 77, 78, 79, 81, 82, 85, 109, 124, 213, 221

T

Taos, New Mexico Territory 3, 28, 32, 104
Thornton, Francis Cholmondeley (Cambridge graduate) 233, 279
Tocqueville, Alexis de (French traveler) xvii, 30, 58
Trinchera Estate, Colorado Territory 101, 102, 103, 115
Trinidad, Colorado Territory 2, 26, 28, 32, 33, 66, 125, 284

U

Union Pacific Eastern Division (see Kansas Pacific) 16, 23, 24, 69, 93, 99, 100, 101, 102, 273
United States Freehold Land & Emigration Company (see Costilla Estate)

W

Waddingham, Wilson (Canadian entrepreneur) 115
Wertheim & Gompertz (Amsterdam banking house) 16, 17, 93, 94, 98, 107, 110, 111, 117, 120-126, 185

Y

Yoho, Ike (Missourian, Blackmore employee) 17, 129, 229, 273